Communicating as IT Professionals

Jay Liebowitz
Johns Hopkins University

William Agresti
Johns Hopkins University

G. Reza Djavanshir
Johns Hopkins University

PEARSON

Prentice
Hall

Upper Saddle River, NJ   07458

Library of Congress Cataloging-in-Publication Data

Liebowitz, Jay
   Communicating as IT professionals / by Jay Liebowitz, William Agresti, G. Reza Djavanshir.
      p. cm.
   Includes bibliographical references and index.
   ISBN 0-13-146828-6
   1. Information technology.   I. Agresti, William W.   II. Djavanshir, G. Reza.   III. Title.
   T58.5.L549 2005
   004—dc22
                                            2005014678

Acquisitions Editor/AVP: Bob Horan
VP/Editorial Director: Jeff Shelstad
Project Manager: Jeannine Ciliotta
Editorial Assistant: Ana Cordero
AVP/Executive Marketing Manager: Debbie Clare
Managing Editor: Judy Leale
Production Editor: Renata Butera
Permissions Supervisor: Charles Morris
Manufacturing Buyer: Michelle Klein
Art Director: Jayne Conte
Cover Design: Bruce Kenselaar
Cover Illustration/Photo: GettImages
Manager, Print Production: Christy Mahon
Composition/Full-Service Project Management: Progressive Publishing Alternatives
Printer/Binder: Malloy Incorporated
Typeface: 10/12 Times Ten

Credits and acknowledgments borrowed from other sources and reproduced, with permission, in this textbook appear on appropriate page within the text.

Microsoft® and Windows® are registered trademarks of the Microsoft Corporation in the U.S.A. and other countries. Screen shots and icons reprinted with permission from the Microsoft Corporation. This book is not sponsored or endorsed by or affiliated with the Microsoft Corporation.

Pearson Education LTD.
Pearson Education Singapore, Pte. Ltd
Pearson Education, Canada, Ltd
Pearson Education—Japan

Pearson Education Australia PTY, Limited
Pearson Education North Asia Ltd
Pearson Educación de Mexico, S.A. de C.V.
Pearson Education Malaysia, Pte. Ltd

10 9 8 7 6 5 4 3 2
ISBN 0-13-146828-6

To the best educator and scholar I have known—my father, Harold Liebowitz, who passed away during the writing of this book—*JL*

To Risa, Aimee, and Karen—and our family fun together—*WA*

To my wife Gissou, my mother Pourandokht, and all my teachers, students, and friends, especially Jay, Bill, and Jim—*RD*

Brief Contents

Contents

Preface

Why do I have to take an oral and written communications course if I am going into IT (Information Technology)? When we introduced this course, "Technical Oral and Written Communications Skills for IT Professionals," several years ago as a requirement in our MS-Information and Telecommunications Systems for Business (MS-ITS) degree, many of our students were not pleased with the notion of having to take such a course. "What does this have to do with information technology? I haven't had a writing course since Freshman Composition, and I didn't like it then and I won't like it now!"

In spite of feeling under attack, we showed the class numerous surveys and examples indicating that the number one attribute IT employers want in their people is the ability to speak and write well (and also to be a critical thinker). The surveys indicated that this trait is lacking in most IT degree programs.

We explained that graduate education should also improve lifelong learning skills, and oral and written communications fit within this basket. Once the students saw that we were integrating the communications skills with IT topics, they started to understand the value of such a course. This was immediately apparent in the first 20 minutes of the class, since typically only 5 out of 25 students could get an A on a simple freshman grammar quiz!

In reviewing the texts for such a course, we found books that only covered business communications or only focused on IT topics. We were unable to find a book that integrates both areas well. To fill this vacuum, we created *Communicating as IT Professionals*. We were also very pleased to hear in reviews of our book proposal that this book would be needed in both the Computer Science and IT/IS curricula at the undergraduate and graduate levels.

With over 70 years of combined industrial and academic experience, we tried to write a book that touches on many important endeavors facing the typical IT professional. From writing functional requirements to conducting technical reviews to even crafting executive summaries and email, the IT professional is affected by his/her written communications skills. Similarly, whether giving a presentation or meeting company representatives from abroad, the IT professional must present him/herself well.

This book is geared for an upper undergraduate or first year graduate course for the information systems, information technology, or computer science program. The book is consciously written in an easy, familiar manner, with warm-up and classroom exercises sprinkled throughout the chapters.

The professor can decide to teach the course according to our OWL framework, the "wise" approach to communicating. The chapters can be categorized and taught under "Oral Communications", "Written Communications", and "Line of Investigation". The figure below depicts this arrangement:

Oral
- Effective IT Oral Communications
- Cross-Cultural Communications
- Technical Reviews

Written
- The "Write" Stuff
- Eliciting and Writing User Requirements
- Writing Feasibility Studies

Line of Investigation
- Due Diligence as an IT Professional
- IT Consulting
- Ethics for the IT Professional

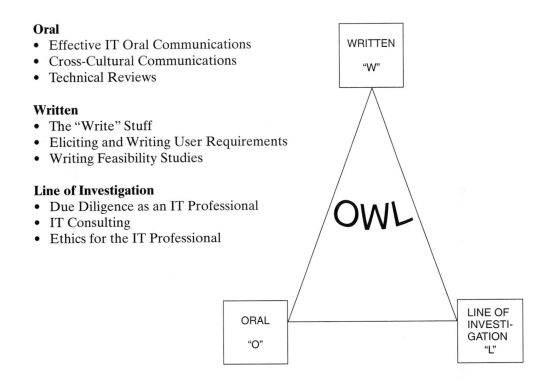

Professors and students also have access to our book Web site at www.prenhall.com/liebowitz for additional materials, including (for professors) an Instructor's Resource Manual.

Acknowledgments

We are indebted to our students in the MS-ITS degree at Johns Hopkins University, as well as to our colleagues and staff in the School of Professional Studies in Business and Education at Johns Hopkins, for their comments and constructive guidance in shaping the book. We want to thank those who reviewed the book for their insightful and helpful comments and suggestions:

Rob Anson, Boise State University

Frederick Gallegos, California Polytechnic State University–Pomona

Denis Gracanin, Virginia Tech

Patricia McQuaid, California Polytechnic State University, San Luis Obispo

Kevin Parker, Idaho State University

Vikram Sethi, Wright State University

We also want to thank all the talented people at Prentice Hall, especially Bob Horan, Lori Cerreto, Jeannine Ciliotta, Renata Butera, Donna King, and Donna Hibbs for their help in making this book a reality.

We couldn't end this preface without thanking our families for allowing us to sneak upstairs early at times to write this book. We hope it provides a refreshing and novel approach to integrating communications into your IT curriculum.

Enjoy!

Jay Liebowitz, D.Sc.
William Agresti, Ph.D.
G. Reza Djavanshir, D.Sc.

About the Authors

Jay Liebowitz is Professor of Information Technology in the Graduate Division of Business and Management at Johns Hopkins University. He is the Program Director of the new Graduate Certificate in Competitive Intelligence. He is Founder and Editor-in-Chief of Expert Systems With Applications: An International Journal, published by Elsevier. Previously, Dr. Liebowitz was the first Knowledge Management Officer at NASA Goddard Space Flight Center, the Robert W. Deutsch Distinguished Professor of Information Systems at the University of Maryland-Baltimore County, Chair of Artificial Intelligence at the U.S. Army War College, and Professor of Management Science at George Washington University. He has published 31 books and many articles dealing with expert/intelligent systems,  knowledge management, and information technology management. He is the Founder and Chair of The World Congress on Expert Systems. Dr. Liebowitz was a Fulbright Scholar, the IEEE-USA Federal Communications Commission Executive Fellow, and was chosen Computer Educator of the Year by the International Association for Computer Information Systems. Dr. Liebowitz received his Doctor of Science degree from George Washington University.

William Agresti is an Associate Professor of Information Technology in the Graduate Division of Business and Management at Johns Hopkins University. His research and professional interests are in software engineering, discovery informatics, and information security management. He held senior technical and management positions at Computer Sciences Corporation, MITRE Corporation, and Mitretek Systems, Inc., where he was Director of the Software Engineering and Economic Analysis Center. Dr. Agresti was Program Director for Experimental Software Systems research at the National Science Foundation and led spacecraft flight dynamics software

development and applied research projects at NASA Goddard Space Flight Center. Dr. Agresti has over one hundred publications, including four best paper awards and serves on the editorial boards of the journals *Empirical Software Engineering, Information Systems Security,* and *IT Professional.* He received a 2002 Excellence in Teaching Award from the Johns Hopkins University Alumni Association. His Ph.D. in Computer Science is from New York University.

G. Reza Djavanshir is an Assistant Professor of Information Technology in the Graduate Division of Business and Management at Johns Hopkins University. Dr. Djavanshir participates in IT Department's activities, including program evaluation and redesign efforts. Prior to joining the Johns Hopkins' SPSPE-Graduate Division of Business and Management he was a member of the Team in BBN/GTE/Telenet Corporation Products Development Division. Dr. Djavanshir was also a Senior Technologist and Vice President of Citicorp's Global Information Systems. Dr. Djavanshir was a Lead Scientist at Mitretek Systems, Inc. where he worked on Business Process Re-engineering and Technology upgrades of the US Postal Service; he also worked on NASA Systems Engineering projects. Dr. Djavanshir has published articles in conference proceedings and journals. He is currently at work on a paper that will look at the failure of IT strategies for Dot Com companies. Dr. Djavanshir obtained his Doctor of Science degree in Systems Engineering from the George Washington University.

1

The "Write" Stuff

Learning Objectives

■ To understand that employers regard communications skills as the top area where employees, especially in the information technology field, are deficient

■ To learn some of the basic tenets of technical writing

■ To learn to write executive summaries and discussion papers

■ To practice "e-mail etiquette" in composing e-mail messages

■ To ask the right questions for critical thinking

Introduction

What typically separates one individual from another in the eyes of the employer? Is it subject-matter expertise? Is it knowledge of the organization's historical background? Or is it the people and "soft" skills?

Many information technology (IT) employers complain that their employees, especially new graduates, have a solid technical background but are lacking in oral and written communications skills. The ability to speak and write well is a critical attribute that is becoming increasingly important in our professional and daily lives. Consider these facts:[1]

According to Phil Pfeiffer's "What Employers Want from Students" (Association for Computing Machinery, http://www.acm.org/membership/student/emplymntart.html), a key recurring requirement from his study of 15 firms was the need for "communications skills." In this study, communications skills cover a wide range of abilities, including:

• strong written and spoken English
• the ability to help customers understand their requirements
• the ability to ask questions—for example, in an interview situation
• the ability to respond to questions quickly and concisely
• the ability to sell oneself
• the ability to create clear metaphors that communicate a system's purpose.

John Rossheim's article[2] indicates that less-tangible skills desired by nearly all employers include management and communications abilities, knowing how to work as part of a team, and a keen sense of business ethics. The IEEE-USA (Institute of Electrical and Electronics Engineers) in its "Testimony on Educating Our Workforce with Technology Skills Needed to Compete in the 21st Century" echoes these findings by stating, "Underlying all of this is the need to develop the critical analytical, communications and problem solving skills that people need to succeed in a fast-changing, technology-driven workplace" (http://www.ieeeusa.org/forum/POLICY/1998/98mar24.html).

Becker et al.[3] in their study of communication skills of technical professionals reconfirmed the need for more communication skills education and training for IS (Information Systems) students.

It is clearly evident that possessing communications skills is paramount for IT workers to have a successful career. Many IT students may feel that they need to know just about the bits and bytes and techno stuff. But in order to move up through the ranks of management, or even to stay on the technology side, proper communications skills are essential. For example, in order to be able to gather user requirements or be the liaison for translating the technology jargon into something that management will adequately understand, communications skills play a key role.

So, you may feel that you already write well, and there is no need to learn more about technical writing. Let's see how much you really know, simply about the basic rules of grammar.

Warm-Up Exercise

Here is a 50-question multiple-choice freshman English final to test how well you know some basic rules of grammar (http://www.uvsc.edu/owl/tests/final2.html). Circle the appropriate answer for each question, taking **only 15 minutes** to complete the quiz. The correct answers are shown at the back of the chapter.

1. The sentences in 1–8 form a paragraph.
   Leonardo da Vinci lived from 1452 to 1519 and he was one of the world's greatest geniuses.
   a. The clauses are correctly punctuated.
   b. The clauses need a comma added.
   c. The clauses need a semicolon added.

2. No one who lived before or after him has achieved so much in so many different fields.
   a. The clauses are correctly punctuated.
   b. The clauses need a comma added.
   c. The clauses need a semicolon added.

3. He was an outstanding painter and architect he also designed bridges, highways, weapons, costumes, and scientific instruments.
   a. The clauses are correctly punctuated.
   b. The clauses need a comma added.
   c. The clauses need a semicolon added.

4. He also invented the diving bell and the tank.
   a. The clauses are correctly punctuated.
   b. The clauses need a comma added.
   c. The clauses need a semicolon added.

5. Although they could not be built with the materials of the time he invented flying machines.
   a. The clauses are correctly punctuated.
   b. The clauses need a comma added.
   c. The clauses need a semicolon added.

6. Da Vinci approached science and art in the same manner that he made sketches to help him solve problems.
   a. The clauses are correctly punctuated.
   b. The clauses need a comma added.
   c. The clauses need a semicolon added.

7. He saw no difference between planning a machine and planning a painting.
   a. The clauses are correctly punctuated.
   b. The clauses need a comma added.
   c. The clauses need a semicolon added.

8. Even though he did a lot of things da Vinci is probably best known for his painting The Mona Lisa.
   a. The clauses are correctly punctuated.
   b. The clauses need a comma added.
   c. The clauses need a semicolon added.

9. In sentences 9–14, select the correct verb form to fill in the blank.
   The strong winds had _____ since early this morning.
   a. blown
   b. blew

10. Jake has _____ to go to the University of Utah next year.
    a. chose
    b. chosen

11. Thousands of angry customers have _____ the Better Business Bureau.
    a. written
    b. wrote

12. The wind chime _____ in the gentle breeze.
    a. swang
    b. swung

13. The cowboy had _____ in many rodeos throughout his life.
    a. ridden
    b. rode

14. Celine Dion _____ with great emotion at the concert.
    a. sung
    b. sang

15. The following sentences make a paragraph. Check the verb tense in the first sentence. Then decide if the verb tense in each of the following sentences is correct or incorrect.
    First sentence: Scientists perform a lot of experiments to observe important things.

For example, scientists raise fleas in labs to learn more about how these pests caused disease in humans.
a. Correct
b. Incorrect/shifts

16. The fleas are kept in special jars that contain sieves.
a. Correct
b. Incorrect/shifts

17. The fleas lay eggs in the jars, and these eggs drop through the sieves.
a. Correct
b. Incorrect/shifts

18. The scientists collected the eggs so they can raise more fleas from them.
a. Correct
b. Incorrect/shifts

19. The jars also have tubes that carry warm water to heat blood that is contained underneath a skin-like sheath.
a. Correct
b. Incorrect/shifts

20. The fleas bit through this sheath to drink the blood, which served as their food.
a. Correct
b. Incorrect/shifts

21. Interestingly, these laboratory breeding grounds are called "fake pups."
a. Correct
b. Incorrect/shifts

22. In sentences 22–31, choose the correct pronoun case for the blank.
Between you and _____, I thought the math exam was really hard.
a. me
b. I

23. Ryan and _____ are sure to take first place in the poetry contest this year.
a. him
b. he

24. Even though Jessica is smarter than _____, she rarely gets A's in her classes.
a. he
b. him

25. Some of _____ students thought the tuition hike was unfair.
a. we
b. us

26. _____ fans thought the game was poorly refereed.
a. We
b. Us

27. Do you know _____ won the race?
a. who
b. whom

28. The president wants to know _____ will volunteer to help.
a. who
b. whom

29. The argument is between his girlfriend and _____.
a. he
b. him

30. Can you go to the party with Daniella and _____?
a. I
b. Me

31. Is that the president? Yes, that is _____.
a. he
b. him

32. Choose the correct adjective or adverb form for the blanks in sentences 32–36.
Professor Smith explained the directions _____ before he passed out the test.
a. quick
b. quickly

33. This is the _____ case of flu I've ever had.
a. baddest
b. worse
c. worst

34. Mark did _____ in his job interview because he wasn't prepared.
a. bad
b. badly

35. My friend Shauna plays the piano really _____.
a. good
b. well

36. That was a _____ good movie, wasn't it?
a. really
b. real

37. In numbers 37–41, one sentence of each pair contains a dangling or misplaced modifier. Choose the letter of the sentence in which the modifiers are used <u>correctly</u>.
a. Walking across the street, a truck turned the corner and narrowly missed the pedestrian.
b. While I was walking across the street, a truck turned the corner and narrowly missed me.

38. a. Feeling the chill in the air, I felt a roaring fire in the fireplace sounded perfect.
b. Feeling the chill in the air, a fire in the fireplace sounded perfect.

39. a. Frightened by the menacing dog, my knees began to shake.
   b. My knees began to shake because I was frightened by the menacing dog.

40. a. Unsure of the best course of action, he had a hard time making a decision.
   b. Unsure of the best course of action, the decision was difficult to make.

41. a. Tired after a full day's work, a nap was what I needed.
   b. Tired after a full day's work, I needed a nap.

42. Choose the correct word for each blank in sentences 42–50.
   You should follow my _____ and go back to school.
   a. advise
   b. advice

43. As soon as Jeremy completes the economics course, he will be _____ to graduate.
   a. already
   b. all ready

44. When the police officer _____ the warehouse, she saw the flames.
   a. passed
   b. past

45. How was I _____ to know the answer to that hard question?
   a. suppose
   b. supposed

46. Diana would rather quit school _____ sell her stamp collection for tuition money.
   a. then
   b. than

47. A week is _____ long for me to be gone during the semester.
   a. to
   b. two
   c. too

48. _____ turn is it to drive to work today?
   a. Whose
   b. Who's

49. _____ coming with us, aren't you?
   a. Your
   b. You're

50. The project is going to take _____ of time.
   a. a lot
   b. alot

▮▮▮ Basic Tenets of Technical Writing

Some people, like Dennis Baron (a professor of English and linguistics at the University of Illinois at Urbana-Champaign), feel that teaching grammar doesn't lead to better writing. Professor Baron believes that in studying grammar, more is good, but writing more is what is really needed to help students' writing performance.[4] There are some key tenets to be followed for good writing: understandability, clarity, simplicity, conciseness, accuracy, and completeness. Let's take a look at each of these areas.

Understandability

Understandability refers to "writing to the audience." Authors should gear their writing to fit the audience's background and needs. The same holds true when giving a speech. Speakers would tailor a speech differently if speaking to an audience of engineers versus a group of senior executives. "Know thy audience" is an important principle to keep in mind when writing (or speaking). If the writing is, for example, too technical the message may be lost. If the writing is too flowery and general, the message may be perceived as lacking depth and considered superficial. A careful balance between breadth and depth must be maintained in order to maximize the understandability of the writing.

Clarity

Clarity deals with how well the writing flows throughout the document or report. Proper use of grammar, segues and transitions, introductory and concluding statements, and other elements are important to maintaining the clarity of the writing. If the writing does not flow well, the message will be jumbled and garbled. Providing structure to the writing, from the perspective of both organization and content, will increase clarity.

Simplicity

An old observation is that if people don't know what they are talking about, they may tend to use "large words" and go into unnecessary detail to mask their lack of knowledge of the subject. Simple, straightforward expression is usually preferred to dissertation mode. Simplicity is elegance, and the ability to write in meaningful, yet simplified, ways is a wonderful talent to develop.

Conciseness

A well-known author once said, "I don't have time to write you a short letter, so here is a long one instead." Being long-winded probably lessens the reader's attention. Try to be concise, to the point, and to condense the material in a meaningful way. As the previous quote suggests, being succinct and concise is not an easy task. It is often easier to use lengthy verbiage than to synthesize and summarize the key thoughts. Writing concisely, as in executive summaries or abstracts, is a special talent that needs to be practiced.

Accuracy

Without question, one must be very accurate in writing. Citing appropriate sources, providing facts, and offering opinions with supportive evidence are important in writing. Contradictory statements, which will confuse the reader, should be avoided. Opinions are fine to express, but the assumptions behind the opinions should be presented to the reader.

Completeness

The last major tenet to keep in mind when writing deals with completeness. Completeness has to do with the fullness of the thoughts presented. In other words, the writer should not express incomplete thoughts and should tie loose ends together in the writing. For example, if a report covers the systems development life cycle and testing is omitted from the description of the life cycle, then this would probably constitute a major omission, for the life cycle would be incomplete. Thus, the testing stage should be included.

As you write, try to keep these basic tenets in mind. Now, let's take a look at some of the typical types of writing that an IT professional should know how to do. These include executive summaries, e-mail messages, and discussion papers. Feasibility studies, proposals, technical reports, and evaluation studies will be covered in subsequent chapters.

▪▪▪ Writing Executive Summaries

Most bosses want to know the essence of what you want to share with them. They typically have very busy schedules and want to be able to pick up the key points of what you have learned in a particular assignment. They want you to be able to condense and synthesize your analysis into your essential findings. How many times have you planned a 30-minute presentation to your senior management only to find that due to schedule constraints, you have now been asked to present the salient points in just 10 minutes?

Executive summaries are included with most reports. In the military, executive summaries are usually no longer than 15 sentences. Oftentimes, military summaries are one page of bullet points. In the same manner, abstracts in technical papers serve as executive summaries. Abstracts are typically no longer than 100–150 words.

Why are executive summaries so difficult to write? First, if you are involved let's say, with a year-long project, you may develop a rather lengthy report on the background, data collection, analysis, and findings. It isn't easy to condense the key information into one page or less. Second, most people tend to be verbose, so synthesizing the information into the critical thoughts can be hard to do. Last, the ability to synthesize ideas is also difficult to acquire. Let's look at some good and poor examples of executive summaries or abstracts.

First Example: Abstract of a Presentation

An Operational Study of Knowledge Management

The focus of the talk will be on an operational study of knowledge management activities in a leading philanthropic organization. As part of this study, an instrument was developed and used to determine knowledge sharing effectiveness in the organization. Based upon interviews and the survey responses, the knowledge sharing effectiveness was formulated in terms of communications flow, knowledge management environment, knowledge measurement, and organizational facilitation. Recommendations were then made which helped to create an improved knowledge management strategy for the organization.

This example is a mediocre type of abstract for a presentation. Its good point is that it gives a general idea of what was done. However, its weak point is that it is too general and doesn't give specific findings and recommendations. An improved abstract for this talk might be the following:

Improved Version of the Abstract

An Operational Study of Knowledge Management

The focus of the talk will be on an operational study of knowledge management activities in a leading philanthropic organization. A knowledge sharing effectiveness survey was developed and administered in the organization, with follow up interviews. Based upon interviews and the survey responses, the overall knowledge sharing effectiveness for the organization was a "C" on an "A to F" scale, in terms of communications flow, knowledge management environment, knowledge measurement, and organizational facilitation. Specific recommendations for knowledge sharing improvement include developing an incentive program for rewarding knowledge sharing behavior, embedding knowledge sharing activities within the daily work life, and concentrating on the people and culture components versus strictly technology.

The purpose of the executive summary is to inform the reader what the report concludes, not what it is about. For example, the following summary, which provides information on what was studied, but not the results of the investigation, can be improved:

> An earthquake occurring near Punkville in 1983 was studied. Evidence from seismology was used to determine the focal mechanism and location of the earthquake. Field investigation confirmed the orientation and mechanism of the faulting. (http://www.mines.utah.edu/~wmep/LE_136/Termproject/Group.html)

An improved version of this summary, which includes a discussion of the results and conclusions, is:

> Seismological records and surface studies indicate that the 1983 Punkville earthquake resulted from dip slip movement on a normal fault. P-first motion directions from 42 seismometers in the region indicate normal motion on a fault striking due north and dipping 45 degrees to the west. Field investigation of the earthquake location revealed a fresh scarp 1 meter high striking north. Trenches dug across the scarp showed a fault dipping 70 degrees west. (http://www.mines.utah.edu/~wmep/LE_136/Termproject/Group.html)

What can be deduced from these examples with respect to writing executive summaries? Follow the format—set up, show up, and shut up. In other words, "set up" in describing the task at hand, "show up" in terms of showing the key findings, and "shut up" after indicating the specific recommendations. Be succinct and write no more than one or two paragraphs for the summary.

EXERCISE

1. Read a report or paper, and write the executive summary or abstract.
2. Find an existing executive summary, and refine it following the guidance presented in this chapter.
3. You have been asked to write an executive summary for your Chief Information Officer (CIO) on the key elements of data mining. Prepare a summary that highlights these key components.

Beware of Spell-Checkers

Dennis Galletta, an information systems professor at the University of Pittsburgh, indicates that spell-checking software is so sophisticated that many people trust it too thoroughly.[5] In a spell-check software study, Galletta found that the software helped students to find and correct errors in a one-page letter, but in some cases, the spell-checking software changed phrases or sentences flagged by the software as grammatically suspicious, even though they were correct. In the study, a passage read, "Michael Bales would be the best candidate. Bales has proven himself in similar rolls." The software suggested changing the verb from "has" to "have" because it thought "Bales" was plural. Also, the spell-checker didn't indicate a problem with "rolls," which should actually have been spelled "roles."

We are not suggesting that spell-checkers should not be used. The writer should just be careful not to rely solely on the spell-checker to pick up errors in the written document. All of us can tell similar stories about where spell-checkers failed. For example, one university letter said that "you must have 'faulty' support" instead of "faculty" support. The spell-checker didn't catch this one. A more embarrassing example is a school letterhead that left out the "l" in "Public Management." Spell-checkers, according to Galletta's study, could damage the work of writers and editors who place too much trust in them. However, in spite of these potential limitations, spell-checkers are a wonderful invention.

Our Top-10 List of Common Errors in English

Over the past 20 years, the authors have graded thousands of essays, tests, papers, reports, and projects. Based on this experience, here is the top-10 list of common errors in English:

10. *Irregardless* instead of *regardless:* "irregardless" is not a word.
9. *Advice* versus *advise:* "Advice" is a noun and "advise" is a verb.
8. *Embarass* instead of *embarrass:* Embarrass has two *r*'s and two *s*'s.
7. *Accomodate* instead of *accommodate:* "Accommodate" has two *c*'s and two *m*'s.
6. *Ocassion* instead of *occasion:* Remember two *c*'s and one *s*.

5. *For all intensive purposes* instead of *For all intents and purposes*: Use the second phrase.

4. *The effect* versus *the affect*: "Effect" is typically used as the noun and "affect" is the verb.

3. *Their* versus *there*: "Their" is possessive.

2. *Principal* versus *principle*: Remember that the "princip<u>al</u> is your pal."

1. *It's* versus *its*: "It's" means "it is"; "its" is possessive.

Think of these the next time you compose a letter, write a proposal, or send an e-mail.

▪▪▪ E-mail Etiquette

Besides writing summaries, the IT professional (as well as everyone today) is actively involved in sending e-mail messages. Everyone has horror stories about experiences with e-mails. For example, did you ever accidentally hit "reply to all recipients" and send your e-mail to everyone, instead of sending it only to the sender of the e-mail? Did you ever respond in a hasty manner with many typos or incorrect grammar? Have you ever responded to a strongly worded e-mail from your boss without taking the necessary time to collect your thoughts? And have you ever not copied or copied someone on an e-mail when you should or should not have done so?

In the professional world, e-mail is like the blood that flows through the body. Everyone has it, uses it, and relies on it. There are some general hints that you should consider when sending e-mail. Here are a few of them.

First, don't always just "react" to e-mail. Give some thought to what you are writing, even though e-mail is considered to be an informal way of communicating. Using improper grammar or spelling and expressing incohesive thoughts may not present you in the best light.

Second, count to at least 50 (or don't even reply until the next day, to collect your thoughts and composure) before you respond to hostile, strongly worded e-mail. Some e-mail that you receive from your boss, for example, may set you on edge. Instead of quickly responding with disgust, take some time to collect your thoughts and respond in a professional manner. Provide constructive, diplomatic remarks and convey a professional image.

Third, try to avoid using bold letters, capitals, and other potentially annoying symbols. One problem with e-mail is that recipients could tend to "read into" the message something you did not intend. Be careful how you use certain symbols, as mixed messages may sometimes be created.

Fourth, be cognizant of the individuals you copy on your e-mails. Sometimes you may want to copy people so that they are informed and don't feel you are going behind their back. But you may annoy people if you are constantly copying them on e-mails that you send. Be judicious in your selection of recipients, and sometimes consider using blind copies when appropriate.

Last, don't write long-winded e-mail messages. If you need to have a lengthy discussion, perhaps the phone would be best. Or maybe an attachment would be useful, if appropriate. Many people seem to get annoyed if they have to read a "dissertation"-lengthy e-mail message, so be prudent in how you construct your e-mail.

E-mail Examples

What Not to Do

To: jay1@xyz.com
From: janedoe@xyz.com
Jay: I reviewed your report and I was disappointed in the content and depth of analysis. I expect a lot more out of you. You'll have to stay up all night revising it, as it's due tomorrow morning. Leave it on my desk when you are done. Jane

What Should Have Been Done

To: jay1@xyz.com
From: janedoe@xyz.com
Jay: Hi. Thanks for sending your report to me. I had a chance to review the report and it looks like you have done a good amount of work. The report probably needs to also include a recommendations section and should delve deeper in the analysis. Unfortunately, the report is due tomorrow morning, which will press you a bit. Could we offer you some assistance in trying to complete the report to meet the deadline? We are almost there . . . Jane

Observations: The first e-mail was strongly worded and bordered on a lack of professionalism. Even though many people tend to write e-mails without thinking of the full consequences, this e-mail showed a lack of diplomacy. The second e-mail is written in a softer and more diplomatic tone than the first e-mail. It provides constructive guidance on how to improve the report, reinforces the deadline date, and offers assistance in order to meet the deadline. It doesn't "put down" Jay and gets the message across in a helpful, tactful way.

E-mail Exercises

1. You just received a strongly worded e-mail from your boss about your lack of teamwork skills, and you feel you need to respond. Construct a short e-mail to respond to your boss.
2. You were just sent a blind copy of an e-mail from one of your colleagues in which your boss indicates that he isn't pleased with your performance. Should you respond by e-mail to your boss or colleague, meet in person with your boss, or not take any action?
3. Write an e-mail that tries to capture the attention of a potential source for funds for developing your new software concept.

▪▪▪ Writing Discussion Papers

Besides composing e-mail messages and writing executive summaries, a typical type of writing engaged in by IT professionals involves discussion papers. A discussion paper is often used to summarize some of the thoughts expressed by the IT professional and the client/customer with respect to the type of work to be performed. It is usually an informal letter that precedes the submission of a formal proposal to the client. The letter serves as a "discussion paper" to highlight the key issues covered in meetings between the IT professional and the client.

In his book *Managerial Consulting Skills,* Charles Margerison typically uses the discussion paper approach to match the expectations of the IT professional/consultant and the client, before a formal contract proposal is sent by the IT professional.[6] The discussion paper serves as a review of understandings and options and enumerates some ideas for further discussion per the initial conversations with the client. This document is not so much a proposal as a summary or review of the discussions that have been held so far.

Then, as part of the discussion paper, various alternatives for accomplishing the task are listed, in order to give the client a range of options for added flexibility. Once agreement and direction are established by the client, then a formal proposal can be submitted by the IT professional to the client for resolution and negotiations. By using the discussion paper as the mechanism for input by the client, the proposal and eventual contract easily emerge from the process. Margerison greatly favors this informal discussion paper route versus submitting a formal proposal right away without sufficient data, which puts the client in an awkward take it-or-leave-it position. An example of a discussion letter follows.

Sample Discussion Letter/Paper

September 8, 2005

Dear Janet:

It was a pleasure meeting with you today to learn about the challenges facing you as you embark on your knowledge management journey for your organization. As you discussed, you have a great need for developing metrics to measure the success of your knowledge management pilots, especially your online communities of practice. Your online communities have been in use for the past six months and you and other senior management would like to know how successful they have been towards creating some value-added benefit to the organization.

As we discussed, I have been doing work in this area for quite a while. One approach that could be used is to develop key system, output, and outcome measures and relate them to your online communities. Surveying the members of the communities and the online community facilitators, through a Web-based survey, would help to collect some of the necessary data. Focus groups could be used here as well.

Another approach could be to observe the discussions in the communities and see what types of anecdotes and vignettes are generated in terms of how the advice from the online community interaction has helped the community members. This would be more of an ethnographic study, but could generate some interesting measures, success stories, and lessons learned.

As you had indicated in our discussions, both approaches have advantages and limitations, but the first approach may provide more specific data and feedback for developing metrics for how well these online communities have been performing. Each approach would probably take about 3 months to conduct, which seems to be aligned with your schedule.

Kindly let me know if I have properly summarized our understandings. If so, I will be happy to submit a formal proposal to initiate the work.

Best regards.

Sincerely,

Jay Liebowitz

▪▪▪ Asking the Right Questions

Whether writing discussion papers or simply interviewing potential users of IT systems, the ability to be a critical thinker and ask the right questions is an important skill to possess. According to Neil Browne and Stuart Keeley's book *Asking the Right Questions,* critical thinking refers to[7]

- An awareness of a set of interrelated critical questions;
- An ability to ask and answer critical questions at appropriate times;
- A desire to actively use the critical questions.

Being cognizant of asking possible interrelated critical questions contributes to becoming a critical thinker. For example, if a U.S. company decides to offshore its IT help desk operations to India, the underlying critical question is "Will this IT offshoring be a cost-saver for the company?" Interrelated critical questions may be "Is the company concerned with trying to improve the U.S. economy by keeping IT jobs in the United States?" and "Should the company teach the appropriate U.S. dialects to the IT help desk personnel in India so Americans may not know that they are really calling for help in India?" The first interrelated critical question deals with the larger picture of keeping IT jobs and employment intact in the United States, thereby stimulating the American economy. The second interrelated question relates to whether IT users will feel comfortable in contacting someone for help outside of the United States. Knowing when to ask and answer such questions is part of the analysis stage in determining the feasibility of IT offshoring. Possessing an active desire to use critical questions provides the stimulation and intellectual curiosity to make appropriate decisions.

According to Browne and Keeley, there are 11 key questions to ask as part of the critical thinking process:

1. What are the issues and the conclusion?
2. What are the reasons?
3. Which words or phrases are ambiguous?
4. What are the value conflicts and assumptions?
5. What are the descriptive assumptions?
6. Are there any fallacies in the reasoning?
7. How good is the evidence?
8. Are there rival causes?
9. Are the statistics deceptive?
10. What significant information is omitted?
11. What reasonable conclusions are possible?

Let's take a look at an example to see how these questions can be applied as part of the critical thinking process in order to improve communications and decision making.

An Example of Critical Thinking

The CIO (Chief Information Officer) of the company that employs you just returned from a business trip; on the flight home, she was reading an article about knowledge management. The article discussed how organizations were using knowledge management strategies in order to better leverage knowledge internally and externally. They were reaping benefits through knowledge management by increasing innovation, improving customer relations, and increasing employee morale. The article highlighted the use of a lessons-learned/best-practices system that allowed employees to share their knowledge and helpful tips with each other.

Your CIO has asked you to look into the possibility of having a similar lessons-learned system for the company. She asks you to read the article and critically review it to determine if a lessons-learned system would be worthwhile and used by the employees. After reading this article, you set out to apply your critical thinking skills to help in your decision-making process.

The first critical thinking question is to determine the issue and conclusion presented in the article. The issue will sometimes be revealed to the reader by the writer. For example, an excerpt from the article read by the CIO is as follows:

> Many organizations are using lessons-learned systems in order to not reinvent the wheel and to increase knowledge sharing in the organization. Lessons-learned systems have been applied in such situations as having Xerox repair technicians exchange tips for repairing Xerox copiers, having NASA project team employees share lessons learned in project management, and engaging Hallmark employees and customers in online communities for generating new ideas and sharing insights. For organizations to succeed in the competitive knowledge economy, they must be willing to have their employees "work smarter" and in more productive ways. Lessons-learned systems are one such way for promoting a knowledge-sharing culture in the organization and stimulating innovation.

In reviewing this excerpt, you may decide that the author is saying that the issue at hand is organizations need to better share what they know to be competitive in the years ahead. The conclusion may be that having lessons-learned systems is a viable way to instill knowledge sharing within an organization.

After determining the issue and conclusion, the next step is to uncover the communicator's reasons. Browne and Keeley, list some words that identify reasons:

> for the reason that . . .
> in addition . . .
> because of the fact that . . .
> in view of . . .
> for example . . .
> is supported by . . .
> researchers found that . . .

Let's take a look at another passage in the article:

> Building and nurturing a knowledge-sharing culture in an organization can reap great rewards. For example, one NASA project team avoided 9 months and $10 million of rework by learning from their lessons-learned system that certain satellite testing equipment shouldn't be used at a particular facility due to vibration testing control problems. Without sharing this knowledge through the lessons-learned system, it may have been difficult to have learned this information, especially since the resident project team and testing facilities were 3,000 miles away from each other.

From this passage, one reason for the need to share knowledge and use lessons-learned systems is to not re-create the same problem. Identifying the reason can be triggered by the "for example" sentence in this passage.

After studying the reasons why knowledge-sharing and lessons-learned systems may be useful in organizations, you should next look at words or phrases that may be ambiguous. In other words, are concepts and ideas well defined in the article and is there any loaded language? For example, if the article stated that "knowledge management produces value-added benefits," is there evidence in the article that shows what value-added benefits are derived? Perhaps the article states that "knowledge sharing is a revenue enhancer"; "revenue enhancer" has a positive connotation. You should also realize that some negative aspects of sharing knowledge are suggested. One such issue may deal with the reluctance of employees to share what they know because they may feel they would lose their competitive edge.

The fourth question to ask yourself is "What are the value conflicts and assumptions?" Browne and Keeley name "competition-collaboration" as a value conflict. For example, males may tend to compete and females may tend to collaborate. These tendencies may affect how well knowledge sharing can take place in your organization. Such value conflicts may be expressed as "Should I share my experiences and rules of thumb through a lessons-learned system so that all employees (and potential internal competitors) could have access to my gems of knowledge? It would be nice to collaborate in this manner, but at the same time, I may be at risk of losing my competitive edge that has taken many years of experience to learn."

The next questions as part of the critical thinking process are intended to determine if there are descriptive assumptions and any fallacies in the reasoning process. Descriptive assumptions refer to hidden beliefs, and some of these beliefs may not be valid according to your worldview. For example, let's assume the article states:

> Lessons-learned systems are most valuable when they use a push approach to send appropriate new lessons to the user when those lessons match the user's interest profile.

In this passage, there is a descriptive assumption that users should like a lessons-learned system because it can proactively disseminate lessons to them. However, this assumption may not be true, because users may get annoyed if lessons get constantly sent to them on a daily basis. Perhaps the compromise is to send appropriate new lessons to users on some periodic basis (e.g., weekly, biweekly, monthly) at the user's discretion to avoid user information overload.

Besides descriptive assumptions, you should check for fallacies in reasoning. For example, the knowledge-sharing article may imply that technology is the key element in making knowledge management work in an organization. This is probably a faulty statement, as most people believe that people, process, and cultural issues usually trump technology in relation to knowledge management. Technology is an enabler for knowledge management, but the cultural issues in creating an environment (e.g., through an incentive system) for encouraging knowledge sharing in an organization are regarded as being more important than knowledge management technologies alone. Thus, the knowledge-sharing article probably has a false assumption and faulty reasoning.

Looking for the goodness of the evidence, rival causes, and deceptive statistics should also be part of the critical thinking process when reviewing an article or listening to a speaker. For example, if a small sample size or low response rate is used in the analysis, then the conclusions may be speculative or unfounded. The goodness of the evidence is based partly on the research methods applied. Is case study analysis or a formal hypothesis-testing method used in the study? It may be difficult to generalize using a case study approach, whereas a more quantitative method, like hypothesis testing, may be preferred in a given situation. You should also be aware of assigning correlation or causation where none exists. Think about the possibility of rival causes by asking yourself, "Can I interpret the evidence in another way?" Be careful of evidence that shows only percentages—look for the absolute numbers upon which the percentages are based. For example, showing a 100 percent increase may suggest something spectacular, but what if the data only increased from 1 to 2? These raw numbers show a small sample size; if you looked only at the percentage increase, then you may conclude the results were dramatic.

The last two questions to ponder when applying critical thinking processes relate to what significant information is omitted and what reasonable conclusions can be drawn. For example, if a survey is used and the sample size and response rate are omitted, then this may be an omission of significant information. Additionally, be careful that quotes aren't taken out of context. When reading an article or listening to a presentation, think about what alternative conclusions can be reached based upon the information presented. Compare the author's conclusions with other possible conclusions that could be derived from the evidence presented in the article or speech.

SUMMARY

This chapter tried to convey a number of key ideas. First, being able to write well is a critical skill to possess in any discipline, including information technology. Second, knowing the rules of grammar and writing often will increase the chances of improving one's writing. Think about the various common mistakes made in writing, and beware of strict reliance on spell-checkers. As much of one's writing on a daily basis is through e-mail, remember to apply the various tenets of writing and proper etiquette to e-mail. Being able to synthesize one's thoughts in an executive summary or abstract is no easy feat. Practice will help achieve proficiency in writing these summaries. Third, writing discussion papers may prove to be invaluable in terms of winning contracts. Last, asking the right questions will facilitate critical thinking and a better understanding of what the speaker or writer is conveying.

EXERCISES

1. Two of the key issues facing today's Chief Information Officers are cost reductions and security. Write an executive summary, intended for your chief information officer, that highlights the factors underlying the issues relating to cost reductions and IT security.
2. As a middle manager in your organization, you have been told that much of your staff's IT work will now be outsourced to India. You have some strong concerns about going in this direction. Construct an e-mail to your boss that expresses your feelings about this situation.
3. You have been invited to work 10 weeks full time on a student summer research fellowship in a state other than where you go to school and live. Unfortunately, due to some recent family conflicts, you are unable to work on-site at the fellowship's research location. Craft an e-mail that summarizes your situation and leaves open the possibility of exploring other opportunities or arrangements for working with this organization.

4. An organization is interested in having you do some IT consulting work to help them develop an enterprise-wide IT strategy. Before submitting a formal proposal, you want to further clarify the scope of the work involved through writing a discussion paper. Write a brief discussion paper that further delineates the expectations of the organization and yours as the consultant.

5. You just received an e-mail from the IT department, copied to your boss, that accuses you of inappropriately accessing non-work-related sites during working hours. You feel strongly that you haven't done anything improper and proceed to craft an e-mail to express your feelings.

ANSWERS TO WARM-UP EXERCISES ▪▪▪▪▪▪▪

1. b	18. b	35. b
2. a	19. a	36. a
3. c	20. b	37. b
4. a	21. a	38. a
5. b	22. a	39. b
6. a	23. b	40. a
7. a	24. a	41. b
8. b	25. b	42. b
9. a	26. a	43. b
10. b	27. a	44. a
11. a	28. a	45. b
12. a	29. b	46. b
13. a	30. b	47. c
14. b	31. a	48. a
15. b	32. b	49. b
16. a	33. c	50. a
17. a	34. b	

ENDNOTES ▪▪▪▪▪▪▪

1. Liebowitz, J. (January–February, 2004). "Teaching the Importance of Communications in IT." *IT Professional.* IEEE Computer Society. pp. 38–42.
2. Rossheim, J., *The Skills Gap and the American Workforce.* http://www.featured reports.monster.com/laborshortage/skills.
3. Becker, J., R. Insley, and M. Endres (April 1997). "Communication Skills of Technical Professionals: A Report for Schools of Business Administration." *Computer Personnel.* Association for Computing Machinery Special Interest Group in Computer Personnel Research (ACM SIGCPR).
4. Barron, D. (May 16, 2003). "Teaching Grammar Doesn't Lead to Better Writing." *Chronicle of Higher Education.*
5. Galletta, D. (March 14, 2003). http://www.globetechnology.com.
6. Margerison, C. (2001). *Managerial Consulting Skills: A Practical Guide.* UK: Gower Publishing.
7. Browne, N., and Keeley, S. (2001). *Asking the Right Questions: A Guide to Critical Thinking,* 6th ed. Englewood Cliffs, NJ: Prentice Hall.

Eliciting and Writing User Requirements

Learning Objectives

- To learn the techniques of listening effectively
- To understand and apply various methods for eliciting user requirements
- To learn how to write functional requirements and understand their role in a software requirements specification document

Introduction

According to Terry Pack, program coordinator for the Professional Master's Program in Natural Sciences at Rice University, a major part of any business position requires an ability to listen.[1] Listening effectively and knowing various techniques for eliciting user requirements are key skills needed not only in the business world but also in the information technology field and everyday life. A *Washington Post* article by Amy Joyce conveyed a similar message, indicating that communication ability, consistency, and respect for employees are critical traits that make one boss better than another.[2] Honesty was also identified as a leading trait that makes someone a good boss.

Let's now take a look at listening skills as well as techniques for determining user requirements needed for information systems projects.

Listening Effectively

Many physicians are good diagnosticians because they "listen" to what the patient is saying, especially when taking a history of the patient and having the patient describe symptoms. In the same manner, systems analysts also need to be effective listeners and interviewers in order to gather the set of user requirements for systems design and development.

Many individuals apply "active listening" skills. Active listening has four components: clarifying, paraphrasing, reflecting feelings, and summarizing. Specifically, according to Mark Gorkin, these steps are[3]

- "Clarifying: asking the other party to provide more information, to elaborate upon their statement or answer specific questions;
- Paraphrasing: repeating the other's message in the person's words or your own words;
- Reflecting feelings: inquiring about or acknowledging overt or underlying feelings that are attached to the other party's communication;
- Summarizing: reviewing what has just been told."

In the sales environment, active listening skills can consist of the following: "often looks to paraphrase to test one's interpretation of what had been said; ensures one is in the right frame of mind for all important sales discussions; allows people to finish what they are saying without interruption; fully focuses one's attention and concentrates on what is being said; ensures that one's body language is positively conducive to active listening."[4]

According to the University of Minnesota-Duluth *Student Handbook*, "the average college student spends about 14 hours per week in class listening (or perhaps I should say "hearing"—there is a difference!) to lectures." The *Handbook* recommends various listening strategies for listening in class that can be generalized to other listening situations[5]:

- "Maintain eye contact with the instructor. Of course you will need to look at your notebook to write your notes, but eye contact keeps you focused on the job at hand and keeps you involved in the lecture.
- Focus on content, not delivery. Have you ever counted the number of times a teacher clears his/her throat in a fifteen minute period? If so, you weren't focusing on content.
- Avoid emotional involvement. When you are too emotionally involved in listening, you tend to hear what you want to hear—not what is actually being said. Try to remain objective and open-minded.
- Avoid distractions. Don't let your mind wander or be distracted by the person shuffling papers near you.
- Treat listening as a challenging mental task. Listening to an academic lecture is not a passive act—at least it shouldn't be. You need to concentrate on what is said so that you can process the information into your notes.
- Stay active by asking mental questions. Active listening keeps you on your toes. Here are some questions you can ask yourself as you listen. What key point is the professor making? How does this fit with what I know from previous lectures? How is this lecture organized?
- Use the gap between the rate of speech and your rate of thought. You can think faster than the lecturer can talk. That's one reason your mind may tend to wander. All the above suggestions will help you keep your mind occupied and focused on what is being said. You can actually begin to anticipate what the professor is going to say as a way to keep your mind from straying. Your mind does have the capacity to listen, think, write and ponder at the same time, but it does take practice."

▪▪▪ Knowledge Acquisition

With improved abilities to listen, eliciting requirements from users should be greatly facilitated. This will aid the process of "knowledge acquisition" from the users or experts, which has always been a primary bottleneck in the development of expert systems (i.e., computer programs that emulate the behavior of experts in well-defined tasks). There are many reasons for this bottleneck. One key reason is the knowledge engineering paradox, which states that the more expert an individual, the more compiled is his or her knowledge and the harder it is to elicit or uncover it. Think of asking a driver who has been driving for 30 years the steps he uses to start his car. Then, think of asking a high school student taking a driver's education course. Invariably, the experienced driver will omit several steps, such as adjusting the mirrors and seat and the like, whereas, the high school student learning how to drive will give you all of the steps in the sequence one by one. The experienced driver already has this knowledge ingrained in his head and performs the starting of the car without thinking. His knowledge is compiled, whereas the high school student's knowledge of starting the car isn't yet intuitive. Thus, the knowledge engineering paradox is fulfilled, because it is harder to uncover the compiled knowledge of the experienced driver because he may not be aware of some of the steps he takes, considering them to be simply common sense.

Other key reasons why knowledge acquisition is difficult deal with human biases in judgment (e.g., the recency bias where people are influenced by the most recent events), lack of interviewing skills, inability to decipher large volumes of knowledge acquisition transcripts, and other factors.

Let's take a look at some knowledge acquisition techniques that may prove helpful in eliciting user requirements. Then, we will discuss these requirements and how to incorporate them into the writing of functional user requirements.

Knowledge Acquisition Techniques

The typical methods for extracting knowledge from experts or users are conducting interviews and recording verbal walkthroughs (called *protocol analysis*). Interviews are easy to use and provide instant feedback. Interviewing can be structured or unstructured. For structured interviews, various techniques can be applied. The "method of familiar tasks" can be used to pose typical scenarios to interviewees to find out what their decision-making process is using the scenario. Once the interviewee feels comfortable, then the interviewer can attempt to elicit the rules of thumb gained by expert experience (called *heuristics*) to determine the shortcuts the interviewee may be taking to arrive at a conclusion. Limited information tasks, constrained processing tasks, and the tough-case method are techniques that can be applied to uncover the heuristics. With limited information tasks, the interviewer doesn't give all the typical information that the expert generally uses to reach a decision; the idea is to see what shortcuts the expert may be taking. In constrained processing tasks, the amount of time the expert has to reach a decision is constrained—for example, if the expert typically needs 10 minutes to develop a decision, then the interviewer may give the expert 5 minutes to solve the task—in order to seek out the heuristics the expert uses. In the tough-cases method, the interviewer describes less frequent scenarios (which still must be considered) to the expert to discover how the expert reasons through them. The success of a structured interview relies on the interviewer (sometimes called the *knowledge engineer*) being well acquainted with the domain terminology, having good interviewing skills, and being able to improvise if needed.

Unstructured interviews can also be used to elicit knowledge. The format and line of questioning are not planned in advance. An unstructured interview could be conducted while the expert is at work and the interviewer is observing and questioning the expert's various actions. Some potential difficulties in unstructured interviewing are that experts may repeat and/or contradict themselves, may misuse words associated with logic, and may skip details and leave the interviewer in the dark.

Protocol analysis, called *verbal walkthroughs*, is another knowledge acquisition technique used for eliciting expert or user knowledge. Here, behavior is recorded as the expert engages in normal task behavior with specific typical cases, and this protocol is transcribed and analyzed. The expert or interviewee talks aloud constantly from the time the problem is presented until the solution is reached. The interviewee is instructed not to plan out the answer, but to keep on talking. He or she is asked to verbalize both orally encoded information and other kinds of thought. The interviewee is also asked to follow rapidly changing thoughts dynamically. The interviewer doesn't intervene in the elicitation process unless the interviewee is silent for a long period of time (then the interviewer asks the subject to talk). Empirical studies have revealed, however, that protocol analysis is less effective than interviewing.

WARM-UP EXERCISE

Choose a partner and pick a subject with which both of you have some familiarity, like why you selected the university or your area of study, how to hit a particular tennis serve, or how to cook a favorite meal. Role-play as the interviewer (knowledge engineer) and the expert. Then, switch roles. Apply the listening and knowledge acquisition methods just discussed. Write down a list of if-then rules that result from your discussions.

▪▪▪ Writing Functional Requirements

A requirement is the description of customers' needs, desires, and preferences for products, services, or a system. Therefore, writing well-articulated requirements is the most important task in any technical project. Developing a good requirements document depends on the analyst's oral communications and writing skills to discover, elicit, analyze, articulate, and write the requirements. A well-written requirement must be testable and traceable. It should also provide a concise description of the functions and attributes of the product, service, or system in a structured manner. Functional requirements are an important communications tool for users, programmers, testers, and managers.

A functional requirement is the description of an action that the product, service, or system shall take in order to satisfy its mission. Functional requirements are written using action phrases after the word *shall*. For example, "the system shall compute each student's GPA." A nonfunctional requirement describes the features and attributes that a product, service, or a system *should* have.

TABLE 2-1   Cost to Fix an Error

Error Found in:	High Cost Multiple
Requirements development phase	1
Design phase	Up to 6
Coding or programming phase	Up to 10
Testing and integration	Up to 40
Customer's acceptance testing	Up to 70
Operation	Up to 1,000

Eliciting correct requirements is a critical task in any technical project. Sometimes, the project team members write a requirements document that results in developing and delivering a product, service, or system that doesn't meet the customer's expectations. A small mistake in eliciting the correct requirements can result in significant problems and staggering costs to correct them. According to Barry Boehm, a leading expert in software engineering, the cost of fixing errors in requirements that were not discovered until later stages in software development process can be devastating (see Table 2-1).[6]

According to Boehm, an undetected and miscommunicated requirement uncovered in a software system's operations phase may cost up to 1,000 times more than if it were corrected during the requirement elicitation and development phase.

No matter what the product, service, or system, there must be a set of user functional requirements. In information systems application, functional requirements relate to what the system should be able to do and what the system should look like to the user. As such, there are usually "shall" and "should have" functional requirements. The "shall" requirements are mandatory, "*must* have" requirements. The "should have" functional requirements are "nice to have" types of requirements. For example, if we are designing a car, a "shall" functional requirement would be to include air bags. A "should have" functional requirement may be to include a navigator system within the car.

Functional requirements should be written in a crisp, clear manner. They should be written in the "shall" and "should have" formats and should be modularized by requirement numbers and subnumbers (i.e., 1.0, 1.1, 1.2, etc.). The functional requirements for the NASA Resume Management Module are shown here as a good example to follow. A generic software requirements specification document is also included, which can be used as a helpful guide when incorporating functional requirements into a software requirements specification document.

The Nuances of Writing Functional Requirements

Many designers confuse a functional requirement and a nonfunctional requirement (such as a performance requirement). A simple rule to keep in mind to distinguish between these two sets of requirements is this: A functional requirement answers "what" kinds of questions, whereas a performance requirement answers "how" types of questions. For example, if we were designing a competitive intelligence

National Aeronautics and Space Administration

Functional Requirements

for the

Resume Management Module

Approved by the

HUMAN RESOURCES PROJECTS STEERING COMMITTEE

September 1, 2000

[http://ifmp.nasa.gov/doc/hr/RMSFunc_Req_9.1.00.doc]

Resume Management Functional Requirements

RM 1 The system shall import position descriptions and create vacancy announcements

> RM 1.1   The system shall import a position description (statement or document) from an external system.

> RM 1.2   The system shall assist the user in constructing vacancy announcements that incorporate position descriptive information, qualifications information and instructions to applicants.

> RM 1.3   The system shall maintain a sortable, searcheable and retrievable database of vacancy announcements by fiscal year, open dates, title/series/grade, and organization code.

RM 2 The system shall have the capability to link electronically to OPM's USAJOBS in order to post vacancy announcements and receive resumes electronically.

> RM 2.1   The system shall be able to convert the vacancy announcement into RTF, ASCII and HTML format and transmit the vacancy announcement to web sites, NASA and government bulletin boards, academic institutions, and publications.

> RM 2.2   The system shall have the capability to upload vacancy announcements to OPM's USAJOBS.

> RM 2.3   The system shall have the capability to receive résumés electronically from OPM's USAJOBS web site & add applicant data to the database without manual intervention.

RM 3 The system shall receive resumes in multiple formats from internal and external candidates.

RM 3.1   The system shall be able to process a résumé in email format.

RM 3.2   The system shall be able to scan and process résumés received on paper.

RM 3.3   The system shall support the application of a single résumé entry to multiple vacancy announcements.

RM 3.4   The system shall provide for the ability to replace an existing résumé on or before the closing date.

RM 3.5   The system shall provide a simplified resume entry format that starts with basic Federal system questions (veterans preference, ICTAP, competitive status, highest grade and type of appointment while in that highest grade), followed by space to paste in resume in a one step operation.

RM 4 The system shall extract and store key information about applicants and their experience, skills and competencies

RM 4.1   The system shall provide the capability to manually override system generated output created during the résumé scanning process.

RM 4.2   The system shall be able to link qualified résumés with Form DD-214, RIF notice, CTAP/ICTAP letter and/or Notification of Personnel Action from previous federal employment.

RM 4.3   The system shall identify and reject duplicate résumés.

RM 4.4   The system shall be able to maintain résumés in an inactive status.

RM 4.5   The system shall support purge of résumés based on user selected parameters.

RM 5 The system shall enable automated identification of best qualified candidates for referral to hiring managers.

RM 5.1   The system shall support multi-tiered evaluation criteria to subset résumés first by vacancy announcement number, then by submitter's qualifications.

RM 5.2   The system shall provide users with résumé selection/prioritization criteria based on interpretation of vacancy announcement qualification specifications.

RM 5.3   The system shall allow the user to accept, modify, or replace system generated résumé selection/prioritization criteria.

RM 5.4   The system shall allow the user to save résumé selection/prioritization criteria to be used with respect to other similar vacancy announcements.

(Continued)

(*Continued*)

RM 5.5   The system shall have the capability to read and screen résumés and apply key words and phrases to identify the best qualified applicants (taking into account all applicable regulatory requirements, incl. ICTAP/CTAP, veteran preferences, job criteria, education, selective factors, specialized experience).

RM 5.6   The system shall have the capability to read and screen résumés and apply key words and phrases to identify minimum qualifications (taking into account all applicable regulatory requirements, incl. ICTAP/CTAP, veteran preferences, job criteria).

RM 5.7   The system shall have the capability to read and screen résumés and apply key words and phrases to identify priority considerations through user defined criteria (taking into account all applicable regulatory requirements, incl. ICTAP/CTAP, veteran preferences, job criteria).

RM 5.8   The system shall be able to maintain historical files documenting the recruitment and staffing process.

RM 5.9   The system shall determine candidate certification order and produce certificates of eligibles through the application of proper veterans preference rules and tie-breaking methods.

RM 6   The system shall collect, store, and make available for analysis data needed to determine\ staff competencies in the current workforce.

RM 6.1   The system shall have the capability to read and screen résumés of all current employees and produce a dataset of the skills and competencies possessed within the workforce

RM 6.2   The system shall provide a Web-based, self-service means for employees to maintain résumé information.

RM 7   The system shall enable electronic workflow between human resources staff and serviced organizations

RM 7.1   The system shall be able to transmit qualified résumés to the hiring manager via NASA email or the internet.

RM 7.2   The system shall enable managers to receive, send, and act upon referral lists and résumés.

RM 7.3   Hiring managers shall be able to access the system and retrieve qualified résumés.

RM 7.4   The system shall provide flexibility in defining internal operational procedures and in supporting agency requirements.

RM 8 The system shall provide notifications and status information to applicants and hiring managers

RM 8.1   The system shall have the capability to automatically reply with electronic notifications to applicants who supply email addresses.

RM 8.2   The system shall have the capability to automatically generate paper notifications to applicants upon receipt of résumés.

RM 8.3   The system shall enable users to generate disposition notifications to selected and non-selected applicants.

RM 8.4   The system shall be able to generate a customized job offer letter to be sent to the candidate with data and conditions of employment.

RM 8.5   The system shall provide letter templates that are tailored to specifics of a job offer (e.g., superior qualifications, set-pay, recruitment or relocation bonuses, outside hire move benefits, benefits, reassignment, other entitlements)

RM 8.6   The system shall be able to automatically generate a customizable notification to non-selected candidates.

RM 8.7   The system shall be able to generate final notification to be sent to a prospective employee based on the outcome of preliminary activities.

RM 9 The system shall validate user input

RM 9.1   The system shall be able to provide capability to customize data input, processing rules, and edit criteria.

RM 9.2   The system shall provide real time notification to users of incorrect or missing data.

RM 9.3   The system shall allow and control access based on the roles and security requirements for anticipated system users.

RM 10 The system shall provide ad hoc reporting

RM 10.1   The system shall be able to provide the capability to allow users to customize output for reporting.

RM 10.2   The system shall support use of ad hoc query tools to create customized reports.

RM 11 The system shall be federalized

RM 11.1   The system shall comply with statutory and regulatory requirements (5 CFR Parts 2, 4, 7, 211 thru 250, and 300 thru 340; 29 CFR 1607; 5 USC Part III, Subpart A, and Subpart B) when processing transactions and providing decision support capabilities in accomplishing recruitment and staffing. (This includes, for example, priority placement entitlement, time-in-grade restrictions,

(Continued)

(*Continued*)

        and minimum qualification criteria for processing recruitment and staffing actions, veterans preference, type of appointment, length of service, and performance data)

RM 11.2   The system shall be comprised of mature, "federalized" commercial-off-the-shelf (COTS) software packages that are on a GSA schedule.

RM 11.3   The software packages shall have a proven track record of use by other government agencies who also follow 5 CFR and 5 U.S.C.

[http://www.processimpact.com/process_assets/srs_template.doc]

Software Requirements Specification (SRS)*

for

<Project>

Version 1.0 approved

Prepared by <author>

<organization>

<date created>

*Permissible to print this template as long as the web site above is given.

Table of Contents

Revision History

Name	Date	Reason For Changes	Version

1.   Introduction

1.1   Purpose

<Identify the product whose software requirements are specified in this document, including the revision or release number. Describe the scope of the product that is covered by this SRS, particularly if this SRS describes only part of the system or a single subsystem.>

(Continued)

(Continued)

1.2 Document Conventions

<Describe any standards or typographical conventions that were followed when writing this SRS, such as fonts or highlighting that have special significance. For example, state whether priorities for higher-level requirements are assumed to be inherited by detailed requirements, or whether every requirement statement is to have its own priority.>

1.3 Intended Audience and Reading Suggestions

<Describe the different types of reader that the document is intended for, such as developers, project managers, marketing staff, users, testers, and documentation writers. Describe what the rest of this SRS contains and how it is organized. Suggest a sequence for reading the document, beginning with the overview sections and proceeding through the sections that are most pertinent to each reader type.>

1.4 Project Scope

<Provide a short description of the software being specified and its purpose, including relevant benefits, objectives, and goals. Relate the software to corporate goals or business strategies. If a separate vision and scope document is available, refer to it rather than duplicating its contents here. An SRS that specifies the next release of an evolving product should contain its own scope statement as a subset of the long-term strategic product vision.>

1.5 References

<List any other documents or Web addresses to which this SRS refers. These may include user interface style guides, contracts, standards, system requirements specifications, use case documents, or a vision and scope document. Provide enough information so that the reader could access a copy of each reference, including title, author, version number, date, and source or location.>

2. Overall Description

2.1 Product Perspective

<Describe the context and origin of the product being specified in this SRS. For example, state whether this product is a follow-on member of a product family, a replacement for certain existing systems, or a new, self-contained product. If the SRS defines a component of a larger system, relate the requirements of the larger system to the functionality of this software and identify interfaces between the two. A simple diagram that shows the major components of the overall system, subsystem interconnections, and external interfaces can be helpful.>

2.2 Product Features

<Summarize the major features the product contains or the significant functions that it performs or lets the user perform. Details will be provided in Section 3, so only a high level summary is needed here. Organize the functions to make them understandable to any reader of the SRS. A picture of the major groups of related requirements and how they relate, such as a top level data flow diagram or a class diagram, is often effective.>

2.3 User Classes and Characteristics

<Identify the various user classes that you anticipate will use this product. User classes may be differentiated based on frequency of use, subset of product functions used, technical expertise, security or privilege levels, educational level, or experience. Describe the pertinent characteristics of each user class. Certain requirements may pertain only to certain user classes. Distinguish the favored user classes from those who are less important to satisfy.>

2.4 Operating Environment

<Describe the environment in which the software will operate, including the hardware platform, operating system and versions, and any other software components or applications with which it must peacefully coexist.>

2.5 Design and Implementation Constraints

<Describe any items or issues that will limit the options available to the developers. These might include: corporate or regulatory policies; hardware limitations (timing requirements, memory requirements); interfaces to other applications; specific technologies, tools, and databases to be used; parallel operations; language requirements; communications protocols; security considerations; design conventions or programming standards (for example, if the customer's organization will be responsible for maintaining the delivered software).>

2.6 User Documentation

<List the user documentation components (such as user manuals, on-line help, and tutorials) that will be delivered along with the software. Identify any known user documentation delivery formats or standards.>

2.7 Assumptions and Dependencies

<List any assumed factors (as opposed to known facts) that could affect the requirements stated in the SRS. These could include third-party or commercial components that you plan to use, issues around the development or operating environment, or constraints. The project could be affected if these assumptions are incorrect, are not shared, or change. Also identify any dependencies the project has on external factors, such as software components that you intend to reuse from another project, unless they are already documented elsewhere (for example, in the vision and scope document or the project plan).>

3. System Features

<This template illustrates organizing the functional requirements for the product by system features, the major services provided by the product. You may prefer to organize this section by use case, mode of operation, user class, object class, functional hierarchy, or combinations of these, whatever makes the most logical sense for your product.>

(Continued)

(Continued)

3.1 System Feature 1

<Don't really say "System Feature 1." State the feature name in just a few words.>

3.1.1 Description and Priority

<Provide a short description of the feature and indicate whether it is of High, Medium, or Low priority. You could also include specific priority component ratings, such as benefit, penalty, cost, and risk (each rated on a relative scale from a low of 1 to a high of 9).>

3.1.2 Stimulus/Response Sequences

<List the sequences of user actions and system responses that stimulate the behavior defined for this feature. These will correspond to the dialog elements associated with use cases.>

3.1.3 Functional Requirements

<Itemize the detailed functional requirements associated with this feature. These are the software capabilities that must be present in order for the user to carry out the services provided by the feature, or to execute the use case. Include how the product should respond to anticipated error conditions or invalid inputs. Requirements should be concise, complete, unambiguous, verifiable, and necessary. Use "TBD" as a placeholder to indicate when necessary information is not yet available.>

<Each requirement should be uniquely identified with a sequence number or a meaningful tag of some kind.>

REQ-1:
REQ-2:

3.2 System Feature 2 (and so on)

4. External Interface Requirements

4.1 User Interfaces

<Describe the logical characteristics of each interface between the software product and the users. This may include sample screen images, any GUI standards or product family style guides that are to be followed, screen layout constraints, standard buttons and functions (e.g., help) that will appear on every screen, keyboard shortcuts, error message display standards, and so on. Define the software components for which a user interface is needed. Details of the user interface design should be documented in a separate user interface specification.>

4.2 Hardware Interfaces

<Describe the logical and physical characteristics of each interface between the software product and the hardware components of the system. This may include the supported device types, the nature of the data and control interactions between the software and the hardware, and communication protocols to be used.>

4.3 Software Interfaces

<Describe the connections between this product and other specific software components (name and version), including databases, operating systems, tools, libraries, and integrated commercial components. Identify the data items or messages coming into the system and going out and describe the purpose of each. Describe the services needed and the nature of communications. Refer to documents that describe detailed application programming interface protocols. Identify data that will be shared across software components. If the data sharing mechanism must be implemented in a specific way (for example, use of a global data area in a multitasking operating system), specify this as an implementation constraint.>

4.4 Communications Interfaces

<Describe the requirements associated with any communications functions required by this product, including e-mail, web browser, network server communications protocols, electronic forms, and so on. Define any pertinent message formatting. Identify any communication standards that will be used, such as FTP or HTTP. Specify any communication security or encryption issues, data transfer rates, and synchronization mechanisms.>

5. Other Nonfunctional Requirements

5.1 Performance Requirements

<If there are performance requirements for the product under various circumstances, state them here and explain their rationale, to help the developers understand the intent and make suitable design choices. Specify the timing relationships for real time systems. Make such requirements as specific as possible. You may need to state performance requirements for individual functional requirements or features.>

5.2 Safety Requirements

<Specify those requirements that are concerned with possible loss, damage, or harm that could result from the use of the product. Define any safeguards or actions that must be taken, as well as actions that must be prevented. Refer to any external policies or regulations that state safety issues that affect the product's design or use. Define any safety certifications that must be satisfied.>

5.3 Security Requirements

<Specify any requirements regarding security or privacy issues surrounding use of the product or protection of the data used or created by the product. Define any user identity authentication requirements. Refer to any external policies or regulations containing security issues that affect the product. Define any security or privacy certifications that must be satisfied.>

5.4 Software Quality Attributes

<Specify any additional quality characteristics for the product that will be important to either the customers or the developers. Some to consider are: adaptability, availability,

(Continued)

(*Continued*)

correctness, flexibility, interoperability, maintainability, portability, reliability, reusability, robustness, testability, and usability. Write these to be specific, quantitative, and verifiable when possible. At the least, clarify the relative preferences for various attributes, such as ease of use over ease of learning.>

6. Other Requirements

<Define any other requirements not covered elsewhere in the SRS. This might include database requirements, internationalization requirements, legal requirements, reuse objectives for the project, and so on. Add any new sections that are pertinent to the project.>

Appendix A: Glossary

<Define all the terms necessary to properly interpret the SRS, including acronyms and abbreviations. You may wish to build a separate glossary that spans multiple projects or the entire organization, and just include terms specific to a single project in each SRS.>

Appendix B: Analysis Models

<Optionally, include any pertinent analysis models, such as data flow diagrams, class diagrams, state-transition diagrams, or entity-relationship diagrams.>

Appendix C: Issues List

< This is a dynamic list of the open requirements issues that remain to be resolved, including TBDs, pending decisions, information that is needed, conflicts awaiting resolution, and the like.>

information system to determine possible relationships and patterns in the external marketplace that affect our organization, we would be interested in "what the system would do for us" (functional requirements) versus "how it worked" (performance requirements). For example, functional requirements for a competitive intelligence system for a biotechnology company may relate to being able to collect and communicate competitive insight and information (e.g., competitive landscapes, competitor profiles, drugs in research, clinical trial activities, etc.) in response to project needs. A performance requirement for such a system may indicate that the competitive intelligence (CI) system must use regression techniques within a 95% confidence level for correlation analysis. The functional requirement discusses the "what" aspect of the CI system; the performance requirement explains the "how" element associated with the CI system.

Another simple heuristic for writing functional requirements is to keep the written functional requirement concise and verifiable. The functional requirement should be clearly written and should generally not be a compound sentence. The functional requirement should also be verifiable since a key reason for writing the functional requirements is to be able to trace the system design back to the requirements in order to make sure "the system is being built right" and "the right system is being built."

Here are some examples of poorly written functional requirements for designing an automated teller machine (ATM) application:

- The ATM shall support the following operations: cash deposit (add some dollar amount to account balance), cash withdrawal (deduct some dollar amount from account balance), and account balance inquiry (get current account balance). *[This functional requirement should be decomposed into separate requirements for each individual function (i.e., cash deposit, withdrawal, and account balance inquiry).]*
- The ATM shall run in its own process and will handle remote requests from a client running in some other process. *[This functional requirement is too nebulous—what is its own process and running in some other process?]*
- The ATM shall have a fully functional user interface for PIN verification, cash withdrawal, cash deposit, and balance inquiry. The user should be able to cancel a transaction at any time. *[What is meant by a fully functional user interface? These two sentences should be broken out into two separate functional requirements.]*
- The ATM software shall control the hardware in the ATM—keyboard and monitor/touch panel, card swipe reader, cash dispenser, deposit acceptance, two printers (receipt printer and a printer to write transaction data on deposited envelopes), a telephone dialer port for connection to the bank host computer, a TCP/IP networking port for connection to the Internet, and a video camera. *[This functional requirement is too lengthy. The various hardware components should be decomposed into sublevel functional requirements].*
- The ATM shall control the entire transaction: verification of PIN, assembling all transaction information (name, account, bank, transaction type), all communications with the host, accepting or dispensing cash, printing the receipt, etc. All account and cash information is sent over the telephone port. All transactions will be time stamped. *[Too many compound functional requirements; never use etc.—not testable].*
- The ATM shall support an audit trail for all activities sent to the bank's central computer. *[Sufficiently written functional requirement; however, "audit trail" would need to be defined somewhere in the functional requirements document.]*

A final helpful hint for writing functional requirements is to think in terms of chunks. In other words, if "PIN (personal identification number) verification" should be a major function of an ATM, think of other major functions (e.g., cash deposits, withdrawals, account balance inquiry, etc.) that should also be included. Then, decompose these major functions into sublevel requirements, for example:

1.0 The ATM shall perform PIN verification.
  1.1 The ATM shall ask the customer to insert the bank card into the ATM.
  1.2 The ATM shall ask the customer to enter the PIN number.
  1.3 The ATM shall verify the customer's PIN with the bank's central database.

    1.4 The ATM shall allow the customer to enter transactions if the PIN verification is accepted.

    1.5 The ATM shall return the bank card to the customer if the PIN verification is not valid.

    1.6 The ATM shall keep the bank card if it is recorded as stolen.

SUMMARY ▪▪▪▪▪▪▪

Listening to the needs of the customer and applying knowledge acquisition techniques to elicit customer/user requirements are key activities for an IT professional, especially a systems analyst. This chapter highlighted some of these techniques in preparation for writing functional requirements for IT projects. The "garbage-in, garbage-out" adage comes to mind for systems designed around the wrong requirements. The chapter provides some practical insights and guidance to help in eliciting and writing functional requirements for systems design and development.

ASSIGNMENT ▪▪▪▪▪▪▪

The following assignment combines techniques for listening effectiveness, knowledge acquisition, and writing functional requirements and software requirements specification documents.

Project: Developing Functional Requirements

Your CIO has just briefed you on an idea for a new product that the company wants to manufacture. The product is an automated movie selector that would be available on the Web and in computer kiosks in stores like Blockbusters, Best Buy, and other stores that carry videos/CDs/DVDs. The idea is to develop a software program that would ask a series of questions to help customers select a movie that would best interest them for rent/purchase on that given day. It would also feed into an inventory system to check the availability of the selected movies, so the customer doesn't have to constantly peruse the stacks to see if the movies are there. There would be interactive multimedia built into the program to show excerpts from selected movies, provide audio recordings of what others thought about the movie (similar to an Amazon.com rating/preference scale), and other types of functionality. This program would be available in computer kiosks and via the Web.

Your CIO has asked you to develop a substantive first cut of the functional requirements part of the software requirements specification document for this product. The document must be submitted to the CIO by next week. The CIO has also asked you to be prepared to give a Powerpoint presentation of your findings next week.

EXERCISES ▪▪▪▪▪▪▪

1. Have a group of your fellow students sit in a row together. Have one student whisper in another student's ear a one-sentence user requirement. Have the student who just heard the user requirement whisper the user requirement to the next person in the row. Continue this process until the last person hears the user requirement. Compare that version of the user requirement to the original version, and examine what listening biases may have caused the user requirement to change.
2. Review knowledge acquisition studies comparing protocol analysis with interviewing techniques. Design a 10-minute Powerpoint presentation of your findings.

3. Confusion often occurs over the distinction between functional requirements and nonfunctional requirements. For a new portable digital music device that people can easily use during work and leisure, list 10 functional requirements and 10 nonfunctional requirements for such a device.

4. Discuss the value of writing down functional requirements for traceability purposes.

5. In the rapid prototyping model, requirements generally evolve and are refined as new versions of the prototype are created. Does this development philosophy run counter to defining requirements up front before any system development begins? Discuss your reasoning.

ENDNOTES ▪▪▪▪▪▪▪

1. Pack, Terry. (May 31, 2003). *The Chronicle of Higher Education.*

2. Joyce, Amy. (May 24, 2003). "What Makes a Good Boss?" *The Washington Post.*

3. Gorkin, Mark. http://www.stressdoc.com/listening_and_leading.htm.

4. http://www.hiringsolutions.net.

5. University of Minnesota-Duluth. *Student Handbook.* http://www.d.umn.edu/student/loon/acad/strat/ss_listening.html.

6. Whitten, J., L. Bentley, and K. Dittman. (2000). *Systems Analysis and Design Methods.* Project Management Institute, Carlisle, PA, 5th edition.

SUGGESTED REFERENCES ▪▪▪▪▪▪▪

Robertson, S., and J. Robertson. (1999). *Mastering the Requirements Process.* Addison-Wesley, Reading, MA.

Wiegers, K. (2003). *Software Requirements.* Microsoft Press, Seattle, WA.

3

Due Diligence as an IT Professional

Learning Objectives

■ To understand why you must be prepared as an IT professional

■ To discover why you should learn from others to not reinvent the wheel

■ To understand some research strategies that will help you as an IT professional

Introduction

In the June 11, 2001 issue of *Information Week,* information technology employers were asked, "What are the top skills colleges and universities need to be teaching their IT students that they aren't now?" The top-ranked response was communication/people skills. However, not far behind were troubleshooting and analytical skills. An important part of troubleshooting and analytical skills is knowing what others have done so that you can learn from their successes or failures. In other words, being able to research and learn what others have done can help an IT professional solve problems more quickly and adeptly. Thus, a critical part of an IT professional's job, as well as of any profession, is performing "due diligence" (i.e., "doing your homework").

"Doing your homework" means seeing what has already been accomplished and learning from these efforts. Whether it is doing a literature review for a technical paper, reading analyst reports (e.g., Gartner Group summaries and reports, International Data Corporation reports, etc.), or speaking with colleagues to see what similar efforts others in the organization have accomplished, all of these tasks coincide with doing your homework. Walter Cronkite is reported to have gained such prominence partly by his diligence in preparing by doing his research. In the same manner as Mr. Cronkite, IT professionals need to spend the necessary time to explore what others have done. Certainly, time constraints may limit the extent of research possible; however, not doing the research may cause the project to suffer similar difficulties that other related projects have experienced. For example, one IT consulting firm was developing a corporate database design for a government client. The project team was unaware that a similar project was being developed in the same firm for another government client just one floor up. If the project team had known about this similar project, it could have saved time and money by learning from their colleagues.

In many organizations, best-practices and lessons-learned databases are being used to help employees do their research by learning from others. For example, the National Aeronautics and Space Administration (NASA) has an agency-wide Lessons Learned Information System (LLIS—http://www.llis.nasa.gov) with over 1,500 lessons learned from across 10 NASA centers and 3 related sites. The lessons cover project management, safety, systems engineering, and many other areas of interest to the aerospace industry. Additionally, there is a user profiling feature whereby lessons matching user profile interests will be sent to a user automatically (via an e-mail with URL links) as new lessons are entered in the system. Thus, the user doesn't have to employ the "pull" approach of surfing the Web for related lessons but instead can take advantage of the "push" approach of being automatically sent appropriate lessons that match the user's profile. A public domain version of this Lessons Learned Information System can be found at http://www.llis.nasa.gov by clicking on PLLS (Public Lessons Learned System).

Before we discuss research strategies that the IT professional can apply, let's try a warm-up exercise.

WARM-UP EXERCISE

You are part of a project team that is developing a knowledge management approach to allow individuals in an organization to better share their knowledge. Your focus is on developing and implementing the technology part of this project. Specifically, you are interested in applying project management techniques, building a portal as a gateway to knowledge resources in the organization, and developing online communities of practice so that people with similar interests in the organization have an electronic venue to share ideas and documents. Access the NASA Lessons Learned Information System at http://www.llis.nasa.gov (click on PLLS) and perform a search to see if there are relevant lessons that apply to your situation. Write a one-page executive summary that summarizes your findings.

▪▪▪ Research Strategies

According to Charles Margerison in his book *Managerial Consulting Skills: A Practical Guide*, "many people make the wrong moves because they do not have the right information. They have a tendency to rush into action, before assessing the situation and the options. Therefore, research is action."[1] In a client setting, research can take many forms. Determining and understanding the client's requirements typically involves an inquiry approach. Using this approach, the IT consultant comes to understand the needs of the client and separate out the symptoms from the problems. The consultant must ascertain and probe the various assumptions associated with the client's issues.

As proposed by Gordon Lippitt in his landmark book on *Organizational Renewal*, the consultant should possess the following traits[2]:

- Focus on the problem-solving approach to learning and change: use data, not just hunches.
- Develop interdependence with others, not dependency.
- Practice what we preach in the field of our specialized knowledge.
- Diagnose situations, rather than merely treat symptoms.
- Understand ourselves so thoroughly that we do not let our personal needs get in the way of helping people and organizations to develop.
- Communicate on a reality level in open fashion.
- Admit mistakes and learn from failure.
- Develop interests and skills so as to be able to work with people in a controlling manner.
- Be willing to experiment and innovate.
- Develop a personal philosophy about working and developing people and organizations.
- Be capable of saying, "I don't know."
- Be willing to learn and change.

In terms of due diligence on the part of the IT professional, research strategies can take many forms. One strategy is to conduct searches to discover articles and information related to the problem being studied. With the myriad of electronic databases (e.g., Business Source Premier, ABI Inform, Inspec, Lexis/Nexis, Gartner Research Services, etc.), assuming the organization subscribes to them, retrieval of full-text articles is greatly facilitated by a simple query. Additionally, electronic journal repositories (such as ScienceDirect from Elsevier, JSTOR, Wiley Interscience, and others) can also be accessed to locate articles that relate to the problem at hand. Certainly, popular Web search engines like Google can help locate information that may be appropriate to the situation under study.

Another research strategy that individuals employ is outsourcing the research or study. A consulting firm, university, or company could be hired to perform the necessary "background check" and explore the best practices used by others in solving problems similar to the one being analyzed. Universities are especially well suited to doing literature reviews, performing research and development studies, developing prototypes, and the like. Consulting firms can also perform benchmarking studies to cull out the best practices for applying certain techniques and solving problems. Thus, instead of the IT professional doing the necessary homework, some other entity does it for the organization; however, the organization must feel confident that it understands and learns from the work being contracted out.

Other than doing the homework yourself or having others do it for you, a compromise approach is to partner with an organization in order to leverage each other's knowledge. A partnership can be a wonderful approach to complementing individual strengths. For example, let's assume that a for-profit organization teams up with a university and another company. Various roles can be assigned in such a way that each partner accentuates its strength and allows the other partners to learn from each other. This teaming approach is widely used and typically creates excellent synergies—that is, the whole is greater than the sum of its parts!

Let's now take a look at the research methodologies that have been applied in the information systems field.

▪▪▪▪ Research Methodologies for Information Systems Projects

Two main types of research methods are used in the information systems field: quantitative research methods and qualitative research methods. According to the Association for Information Systems (http://www.isworld.org), quantitative research methods were originally developed in the natural sciences to study natural phenomena. Examples of quantitative methods now well accepted in the social sciences include survey techniques, laboratory experiments (e.g., hypothesis testing), formal methods (e.g., econometrics), and numerical methods (e.g., regression analysis, mathematical modeling). Qualitative research methods were developed in the social sciences to enable researchers to study social and cultural phenomena. Examples of qualitative research methods are action research, case study research, and ethnography. Qualitative data sources include observation and participant observation (fieldwork), interviews and questionnaires, documents and texts, and the researcher's impressions and reactions.

Generally, information systems research methods are either exploratory or explanatory. Exploratory research refers to discovering knowledge without having any predefined conceptions. In the data mining field, which attempts to discover relationships and patterns among large masses of data, the exploratory approach would be called *undirected* data mining. When researchers have some preconceived ideas and want to try to explain or test those ideas, this would be an explanatory research approach. In the data mining world, explanatory approaches are called *directed* data mining, as there are predefined labels and researchers are looking for relationships and patterns among these predefined data elements.

Among the qualitative research methods, the case study approach is often used. Case studies range from those that are purely descriptive, with no measurements made, to those that include elementary descriptions of some behavior (frequencies, means, etc.).[3] The main limitation of case studies is that they can't easily be generalized because the study typically focuses on a specific or limited number of organizations. Action research, another qualitative research method, involves the dual objectives of solving practical problems and contributing to new knowledge through change and reflection (see Kock and Lau, 2001).[4] Action research has been applied quite extensively in the education field and involves the steps of planning, acting, observing, and reflecting. Another qualitative research method used in the information systems field is ethnographic analysis. Also called *narrative analysis*, ethnographic analysis involves examination of cultural events or experiences (observations and interviews with respondents). One major limitation of this approach is that it can be fairly time-consuming.

Quantitative research methods have also often been used in the information systems field. Surveys are frequently used to gather data and develop analyses. For surveys, you need a valid and reliable questionnaire (usually the questionnaire must be pretested), a representative sample, and an adequate response rate. A response rate of at least 80% is considered desirable for in-person surveys. Standards for mail and telephone surveys are somewhat lower, with rates of 65% or better considered acceptable.[5] Correlation studies are also used as quantitative research techniques. These studies attempt to establish relationships between two or more variables. A correlation coefficient describes the strength and direction of the relationship between variables, positive or negative [www.isworld.org]. Regression analysis is used to predict certain variables on the basis of knowledge about other independent variables, or the effects of certain independent variables on a particular dependent variable (e.g., how well Graduate Record Examination scores predict performance in graduate school) [www.isworld.org].

▪▪▪ Solving a Mystery Like a Detective

Why should IT professionals use research methods in their work? In many ways, being a systems analyst, IT manager, or CIO (Chief Information Officer) is similar to being a detective solving a crime. A large part of research is knowing the right question(s) to ask. In order to know what questions to ask, one must be familiar with the current state-of-the-art and IT literature to understand what is already available in the field. This is analogous to a detective determining who did what. A detective must study the crime scene and make some initial hypotheses. The detective will then test the hypotheses by gathering more research, getting lab test results, gaining more knowledge and information through further investigations, and performing further analysis. The detective will then generate new hypotheses and/or confirm previous hypotheses. Ultimately, the detective will solve the case by identifying the culprit and making an arrest.

The detective, like the systems analyst, is using a systems development life cycle methodology. The detective first studies the crime scene and asks initial questions (requirements stage). Then, the detective performs some "analysis and design" by postulating various hypotheses (i.e., generating alternatives) and visualizes how each alternative could have been designed and accomplished. After a trade-off analysis (testing stage), the detective can narrow down the list to the most likely alternative and reveal how it was implemented (implementation stage).

▪▪▪ A Closer Look at Some IS Research Methods

Like a detective, the systems analyst, IS manager, or IS professional must perform due diligence in "doing their homework." The various IS research methods previously highlighted in this chapter often help the IS professional to perform this task by supplying a well-conceived perspective for approaching the problem or opportunity. Whether using surveys, formal methods, ethnographic analysis, case studies, interviews/focus groups, or other research methods, the IS professional can benefit. Let's take a closer look at some of these techniques and some helpful hints on when to use them.

Surveys

Surveys seem to be a popular research method in the IT field, especially for receiving user or customer feedback. A survey should normally be pretested before sending the final version to its intended audience. By conducting a pilot survey, unclear questions can be identified and reworded for the final survey. Additionally, since a survey should take no longer than 20 minutes to complete (otherwise, people may not take the time to complete it and thereby reduce the response rate), pretesting will reveal whether the survey is too long.

Achieving an adequate response rate is always an issue when using surveys. Oftentimes, e-mail or telephone reminders need to be sent as follow-up correspondence to remind people to complete their survey by the stated deadline. Accompanying the survey with a cover letter from an influential person in the organization will encourage a better response rate. Some organizations may even award prizes to those who complete the survey first. One organization held a prize drawing, including Palm Pilots, for the first 100 people who completed its surveys. To make completion easy, many organizations use a web-based survey. Reasonably priced software such as Perseus' Survey Solutions on the Web (http://www.perseus.com) or SurveyMonkey (www.surveymonkey.com) can help in the design, dissemination, and analysis of the survey and results. Be aware that surveys are not always valid in different contexts. The effect of cultural differences, for example, may alter the survey results and prevent generalizing them across cultures.

On the next page is an example of a survey (developed by Jay Liebowitz and colleagues) used in a knowledge audit of a large foundation to determine knowledge flows within the organization and eventually to develop a knowledge management strategy.

Formal Methods

Many IT professionals may opt to use formal statistical methods and mathematical modeling as their preferred IS research method. Hypothesis testing, whereby a null hypothesis and an alternative hypothesis are developed and tested, is often used in the quantitative IS research approach. When developing the hypotheses, be certain that they reflect the essence of what you hope to prove. For example, if we are interested in finding out if CEOs in U.S. companies are usually tall, then we could set up a null hypothesis to say, "Men over 6 feet tall are more likely to become CEOs in U.S. companies than those men under 6 feet." The alternative hypothesis could be "Men over 6 feet tall are NOT more likely to become CEOs in U.S. companies than those men under 6 feet." Are these hypotheses worded correctly? Are we saying that men over 6 feet are likely to become CEOs, or do we want to say that CEOs are typically men over 6 feet? In other words, are we considering the population to be CEOs whom we could line up and measure, or are we including the average man on the street? What about CEOs who could be female? A better null hypothesis might be "Height has no influence on becoming a CEO." The alternative hypothesis might be "Height has an influence on becoming a CEO."

Case Study Research and Ethnography

The case study research approach is a popular technique in IS research and practice. It allows the researcher to study one or several organizations or social groups and typically uses interviews as the primary source of data (along with documentary evidence). According to Myers, the case study approach allows the researcher to immerse him or herself in the life of the social group under study.[6] One key limitation of case studies is that it may be very difficult to generalize the results since the focus of study is usually one or a limited number of social groups/organizations.

KNOWLEDGE ACCESS AND SHARING SURVEY

A key part of developing a knowledge management strategy for the Foundation is to find out how people gain access to and share knowledge throughout the organization. This survey seeks to gather fairly detailed information about the ways in which you access, share, and use knowledge resources in your work. In answering the questions below, please keep in mind the following: answer for yourself, not how you think someone else in your job might answer; answer for how you *actually* work now, not how you wish you worked or think you should work.

We expect that some questions will require you to think carefully about the nature of the tasks you perform and how you interact with people both inside and outside the Foundation day-to-day. Carefully completing this survey will probably take about 20 minutes. *We appreciate your effort in helping us meet a strategic goal designed to make the organization more effective and to make it easier for all of us to do our jobs on a daily basis.*

Please forward your completed survey to _____ by _____. Thank you!

PLEASE PROVIDE THE FOLLOWING INFORMATION:

Name: _____

Which division are you a part of:
❑ Communications
❑ Executive Office & General Counsel
❑ Finance and Administration
❑ Financial Innovation, Planning and Research
❑ Housing & Community Initiatives
❑ Knowledge Access and Technology Strategy

How long have you been a full-time employee at the Foundation?
❑ Less than 6 months
❑ 6 months–less than 1 year
❑ 1 year–less than 3 years
❑ 3 years–less than 5 years
❑ More than 5 years

PLEASE BEGIN THE SURVEY!

1. In the course of doing your job, which resource do you most often turn to *first* when looking for information? *(please check only one)*:

   ❑ E-mail or talk to a Foundation colleague
   ❑ E-mail or talk to a colleague who works outside the Foundation
   ❑ Do a global web search (for example, Google, Yahoo)
   ❑ Go to a known web site (for example, HUD, LiscNet, Geofunders)
   ❑ Search online Foundation resources (for example, Gifts, intranet)
   ❑ Search through documents/publications in your office
   ❑ Post a message on a listserv/online community to which you belong
   ❑ Ask your manager for guidance based on his/her experience
   ❑ Other *(please specify)* _____

2. What would be your second course of action from the above list?
   _____

3. Think about the times when you've been really frustrated by not having a critical piece of knowledge or information you needed to get something done at the Foundation. Give an example, including the nature of the challenge and how the need eventually was met.
   _____
   _____
   _____
   _____

KNOWLEDGE RESOURCES

4. How often **on average** do you use each of the following to do your job?

	DAILY	WEEKLY	MONTHLY	QUARTERLY	NEVER
Foundation-wide database (e.g., Gifts, IMIS, Peoplesoft)	❑	❑	❑	❑	❑
Foundation-operated web site (e.g., web site, intranet)	❑	❑	❑	❑	❑
Department- or division-operated database (e.g., shared calendar)	❑	❑	❑	❑	❑
My own database or contact list file	❑	❑	❑	❑	❑
Foundation policy/ procedures manual or guidelines	❑	❑	❑	❑	❑
Department- or division-specific procedures manual or guidelines	❑	❑	❑	❑	❑
Vendor-provided procedures manual or guidelines	❑	❑	❑	❑	❑
My own notes or procedures	❑	❑	❑	❑	❑

(Continued)

(*Continued*)

5. List up to five resources (hard-copy or web-based) that you use to perform your job and indicate how often you use them. These resources can be journals, magazines, newsletters, books, web sites, and so forth.

	DAILY	WEEKLY	MONTHLY	QUARTERLY
1.	❏	❏	❏	❏
2.	❏	❏	❏	❏
3.	❏	❏	❏	❏
4.	❏	❏	❏	❏
5.	❏	❏	❏	❏

6. How often **on average** do you ask each of the following staff for help with understanding or clarifying how you are to perform your job, solving a problem, getting an answer to a question from a grantee or customer, or learning how to accomplish a new task?

	DAILY	WEEKLY	MONTHLY	QUARTERLY	NEVER
Your immediate supervisor	❏	❏	❏	❏	❏
Your department head	❏	❏	❏	❏	❏
Your division head	❏	❏	❏	❏	❏
Subject-matter expert (in an area of policy, practice, or research)	❏	❏	❏	❏	❏
Technical or functional expert (e.g., accounting, legal, grants administration, technology)	❏	❏	❏	❏	❏
A peer or colleague in your department or division (informal)	❏	❏	❏	❏	❏
A peer or colleague outside your department or division (informal)	❏	❏	❏	❏	❏

7. Name the top three people, in order, to whom you go when you have questions or seek advice in the following areas:

	ONE	TWO	THREE
General advice			
Management and leadership knowledge/advice			
Subject-matter expertise/content knowledge			
Institutional/historical knowledge about the foundation			
Technical/procedural knowledge			

8. List up to five experts *outside* the Foundation whom you access to do your job. For each one, please indicate how often **on average** you contact them.

		DAILY	WEEKLY	MONTHLY	QUARTERLY
1.		❏	❏	❏	❏
2.		❏	❏	❏	❏
3.		❏	❏	❏	❏
4.		❏	❏	❏	❏
5.		❏	❏	❏	❏

KNOWLEDGE USE

9. Which of the following do you *usually* use and/or perform (that is, on a daily or weekly basis) in doing your job? *(Check all that apply.)*

   ❏ Data or information from a known source (e.g., database, files) you have to retrieve to answer a specific question.
   ❏ Data or information you have to gather yourself from multiple sources and analyze and/or synthesize to answer a specific question.
   ❏ Instruction (step-by-step) you provide (i.e., not a document) to a grantee, customer, vendor, or staff person.
   ❏ Direction you provide to a grantee, customer, vendor, or staff person (such as advice, counsel or guidance, not step-by-step).
   ❏ Judgments or recommendations you are asked to make based on data or information that is given to you.
   ❏ Judgments or recommendations you are asked to make based on data or information that you must find yourself.
   ❏ Routine procedure or process for handling information, paperwork, requests, payments, invoices, and so forth (always done the same way).
   ❏ Variable procedure or process for handling information, paperwork, requests, payments, invoices, and so forth (requires some analysis and judgment to select the proper procedure or process to follow).
   ❏ Reports, memoranda, letters, or informational materials for grantees, customers, vendors, or staff that you must compile and/or write.
   ❏ Educational or promotional materials that you must compile and/or write.
   ❏ Proposals you develop to recommend new programs, projects, procedures, or processes.

(Continued)

(Continued)

10. After you have received, gathered, or produced information, instructions, documents, proposals, etc., and completed the task, what do you do with them? (*Check all that apply.*)

❑ Save them in an electronic file in my personal directory
❑ Save them in an electronic file in a shared directory (e.g., s:drive, intranet)
❑ Save them in a personal paper file
❑ Save them in a secure departmental paper file
❑ Save them in an open departmental paper file
❑ Share them or distribute them to others
❑ Delete or toss them
❑ Other *(please specify)* _____

SHARING

11. When you come across a news item, article, magazine, book, web site, announcement for a meeting or course, or some other information that may be useful to other Foundation staff, what are you *most likely* to do? (*Check only one.*)

❑ Tell them about it or distribute a copy to them personally
❑ Post an announcement on the intranet or web site
❑ Send a broadcast e-mail
❑ Send a memo or a copy through the interoffice mail
❑ Intend to share it but usually too busy to follow through
❑ Include it in the Weekly Update
❑ Ignore it
❑ Other *(please specify)* _____

12. What are the constraints you face in being able to access or share knowledge?

_____
_____
_____
_____
_____

13. What critical knowledge is at risk of being lost in your department or division because of turnover and lack of backup expertise?

_____
_____
_____
_____

TRAINING/TOOLS

14. When you want to learn or improve a skill or task, what do you prefer to do? (*Check all that apply.*)

   ❑ Get formal face-to-face training or coursework outside the workplace
   ❑ Get formal self-directed training (e.g., workbook, CD-ROM, online course)
   ❑ Have a specialist train me on-site
   ❑ Train myself (informally, using a manual or tutorial program)
   ❑ Have my supervisor show me how to do it
   ❑ Have a friend or colleague show me how to do it
   ❑ Other *(please specify)* _____

15. What kind of tools or resources do you prefer to help you do your job? (*Check all that apply.*)

   ❑ Person I can talk to in real time
   ❑ Help line or help desk via phone, fax, or e-mail
   ❑ Advice via online communities of practice (on the intranet, listservs, or other sources)
   ❑ Printed documents (for example, resource books, manuals)
   ❑ Electronic documents
   ❑ Audiovisual/multimedia material
   ❑ Special software
   ❑ Web-based utility, directory, or service
   ❑ Other *(please specify)* _____

KNOWLEDGE NEEDS

16. What information or knowledge that *you* don't currently have would you like to have to do your job better? Consider all aspects of your job, including administrative tasks, policies and procedures, interpersonal relationships, and so forth.

   _____
   _____
   _____
   _____
   _____
   _____
   _____
   _____
   _____

(*Continued*)

(*Continued*)

17. What information or knowledge that the Foundation currently does not have do you think it should or will need to have to execute its mission, improve organizational effectiveness, and serve its customers with excellence? (You may answer for specific departments as well as for the Foundation as a whole.)

_____

_____

_____

_____

_____

_____

_____

_____

_____

18. To what extent do you agree with the following statements:

	STRONGLY DISAGREE	DISAGREE	NO OPINION	AGREE	STRONGLY AGREE
I would benefit from having access to documents that contain introductory knowledge that I currently have to acquire from experts directly.	❏	❏	❏	❏	❏
I would benefit from templates to help me more easily capture knowledge (e.g., standard format for documenting what I learned at a conference or meeting).	❏	❏	❏	❏	❏
I would benefit from processes to help me contribute knowledge that I don't currently document or share.	❏	❏	❏	❏	❏
I would benefit from support to determine the most relevant knowledge to share for various audiences and how best to share it.	❏	❏	❏	❏	❏
I have knowledge in areas that I know the Foundation could benefit from but no way to make it available.	❏	❏	❏	❏	❏

KNOWLEDGE FLOW

19. Imagine that you've just won the first Foundation Knowledge-Sharing Award. This award is given to a person who shares his or her mission- or operation-critical knowledge so that the Foundation can be more effective. List the top five

categories of knowledge that earned you this award and the category of staff with whom you shared it (e.g., regional staff, program officers, senior management, D.C. Initiatives, Finance and Administration division)

	KNOWLEDGE CATEGORY	STAFF CATEGORY
1.		
2.		
3.		
4.		
5.		

20. How can the knowledge flow in your area of responsibility be improved?

_____

_____

_____

_____

_____

ADDITIONAL COMMENTS

_____

_____

_____

_____

_____

_____

_____

Thank you for taking the time to complete this survey.
Please forward your survey to _____ by _____.

The ethnographic research approach relies heavily on field observation and usually requires the researcher to spend a long period of time in the field. According to Myers, the data sources used in the case study approach are supplemented by data collected through observation of participants. Both the case study and ethnography allow a rich description of the situation under study. Ethnography, in particular, is one of the most in-depth, intensive research methods. However, a key limitation is that this approach takes much more time than other research methods, mainly due to the observational nature of the process. Additionally, as in the case study approach, the findings may be hard to generalize.

The following table may be helpful in deciding whether to use a qualitative or quantitative IS research method.

	Survey	Hypothesis Testing	Formal & Numerical Methods	Case Study	Ethnography	Action Research
Deductive Reasoning	x	x	x			
Inductive Reasoning				x	x	x
Causation	x	x	x			
Meaning				x	x	x
Objectivity	x	x	x			
Subjectivity				x	x	x
Pre-specified Questions	x	x	x			
Open-ended Questions	x			x	x	x
Outcome-oriented	x	x	x			
Process-oriented				x	x	x
Numerical Estimation/ Statistical Inference	x	x	x			
Narrative Description				x	x	x

Source: Adapted from Casebeer, A., and Verhoef, M. (1997). "Combining Qualitative and Quantitative Research Methods: Considering the Possibilities for Enhancing the Study of Chronic Diseases." *Chronic Diseases in Canada Journal* 18 (no. 3).

▪▪▪ Using Research Methods in Practice: A Case Study

This section discusses a semifictional case study (and class exercise) involving the development of an information and knowledge management strategy for HelpMe Corporation (a pseudonym). As part of this project, surveys were used to gain added insight.

Organizational Background

HelpMe Corporation is a multinational firm with headquarters in Washington, D.C. and offices in 30 countries throughout the world. There are about 500 people in corporate headquarters and approximately 2,000 others in the worldwide field offices. HelpMe Corporation's main business is providing consulting services in the telecommunications and information technology industries. Curiously, the shoemaker's children paradox applies to the company in that although HelpMe provides high-tech consulting advice to many of the Fortune 500 companies, it lacks internal information and knowledge management strategies. One of the major challenges facing the HelpMe Corporation concerns how best to capture, share, and leverage knowledge internally and externally. Through attrition, retirement, and an aging workforce, HelpMe is losing its key intellectual capital. By the end of 2004, 51% of all HelpMe employees were eligible for retirements. In order to combat this "brain drain," HelpMe needs to develop an information and knowledge management strategy to capture, share, and preserve information and knowledge and integrate knowledge management and e-business into HelpMe's new strategic plan.

HelpMe is under the leadership of CEO Janet Sheridan and has three main divisions (Telecommunications Consulting Sector, headed by VP Jason Evans; Emerging Technologies Consulting Sector, headed by VP Kenneth David; and Internal Practices Sector, headed by VP Jay Liebo). (Note that it is fairly well known throughout the company that the CEO and Jay Liebo are "an item" and have been involved romantically for the past 3 months.) HelpMe had revenues of $200 million in 2003 and is forecasting a revenue base shrinkage of 10% by the end of 2004. With the possibility of many senior consultants retiring from HelpMe at the end of 2004, HelpMe needs to do some strategizing and visioning in order to continue to be competitive in the marketplace.

The culture and leadership style throughout HelpMe seem to be more authoritarian versus collaborative and participatory. Additionally, CEO Sheridan rules with an iron hand and seems to micromanage at times—as evidenced by personally approving individual office fax machines. As a result, some creativity on the part of management and employees has been stifled. This has created a culture of being laggards versus leaders in the field. If HelpMe is to continue beyond its current 50 years of longevity, it must be more proactive and needs to create a corporate-wide information and knowledge management strategy.

Methodology for Developing a HelpMe-Wide Information and Knowledge Management Strategy

To do some data collection for developing such a strategy, an information and knowledge management survey was developed to examine all the strategies/approaches/processes, culture, technology resources, and applications within HelpMe. Some general findings based upon the piloted survey were the following:

- People are recognized as being the most important sources of information.
- Half the respondents felt that HelpMe's strategic goals include knowledge management (KM) explicitly, and half the respondents felt there was a KM initiative at HelpMe.
- Those who said there wasn't a KM initiative felt the idea had never been considered or discussed
- Those who said there was a KM initiative felt it was less than 1 year old.
- The main advantages of a KM initiative were perceived as being (1) standardization of existing knowledge in the form of procedures/protocols and (2) facilitation of the reuse and consolidation of knowledge about HelpMe operations.
- The main approaches used to improve knowledge assets and knowledge sharing are cross-functional teams, communities of practice, the intranet, and documentation/newsletters.
- The main approach for improving creation and refinement of knowledge is "lessons-learned analyses."
- The key knowledge that may be lost at HelpMe is knowledge of nonpublished considerations behind HelpMe decisions (i.e., undocumented history of policy/implementation reasons for specific decisions).
- The aspects of the organizational culture that support effective KM are the desire to reach out and provide expertise to other organizations and improved information flows via web site, e-mail, the intranet, databases, and so on.

- The potential inhibitors to KM are time pressures, high turnover of personnel, insufficient resources, and the usual turf protection.
- There is typically little to no organizational buy-in about KM among staff and management.
- There are no formal training programs or formal efforts to support knowledge management; in some cases, KM is supported by on-the-job training and mentoring programs.
- Typically, steps have not been taken to reward and motivate people to encourage a knowledge-sharing environment and knowledge retention.
- Most people regularly use or have access to the intranet and the Internet, but typically don't have, or use, more advanced technologies such as software decision support systems that aid decision makers in their analyses.

The piloted survey was revised and then sent electronically to about 1,000 people at HelpMe, representing all levels of management and staff. A response rate of 80% was achieved. The next section discusses the survey's results.

Survey Analysis

Respondents identified a wide variety of symptoms that suggest a strong need to focus more fully on information and knowledge management at HelpMe. These include

- Employees and managers being too busy "putting out fires now" to think long-term
- Frequent transitions of senior management
- Too busy to have time to chat informally with colleagues
- E-mail being used extensively instead of face-to-face discussions
- Valuable expertise "leaving the company" due to better job offers and retirements
- Professional employees being "transient" in many areas, suggesting the need to capture valuable expertise before those employees leave
- An inadequate training and development budget, which needs to be augmented to maintain and replenish human capital

All of this information suggests a significant need to develop improved information and knowledge sharing, retention, leveraging, and management techniques at HelpMe. The survey responses also provided additional information:

The Most Important Knowledge Carriers at HelpMe Are:	
People	56%
Paper	22%
Magnetic media	13%
Processes	6%
Products/Services	1%
Other	2%

Do Strategic Goals Explicitly Include KM?	
Yes	7%
No	93%

Is There a KM Initiative in Your Organization?	
Yes	16%
No	84%

How Long Has the KM Initiative Been in Existence?	
Less than 1 year	40%
1–2 years	5%
3–4 years	33%
More than 4 years	22%

Ranking of Advantages of KM at HelpMe (percent)						
	Most Important	2	3	4	5	Least Important
Reuse and consolidation of K about operations	24%	19%	18%	10%	13%	3%
Standardization of existing K	26%	14%	14%	13%	6%	12%
Combination of customer K and internal know-how	9%	12%	22%	13%	14%	15%
Acquisition of new K from external sources	21%	12%	18%	10%	7%	15%
Generation of new K inside the organization	17%	27%	15%	13%	8%	7%
Transforming individual K to collective K	50%	13%	8%	8%	3%	6%

Approaches Used to Improve Knowledge Assets (percent)

	Organization-wide	Organizational-unit Specific	Methods (no indication)
Sharing and Combination of Knowledge:			
External or internal benchmarking	8%	10%	6%
Communities of practice	16%	18%	21%
Cross-functional teams	21%	16%	18%
Intranets (including groupware)	21%	5%	18%
Training and education	25%	15%	26%
Documentation and newsletters	20%	13%	22%
Other	1%	2%	2%
Creation and Refinement of Knowledge:			
Lessons-learned analysis	9%	11%	20%
Research and development centers/labs	2%	8%	4%
Explicit learning strategy	6%	5%	6%
Other	0%	1%	1%
Storing of Knowledge (K):			
Storage of customer/stakeholder K	8%	10%	11%
Best-practice inventories	7%	9%	3%
Lessons-learned inventories	8%	13%	8%
Manuals and handbooks	19%	19%	8%
Yellow pages of expertise/knowledge	7%	10%	0%

Degree of Organizational Buy-in for Knowledge Management (percent)

	None	A Little	Some	A lot
Staff				
Professionals/knowledge workers	19%	29%	22%	13%
Operational and clerical	28%	29%	17%	5%
Management				
Senior management	17%	24%	25%	13%
Middle management	17%	23%	25%	15%
First-line supervisory	16%	24%	26%	10%

Has the Organization Taken Steps to Motivate Employees for KM Initiatives?	
Yes	17%
No	83%

Information Technology Used as an Enabler to:	
Investigate, assess, safeguard important K	72%
Use best K to do job well	60%
Learn and innovate to do job better	57%
Reengineer workplace and product system	33%
Better inform public and constituents	68%
Create new products and services	23%
Other	1%

Technologies Used Regularly	
Intranet Technologies	
E-mail	94%
Videoconferencing	23%
Yellow pages expertise	16%
Discussion forums	34%
Shared documents/products	54%
Training and education	44%
Gathering and publication of "lessons-learned/best practices"	26%
Internet Technologies	
Knowledge searching on the WWW	83%
Knowledge exchange with customers	47%
Knowledge and Database Technologies	
Knowledge-based systems (expert systems)	17%
BP/LL best practices/lessons-learned databases	9%
PSS/DSS (performance/decision support systems)	15%
Management info systems (transaction processing)	42%
Data Mining and Knowledge Discovery Techniques	
Extracting knowledge from process data to improve ops	23%
Simulation	12%

The main findings from these responses are

- People were consistently identified as the most important knowledge carriers; this is a good foundation for knowledge management activities and beliefs.
- Knowledge retention and management are not an explicit part of HelpMe's current strategic goals.
- Effective knowledge management transforms individual knowledge into institutional knowledge.
- Training and education were cited as the main approaches for sharing knowledge, yet there has been a very limited budget for formal training and education.
- Lessons-learned analyses were the top method for creating and refining knowledge, yet codifying them into an online repository has rarely been done at HelpMe.
- Manuals and handbooks seem to be the top way of storing operational knowledge.
- There is "a little to some" buy-in, at both the staff and management levels, for the basic tenets of knowledge management.
- HelpMe has not taken steps to motivate or reward employees for creating and contributing to a knowledge-sharing culture.
- Information technology is mainly used at HelpMe to investigate, assess, and safeguard important knowledge.
- Technologies used most frequently at HelpMe include e-mail, knowledge searches on the Web and specialized databases, and management information systems. Very little use is made of decision support tools (e.g., computerized multicriteria decision-making tools), advanced information technologies (e.g., knowledge-based systems that capture and emulate the behavior of human experts in well-defined tasks), and best-practices/lessons-learned databases.

Findings and Recommendations

In order to achieve the goals of HelpMe's new strategic plan, taking into account the survey results, several information and knowledge management initiatives were suggested by an outside consulting firm, including the following:

- Increasing and facilitating employees' access to the information and knowledge they need to perform their jobs efficiently, effectively, and consistently
- Improving the quality and "comfort level" (i.e., reliability, impartiality) of HelpMe decisions
- Capturing and storing, to the fullest extent possible, employee knowledge that is critical to HelpMe's operations and other key HelpMe decisions
- Instilling a culture of information and knowledge sharing and reuse within HelpMe

Applying the Survey Results

The consulting team was assigned to develop an information and knowledge management strategy from the survey results and the other information presented here and to prepare a briefing for HelpMe's board of directors. The team must address the following objectives to develop the strategy:

1. An information and knowledge management plan to meet and implement the four findings and recommendations (i.e., that describes the next steps towards making HelpMe a "knowledge organization" for the 21st century)
2. Methods of gaining and maintaining management and employee support
3. Determining whether the information and knowledge management initiatives have been successful (i.e., metrics to be used to assess the success of the plan)

Effective implementation of objectives 1 and 2 will require the following:

Creation of a More Unified Knowledge Network

Most of the knowledge sharing within HelpMe occurs informally either among individuals in their work units or teams or among peers across work units or groups. This informal personalized knowledge-sharing approach should be encouraged and continued, but the knowledge that is exchanged during these meetings should be made explicit and "codified" into a formal knowledge repository. Knowledge that is not retained and shared can result in repeated mistakes, dependence on a few key individuals, duplicated work, lack of sharing of good ideas, and slow introduction of new solutions.[7] At present, there is no easy way to search across existing knowledge repositories or directories. A nationwide HelpMe knowledge management system should be created with a uniform technology infrastructure. Such a knowledge management system should include proven practices (e.g., best and worst practices), success stories, lessons learned, and rules of thumb (heuristics) gained from experiential learning.

Formalized and Systematized Knowledge Capture

HelpMe's intellectual capital resides largely in its employees. Given the high employee turnover, there is a need to capture the knowledge of HelpMe employees before they leave the company. Widely accessible and thorough documentation of core competencies needs to be created and maintained in one or more repositories.

Strengthening Incentives to Reuse Knowledge

Encouraging HelpMe personnel to reapply successful practices and reuse available knowledge could improve HelpMe's responsiveness. Forming "communities of practice or online communities" (individuals who share similar responsibilities and needs) may also be useful to HelpMe in encouraging the elicitation, sharing, and transfer of knowledge. Some organizations have "Knowledge Fairs" where people with similar interests meet, as part of their work, to network, share experiences, tell stories, and build stronger communities of practice. Additionally, as part of an individual's annual job performance review, employees and managers could be evaluated on how well they are contributing to the knowledge repositories and how well they are applying the knowledge that is available in those repositories in ways that add value to HelpMe's processes.

Organizationally, HelpMe should consider adding a Chief Knowledge Officer (CKO) or charging someone in a senior position with leading the knowledge management initiative and associated knowledge management team. The CKO or equivalent would report directly to the CEO. The CKO should be someone different from the

CIO (Chief Information Officer) due to the different skill set needed and to avoid a strictly technology-focused approach to knowledge management. One of the responsibilities of the CKO could be to make sure that HelpMe is continuously apprised of the latest developments in knowledge management. Consideration should also be given to having "knowledge managers" and "knowledge specialists" in the various business units of HelpMe. Knowledge managers' roles could consist of gathering, reviewing, and overseeing/maintaining knowledge assets for a given area. Knowledge specialists could be subject-matter experts who for a certain amount of time are assigned to gather, analyze, and synthesize a body of knowledge critical to HelpMe.

Culturally, HelpMe may want to consider adding, at some point, a "knowledge performance factor" to annual job performance evaluations. As appropriate, employees could be held accountable for contributing to HelpMe's knowledge stores and for sharing, reusing, seeking, and applying the knowledge from the knowledge repositories. Some organizations, such as Accenture, have even created knowledge-sharing proficiency levels; to be promoted, employees at Accenture must reach a certain level.

Also, parts of each substantial HelpMe project could be to document/encode a set of lessons that were learned from the project into the knowledge management system. This could be made standard practice in the evaluation of, and debriefing on, all important projects.

For knowledge management to work and to build a supportive culture for knowledge sharing, people must be recognized and rewarded for their work in this area. Recognition could be in the form of including the name of each person associated with each lesson learned in the knowledge repositories and then publishing monthly, on the intranet, the most frequently accessed or reused nuggets of knowledge with the author names attached. American Management Systems used this approach in publishing "Best Knews" headlines, and Xerox has used it as well (this has been more motivating than cash incentives). By incorporating a "knowledge contribution and usage" factor into an individual's annual job performance review, people could also be rewarded monetarily for their efforts. Job rotation is another way for employees to better understand HelpMe's various functions and processes and can also serve as additional stimulation for knowledge sharing.

Next Steps Toward Making HelpMe a "Knowledge Organization"

According to one knowledge management study of thirty-one projects in twenty-four companies, the most important factors for successful knowledge management projects were having a knowledge-oriented culture, creating an organizational infrastructure, finding effective motivational tools, and developing senior management support.[8] Toward this goal, the following steps should be strongly considered to transform HelpMe into a knowledge organization:

- Identify a senior-level individual for HelpMe (reporting directly to the CEO) to spearhead knowledge management initiatives and to facilitate the development of a "Knowledge Management Team" across the various business units in HelpMe as a KM Steering Committee (the CKO would chair that committee).
- Establish a group of individuals overseen by the CKO to help develop a HelpMe-wide knowledge management system, provide educational forums on knowledge

management throughout HelpMe, and act as the analyzer and disseminator to ensure that lessons learned will be available to individuals who could benefit from those lessons.

- Start to develop pilot online knowledge management systems, strategically placed within HelpMe, that will include best/worst practices, lessons learned, frequently asked questions and answers, appropriate documentation, cases, and online pools of mission-critical knowledge that has been captured and elicited from experts within HelpMe.
- Bring back some key experts who recently retired in part-time positions to capture their knowledge for permanent inclusion in the knowledge management system.
- Develop a certification/training curriculum on key HelpMe processes and functions.
- Continue to seek increased funding for training and development and develop more formal mentoring programs.
- Routinely have each department present tutorials on hot topics in their respective areas for all interested HelpMe employees to attend.
- Make sure that each department has in-depth manuals of certain processes available via the intranet and that they are updated regularly.
- Use the "team concept" where possible so that people can meet and learn from each other.
- Include a knowledge performance factor as part of the annual job performance appraisal; provide a reward structure to motivate employees to share knowledge.
- Where appropriate, require that lessons learned be encoded during project development and implementation, before final signoff can occur.
- Continue to offer Knowledge Exchanges in key HelpMe core competencies at informal get-togethers to allow communities of practice to network and share their knowledge.
- Make sure that every employee has access to HelpMe's knowledge management system.

HelpMe should also consider undertaking competitive intelligence, identifying key processes and key decision areas, designing and conducting information and knowledge audits, performing knowledge mapping, and so on.

To fulfill objective 3 (measures of success) a number of knowledge-sharing measurements can be compiled. For example,

- Number of new colleague-to-colleague relationships spawned—this will hopefully encourage the exchange of tacit knowledge between individuals
- Reuse rate of "frequently accessed/reused" knowledge
- The number of key concepts that are converted from tacit to explicit knowledge in the online knowledge repositories and are used by members of the organization)
- How many times knowledge is disseminated (i.e., distribution of knowledge) to appropriate individuals
- Number of knowledge-sharing proficiencies achieved
- Number of new ideas generating innovative products, services, or improved processes

- Number of lessons learned and best practices applied to add value (e.g., decreased proposal writing/development time, increased customer loyalty and satisfaction, etc.)
- Number of patents and trademarks produced, the number of articles or books written, and the number of talks given at conferences or workshops or trade shows per employee—the higher the number, the better
- Professional development training dollars, R&D budget dollars, independent R&D dollars per employee—the greater the number, the better
- Number of "serious" anecdotes gathered about the value of the organization's knowledge management systems
- Number of apprentices that employees mentor and the success of these apprentices as they mature in the organization
- Number of interactions with academicians, consultants, and advisors

The set of knowledge management indicators examined by the American Productivity and Quality Center included such measures as the following [www.apqc.org]:

- *Customer Relationships.* Quality customer retention, growth rates.
- *Human Resources.* quality employee retention, rate of investment in intellectual capital (such as training expenditures, employees on sabbatical, employee development plans in progress).
- *Strategic Alliances.* Value added from joint ventures and associations with learning institutions, customers, suppliers, and competitors.
- *Innovation.* new products/services launched, product/service lines exited, prototypes in test, information value added to products/services.
- *Process Improvements.* Best practices imported from elsewhere, best practices exported to others, cycle time and cost reductions, productivity, and quality improvements.

British Petroleum used various knowledge sharing metrics, for example:

- Number of links per respondents
- Frequency of advice seeking
- Individuals with highest number of nominations (i.e., identifies the true experts)
- Ratio of internal to external links (how inward-looking, or otherwise, a business unit is)
- Proportion of total contacts that are inward (how sought-after the knowledge of that business unit is)
- Proportion of total contacts that are outward (which business units seek help the most)
- Number of shared documents published
- Number of improvement suggestions made
- Corporate directory coverage
- Number of patents published
- Number of presentations made

Based on the consulting team's analysis and recommendations, the HelpMe board of directors was very pleased and proceeded to implement some of the suggestions.

⁞⁞ "Doing Your Homework" via a Form of Ethnographic Analysis

Social network analysis (SNA) can be used as a form of ethnographic analysis to map knowledge flows between individuals and departments. According to Cross and Parker, mapping social networks helps in understanding how work really gets done in organizations.[9] Social network analysis can measure relationships between individuals, groups, departments, and various entities and has been used in sociology, anthropology, information systems, organizational behavior, and many other disciplines.

Looking at the results from question 7 in the Knowledge Access and Sharing Survey, we can use SNA to determine who people in an organization seek out for answers to their questions. The knowledge maps included here were drawn with the mapping software Netdraw and UCINET 6. For example, the social networks show the survey responses identifying the top two individuals in the Foundation to whom people go when they have questions or seek general advice. The first diagram makes it easy to identify the key individuals (Kevin S., Peter B., Rob F., and others) who are sought out for "general advice." The size of the nodes in the diagram is proportional to their "betweenness centrality"; that is, the larger the nodes, the more power the individual has because more people depend on that individual to make connections with other people. The small black-colored nodes show the "isolates," who aren't connected. The second graph depicts the multidimensional scaling method, which shows the clusters of connections. Here certain black nodes depict the "cutpoints" whereby if a node were removed, that structure would become unconnected. The larger nodes are shown in the middle (with the smaller nodes on the periphery) to indicate "where the action is" (i.e., where the strength of the connections occurs).

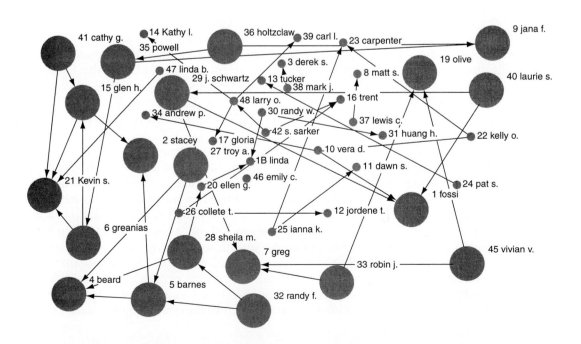

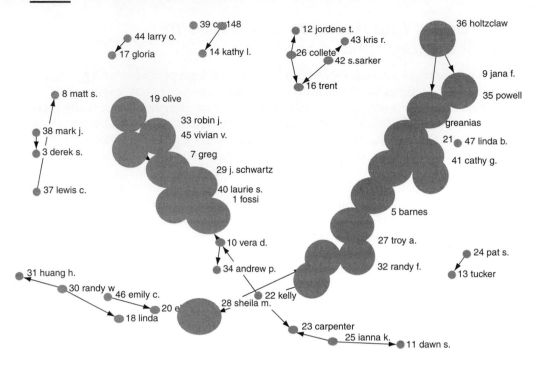

The second graph can also portray groupings to indicate the level of connectedness and interactions between divisions. For example, the grouping with Tina T. (node 16) indicates that all those individuals are within one division and that they seek help within this community. Other divisions seem to seek help from within their own communities/divisions. The graph also shows some gatekeepers, who bridge between different communities, such as Sheila M. (node 28). One area for improvement is better interlinking among the divisions through more interaction between the Executive Office and the various divisions and also having Communications play a greater interconnected role by linking with the various divisions. The Communications Division should probably have a more central role instead of being on the periphery, as depicted in the second graph.

Social network analysis can also be used on the responses to the knowledge audit to see how employees are interacting with each other, based upon their length of service to the Foundation. The following graph depicts the five communities of employees (those who have been at the Foundation less than 6 months, those who have been employed 6 months to less than 1 year, 1 year to less than 3 years, 3 years to less than 5 years, and more than 5 years). The social network shows a healthy relationship in that the employees who are the newest in the organization are seeking advice from employees who are typically fairly senior (more than 5 years at the Foundation). The Foundation may want to consider a mentoring program or "buddy system" whereby those employees who have been working less than 1 year can link up with those employees at the Foundation for 1–3 years (currently, those working less than 1 year at

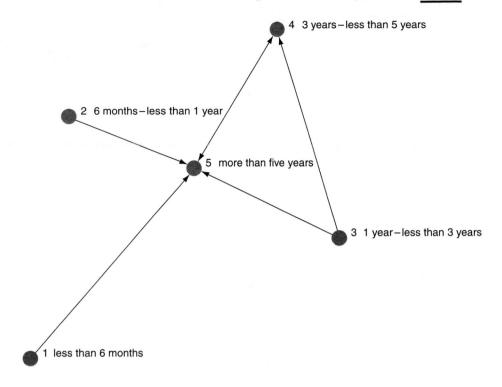

the Foundation aren't generally seeking advice from peers closest to their work experience) in order to further build a sense of belonging.

Through social network analysis and other research methods, the IT professional can be better prepared to handle the client engagement. "Doing the homework," in terms of applying the proper analytical and research techniques, allows the IT professional to be ready to tackle future challenges.

EXERCISES   ▮▮▮▮▮▮▮

1. Use the electronic databases and electronic journals in your library's electronic resources to research the do's and don'ts of IT (information technology) management consulting. Write a paper that discusses what you discover.
2. You have been asked by a client to develop an IT application, but you feel that there is "scope creep" whereby the user requirements for the application keep growing. In other words, the client keeps expanding the original scope of the effort without increasing the resources assigned to the project. How do you tactfully tell the client about this problem?
3. Write a paper on the pros and cons of "not reinventing the wheel" from an IT perspective.
4. Some people claim that using quantitative information systems research methods are better than applying qualitative methods. Prepare to discuss both sides of this claim.
5. Research the pitfalls in using surveys, and write a short paper discussing your findings. Be prepared to present a 15-minute briefing on your results.

ENDNOTES ▪▪▪▪▪▪▪

1. Margerison, Charles. (2001). *Managerial Consulting Skills: A Practical Guide.* Gower Publishing, p. 62.
2. Lippitt, Gordon. (1971). *Organizational Renewal.* Appleton Century Crofts, NY.
3. Myers, Mike. http://www.isworld.org.
4. Knock, N., and Lau, F. "Information Systems Action Research: Serving Two Demanding Masters." *Information Technology & People* 14 (no. 1), pp. 6–11.
5. Babbie, E. (1995). *The Practice of Social Research,* 7th ed. Wadsworth Publishing, Belmont, CA.; Dillman, D. (1978). *Mail and Telephone Surveys: The Total Design Method.* Wiley, NY.
6. Myers, Mike. (1999). "Investigating Information Systems with Ethnographic Research." *Communications of AIS* 2.
7. Cortada, J., and Woods, J., eds. (1999). *The Knowledge Management Yearbook 1999–2000.* Butterworth-Heinemann, Cambridge, MA.
8. Davenport, T., DeLong, D., and Beers, M. (1998). "Successful Knowledge Management Projects." *Sloan Management Review* (Winter).
9. Cross, Rob, and Parker, Andrew. (2004). *The Hidden Power of Social Networks.* Harvard Business School Press, Cambridge, MA.

SUGGESTED REFERENCES ▪▪▪▪▪▪▪

Becerra-Fernandez, I., Gonzalez, A., and Sabherwal, R. (2004). *Knowledge Management: Challenges, Solutions, and Technologies.* Upper Saddle River, NJ, Pearson Prentice Hall.

Chatzkel, J. (2003). *Knowledge Capital*, Oxford University Press, Oxford, UK.

Cortada, J., and Woods, J. eds. (1999). *The Knowledge Management Yearbook 1999–2000.* Butterworth-Heinemann, Cambridge, MA.

Davenport, T., De Long, D., and Beers, M. (1998). "Successful Knowledge Management Projects." *Sloan Management Review*, (Winter).

Davenport, T., and Prusak, L. (1998). *Working Knowledge.* Harvard Business School Press, Cambridge, MA.

Groff, T, and Jones, T. (2003). *Introduction to Knowledge Management: KM in Business.* Elsevier Butterworth-Heinemann, Burlington, MA.

Holsapple, C., ed. (2003). *The Handbook on Knowledge Management.* 2 volumes. Springer-Verlag, Berlin.

Liebowitz, J. (2004). *Addressing the Human Capital Crisis in the Federal Government: A Knowledge Management Perspective.* Elsevier Butterworth-Heinemann, Burlington, MA.

Liebowitz, J. (2001). *Knowledge Management: Learning from Knowledge Engineering.* CRC Press, Boca Raton, FL.

Liebowitz, J. (2000). *Building Organizational Intelligence: A Knowledge Management Primer.* CRC Press, Boca Raton, FL.

Liebowitz, J., ed. (1999). *The Knowledge Management Handbook.* CRC Press, Boca Raton, FL.

Liebowitz, J., and Beckman, T. (1998). *Knowledge Organizations: What Every Manager Should Know.* CRC Press, Boca Raton, FL.

Leedy, P., and Ormrod, J. (2001). *Practical Research: Planning and Design,* 7th ed. Prentice Hall, Upper Saddle River, NJ.

Morey, D., Maybury, M., and Thuraisingham, B. eds. (2000). *Knowledge Management: Classic and Contemporary Works.* MIT Press, Cambridge, MA.

Saint-Onge, H., and Armstrong, C. (2004). *The Conductive Organization: Building Beyond Sustainability*, Elsevier Butterworth-Heinemann, Burlington, MA.

CHAPTER 4

Writing Feasibility Studies

Lesson Objectives

■ To learn the importance of performing feasibility studies

■ To acquire skills in writing feasibility studies

■ To apply feasibility assessment methodologies

What Is a Feasibility Study?

Whether developing an information systems project or determining the best site to establish an office, a feasibility study is typically used as part of the preparation stage in the decision-making process. A feasibility study is usually conducted to assist decision makers in determining whether or not to implement a particular project or program. Such a study is, according to one definition, an evaluation or analysis of the potential impact of a proposed project or program. For example, the sections of a feasibility study to determine whether to use a centralized foodservice system could consist of the following[1] :

1. Executive Summary
2. Background Information
3. Proposed Centralized Foodservice System
   a. Description of the Proposed System (Solution)
   b. Advantages and Disadvantages of the Proposed System
   c. Staffing
   d. Space Requirements
   e. Basic Layout of the Central Kitchen and Satellite Kitchens
   f. Equipment Needs and Costs
   g. Computer Hardware and Software Requirements
   h. Site Possibilities
4. Comparison of Current and Proposed Alternative Systems or Solutions
5. Project Schedule
6. Final Recommendation

A feasibility study attempts to determine the practicality of a project.[2] The simplest form of a feasibility study answers the yes-or-no question: "Should we undertake the project?" More complex studies answer a more difficult question, "Which (if any) of several projects should we undertake?" A feasibility study is research that gives you preliminary information regarding your business idea's potential to succeed in the marketplace.[3] In the context of writing a feasibility study to determine whether your business idea is a good one, the feasibility study would study, analyze, and discuss the product or service being proposed, the owners and management, the market, the competition, and the budget. In this context, the goal of the feasibility study is to give the entrepreneur a clear evaluation of the potential for sales and profit for a particular idea.[4]

▪▪▪ Why Are Feasibility Studies Important for IT Professionals?

IT professionals are taught that requirements and analysis are the first components of the systems development life cycle. Part of the analysis phase includes performing a feasibility study to determine "proof-of-concept" or to investigate the various alternatives for systems development. For example, if you are building a scheduling system, you would want to see if scheduling systems have been built in your domain of application. If so, what techniques were used to handle the scheduling—optimization approach, heuristic method, hybrid approach, or others? The feasibility study should consider the various alternative scheduling methods and then recommend the best approach to use for the scheduling system. According to the Greenwood Consulting Group,[5] a feasibility study should

- Reiterate what problem or opportunity you are addressing
- State your proposed solution or approach
- Indicate why this is the best possible solution to your problem or opportunity
- Discuss the "technical risks" of your proposed approach
- State how you will decide whether your solution or approach is feasible, and how you will measure feasibility
- Justify your feasibility measure

The feasibility study usually looks at various types of feasibility: technical, economic, legal, operational, and schedule. Technical feasibility examines the function, performance, and constraints that may affect the ability to achieve an acceptable solution. Economic feasibility is an evaluation of development cost weighed against the income or benefit derived from the system or product developed. Legal feasibility determines any infringement, violation, or liability that could result from development of the system. Some feasibility studies explore market feasibility in terms of examining the competition and determining how successful the proposed product, service, or approach would be in the marketplace. Operational feasibility determines how well the proposed system or solution will work in a given organization. It also studies how people (users, operators, and support or maintenance staff) interact, use, operate, and feel about the proposed system. Finally, schedule feasibility determines how reasonable and doable the project schedule is in terms of meeting the milestones and deadlines.

Technical Feasibility

Technical feasibility determines how reasonable and practical it is to design and develop the proposed system or solution in terms of the availability of technology, parts, tools, equipment, infrastructure, resources, expertise, hardware, and software components. In general, technical feasibility responds to the following major questions during the design and development process of a given system:

1. Does the technology for building the proposed system exist, and if so, is it proven and mature?
2. Do the required expertise and skill sets exist (either inside or outside the company) to design and develop the proposed system, and if so, are they affordable in terms of planned budget and schedule?

In terms of "proof of concept" or analyzing whether the approach has merit, technical feasibility becomes an important measure. Technical feasibility looks at whether the idea has a good chance of succeeding from a technical perspective. It also determines how practical the proposed solution is in terms of availability of technical resources, expertise, adopted standards, and infrastructure. For example, a chemist at a well-known government laboratory had taken a course on expert systems development (an expert system is a computer program that emulates the behavior of an expert in a well-defined domain of knowledge). The chemist, as part of his duties in the laboratory, became involved in procurement and contracting activities in order to hire contractors to help with his research. The chemist felt that an expert system would be appropriate to help him and other contracting officer's technical representatives (COTRs) answer questions relating to the pre-award phase of a contract, such as what forms should be included in a procurement request package, to whom these forms should be routed, what type of synopsis must be written to announce the solicitation for proposals, and other considerations. The chemist sent a memo to the laboratory's artificial intelligence group to see whether this idea of developing an expert system to help COTRs in the pre-award phase of contracts was feasible. The artificial intelligence group looked first at technical feasibility. In other words, would this type of problem be amenable to an expert system solution? Such technical factors as whether this problem involved mostly cognitive skills, whether the application occurred frequently, whether the problem involved mostly symbolic processing, whether there was an expert who was willing and able to work on this project, and a host of other related technical questions were considered.

Technical feasibility can be decomposed into various technical criteria that need to be met in order for the project idea to be successful. Some of the technical questions to be answered are

- Does the proposed approach or solution lend itself to the problem characteristics?
- Has this type of technical approach been applied previously to similar problems?
- What are the technical risks and associated risk mitigation strategies associated with this project?
- What are the technical backgrounds and knowledge areas needed, on the part of the project team, in order for this project to succeed?
- What types of technologies must be applied to make this project successful?

In the expert system example, the contracting domain had the problem characteristics that were amenable to an expert system solution. Additionally, others had applied an expert system approach successfully to procurement and contracting applications. A knowledge engineering project team could be developed for which a project manager, knowledge engineers (i.e., expert system developers), and a domain expert were available and interested in working on this project. The project also had the financial and moral support of the sponsor—the director of the contracts division in the laboratory. The director wanted the expert system to be deployed on PCs since most people had access to personal computers. Additionally, expert system shells (i.e., development toolkits) existed that could be used to aid in the development process, instead of programming everything from scratch. This would reduce some of the technical risks and speed up the prototyping process. Other technical risks were negligible and could be easily mitigated.

Economic Feasibility

In addition to the technical feasibility of a proposed approach or solution, economic feasibility must also be determined. Economic feasibility refers to the viability of the proposed idea from a financial perspective through analyzing whether the benefits of a proposed system or solution are worthwhile. Economic feasibility is conducted as soon as the proposed system requirements specifications are developed. An approach or solution could be technically feasible but may be infeasible from a cost viewpoint. Financial constraints are present with most projects because usually funds are limited. Thus, a thorough cost-benefit study must be performed to determine the financial viability of the proposed idea. Many analysts use a return-on-investment approach to do this. For example, an organization interested in developing a knowledge management (KM) strategy throughout its divisions calculated the following costs for the first 2 years of the knowledge management plan:

Year 1 Costs	
KM Monthly Seminars: 6 local/6 outside (travel expenses, possible honoraria):	$3,500
KM Council Meetings: monthly (materials):	600
KM Department (Chief Knowledge Officer @ $95,000/yr; 1 staff @ $85,000/yr; KM Specialist ($30,000—will help develop the knowledge portal):	210,000
KM Facilitated Workshop: Online Expertise Locator:	20,000
3 mo. × $10,000/mo. × 2 persons (labor costs):	60,000
Online Community of Practice with Lessons-Learned Pilot: 6 mo. × $10,000/mo. × 1 person × ½ time (facilitator/moderator) = $30,000 + $30,000 launch + [$5,000/mo. × 6 mo. for basic features using CoP (community of practice) software] + $10,000 (customization):	100,000
User Fees for Software ($200/user × 500 persons in Code X):	100,000
Expert and Knowledge-Retention System Pilot:	100,000
Technical Database–LiveLink Integration (importing contents of the Technical Database into LiveLink and integrating a few knowledge-management-related databases and capturing/storing selected KM-related documents):	500,000*
Measure and Evaluate KM Pilots: 1 mo. × $10,000/mo. × 1 person:	10,000
Develop Knowledge-Sharing Proficiencies and Institutionalize Them within Annual Appraisal Form:	10,000
Conduct Focus Groups Throughout All Directorates on Change Management/KM Processes: Outside specialist (every other month at $3000/day):	18,000
TOTAL for Year 1	$1,132,100

*Please note: May want to defer to Year 2.

Year 2 Costs	
Extend the Expertise Locator to all Directorates ($150/user × 3,300 persons):	$495,000
Extend the Online Communities and Collaboration—5 more major online communities: ($30,000/yr/facilitator × 5)	150,000
Expand the Lessons-Learned Repository to all Directorates (7 people × 1 yr × $85,000/yr):	595,000
Continue to Develop Expert and Knowledge-Retention Systems in 10 Critical Areas ($30,000/area × 10 areas):	300,000
Expanding the Technical Database with LiveLink via Further Integration to Include Other Relevant KM-related Databases and Resources:	800,000
Give Awards/Tie Knowledge Sharing to Merit/Reward:	Not Sure Yet
KM Dept. (Chief Knowledge Officer @ $95,000/yr; 2 staff @ $85,000; KM Specialist @ $10,000):	275,000
TOTAL for Year 2 (not including awards/merit)	$2,615,000

The payback period, which looks at when the organization would recoup its costs, was calculated at about 3 years. After 3 years, the organization would realize benefits of about $2 million a year. The organization felt that knowledge management was important enough to implement in the organization and felt comfortable with its financial viability and projections.

Part of the challenge of performing an economic justification is how to handle the "intangibles." Intangible assets may be human capital, structural capital, relationship capital, or competitive capital. Human capital is "people power," namely, what is in the heads of the employees in terms of knowledge and experiential learning. Structural capital is assets that can't be easily taken home from the office, such as intellectual property rights or certain types of databases. Relationship capital, sometimes called *social* or *customer capital*, is knowledge gained from customers or stakeholders. Competitive capital, especially "competitive intelligence," deals with branding or the competitive edge that an organization has over others. These four types of capital should be considered as part of the economic justification. Skandia, an international financial services firm headquartered in Sweden, produces an Intellectual Capital Navigator report that quantifies human, structural, and social capital at Skandia, and it sends this report along with its annual financial report to its stockholders. In the United States, the Securities and Exchange Commission (SEC) wants companies to quantify their intangible assets in their 10K annual reports, rather than lumping these intangibles under "goodwill" in a balance sheet.

Operational Feasibility

Operational feasibility determines how well the proposed system or solution will work within the intended environment. Whitten and Dittman argue that operational feasibility is people-oriented whereas technical feasibility is technology, hardware, and software-oriented.[6] This means that operational feasibility must take into account how the users, systems administrators, operators, and maintenance and support staff would feel about the proposed system. Therefore, when assessing the operational feasibility of a system, close attention should be paid to the following issues:

- The end users are provided with their desired outputs or services.
- The system is reliable and meets its reliability, availability, and maintainability requirements.
- Management, users, operators, and support and maintenance staff supports the system. People may resist change. If they do, how this resistance to change can be overcome by reasonable and acceptable effort will be critical to the success of the system.
- The system can be easily learned and used by its operators and end users. Ease of use is an important issue in determining the operational feasibility of a proposed system. How long training will take and how much it will cost to train people to operate, use, support, and maintain the proposed system should be determined.

Schedule Feasibility

According to Baccarini et al., one of the highest risk areas in information technology projects is meeting the project's schedule, milestones, and deadlines.[7] Schedule feasibility determines whether the project schedule, milestones, and deadlines are acceptable. Missing a deadline can be very costly, and sometimes penalties are incurred. Therefore, you should study and analyze the schedule feasibility of a project to make sure that the proposed solution(s) and deliverables will be on time.

Legal Feasibility

Legal feasibility refers to the possible violations and liabilities that could result from the proposed product or service, once developed. For example, developing an expert system to diagnose children's medical problems could possibly lead to litigation if the system produced faulty advice that was relied upon by the user. Even with disclaimers to limit the liability, certain products may not be worthwhile to develop from a legal feasibility standpoint. When Disneyland Paris was being built (at that time, it was called EuroDisney), the insurance laws were quite different in France from those in the United States; this should have been factored into the legal feasibility of developing the Disney park in Paris. It would be worthwhile to have the appropriate lawyers as part of the feasibility study team to provide counsel on legal issues relating to product/service design.

Market Feasibility

In developing a product or service to be sold, market feasibility is a critical piece of the up-front analysis. Any entrepreneur who develops a business plan and asks for venture capital will need to provide a detailed market feasibility study. This study would include such things as the potential market for the proposed product/service, the competitors in that market, demand and supply projections, justification for why this product/service would be successful from a marketing viewpoint, and other market-related considerations. The market feasibility component of the overall feasibility study should address the following categories in detail[8]:

The Market
Who is your market? What is the demographic? Is the market strong? Is it growing? What challenges are facing the market? How will you reach the market? What are the costs involved in reaching this market?

The Competition
Who is the direct competition? Who is the indirect competition? How does your product compare to theirs? What is your unique selling point? Can your competitors readily duplicate your product or service? How are they likely to react when you enter the market?

EXERCISE

Your brother-in-law, the chief designer of Cars R Us (a niche marketing car manufacturer), has asked your help in his latest project. He would like you to write a feasibility study for the following application:

> Due to Washington, DC being the third most traffic-congested area in the United States, commuters have often remarked that there isn't sufficient road infrastructure to support all the vehicles in the DC-Baltimore area. To address this concern, one of the car manufacturers (Cars R Us) has recently announced that it is developing a "James Bond" car. At the press of a button, this car will be equipped to have collapsible helicopter blades that can be unfolded so that cars can fly above the traffic (of course, concerns also arise with having traffic congestion and accidents in the air space if these types of cars become affordable and plentiful). Other high-tech features of this car are being discussed in order to either maximize comfort in the car if stuck in traffic or provide other creative functionalities in the car to circumvent road congestion. One of the main constraints is that the car's entry price in the market will probably be initially for the high-end buyers, but ultimately the hope is to eventually lower the car price to make it more affordable for the everyday consumer.

Your brother-in-law needs to show the feasibility study of this new car design to the CEO of Cars R Us by next week. You have agreed to help him, primarily out of favor to the family. This also sounds like an exciting idea that could perhaps make you "rich and famous." Your brother-in-law has asked you to give him a written feasibility study for this innovation and to prepare a 10-minute Powerpoint presentation as well (turning in a hard copy of the Powerpoint slides). You reply, "It sounds like fun!"

Be Careful of Numbers When Conducting Feasibility Studies
USA Today (Ellen Horrow and Alejandro Gonzalez, Jan. 2, 2004) indicated that the Rose Bowl generates the biggest crowds. The average attendance in the BCS bowl games in the 5 years, 1999–2003 (stadium capacity in parentheses), was

> Rose: 92,525 (96,576)
> Fiesta: 75,809 (73,471)
> Sugar: 74,429 (76,791)
> Orange: 72,965 (72,230)

In reading these statistics, there are two possible misrepresentations. First, for the Orange Bowl figures, the average attendance exceeded the stadium's capacity. This figure may be questionable, unless people stood without having a designated seat or two people sat in the same seats.

Second, it would make sense that given these numbers, the Rose Bowl would attract the biggest crowd because it has the largest stadium capacity versus the others. It would have been better to perhaps compute a percentage in terms of the "occupancy rate" (e.g., average attendance/stadium capacity) than to just base the results on the raw attendance figures.

▪▪▪ Applying Feasibility Assessment Methodologies

Various feasibility assessment methodologies can be used in a feasibility study. One popular one is cost-benefit analysis. Benefits could include cost savings, cost avoidance, increases in revenue, intangible benefits (e.g., improved consistency in decision making or increasing the synergy among departments in the organization), and benefits observed from existing systems.[9] Cost factors include tangible costs (e.g., capital costs, recurrent costs), intangible costs, and risk factors. The key question that user management needs to answer by analyzing the costs and benefits of the proposed information system is: "Given my wish list for the system and the envisaged benefits of the proposed system, am I willing to pay the estimated price and operate with the listed potential risks?"[10]

Another approach to feasibility assessment is the Analytic Hierarchy Process (AHP). AHP, developed by Thomas Saaty at the University of Pittsburgh, applies a multicriteria decision-making approach consisting of ratio scales versus ordinal scales to make comparisons. Ratio scales (e.g., saying "proposal 1 is twice as strong as proposal 2") are probably preferred over simply assigning a single or aggregate number to rate a particular choice. Using the AHP, the goal is placed at the top of the hierarchy, then criteria and subcriteria are listed, and finally alternatives at the lower level of the hierarchy. Through pairwise comparisons using Saaty's scale of relative importance (shown next), the decision maker first compares the criteria with respect to the goal in order to determine the relative weight of importance of one criterion over another.

Then, the alternatives are compared with respect to each criterion to determine the relative weights of the alternatives interms of each criterion. Afterwards, a synthesis of the weights of the criteria and the associated weights of the alternatives per criterion is calculated to give the overall weights of preferences for the various alternatives.[11]

Scale of Relative Importance
1: Equal in Importance
3: Moderate Importance
5: Strong Importance
7: Very Strong Importance
9: Extreme Importance
2, 4, 6, and 8 are intermediate values between the ranges.

A software package called Expert Choice (www.expertchoice.com) is an automated version of AHP. Following is an example of using the AHP–Expert Choice approach to evaluate software packages.

AHP Example of Evaluating Software Packages

Let's suppose you have been tasked to determine the most appropriate software to use for your particular project. We can apply the AHP methodology to help in this evaluation. Of course, the Expert Choice software program automates the process, but we'll explain how the AHP methodology works. The goal will be to determine the best software to use for your project. The criteria are "meets project technical requirements," "financial considerations," "prestige in the field," and "vendor support." The alternatives are Software A, Software B, Software C, and Software D.

You as the evaluator, would start entering your verbal judgments to weight the criteria and then would weight the alternatives versus each criterion as follows: "With respect to the goal, is "meets project technical requirements" more important than "financial considerations," and if so, how much more important? Saaty's scale of relative importance would be used to translate the verbal judgments into numeric values.

You would then enter all the pairwise comparisons for the criteria, which would result in weighted criteria that add up to 1. In this example, your preferences for the criteria, with respect to the goal, are

	Prestige in the Field	Vendor Support	Financial Considerations	Meets Project Technical Requirements
Prestige in the Field	1	3	1	1/3
Vendor Support	1/3	1	1/3	1/3
Financial Considerations	1	3	1	1
Meets Project Technical Requirements	3	3	1	1

Now, the overall weight that is assigned to each criterion must be determined. This is calculated by dividing each entry by the sum of the column in which it appears [http://mat.gsia.cmu.edu/mstc/multiple/node4.html]. For example, the Prestige in the Field/Prestige in the Field entry would end up as 1/(1 + 1/3 + 1 + 3) = 0.188. The other entries are as follows:

	Prestige in the Field	Vendor Support	Financial Consideration	Meets Project Technical Requirements	Average
Prestige in the Field	.188	.333	.300	.124	.223
Vendor Support	.062	.100	.100	.124	.096
Financial Consideration	.188	.333	.300	.375	.287
Meets Project Technical Requirements	.563	.333	.300	.375	.394

The average weights of the criteria suggest that the most important criteria according to your judgments are in order, meets project technical requirements (about 39 percent), financial considerations (about 29 percent), prestige in the field (about 22 percent), and vendor support (about 10 percent). Note that the percentages should add up to 100 percent.

The next step is to weight the alternatives versus each criterion using pairwise comparisons. The same procedure is followed. The relative scores for each of the alternatives versus the criteria are as follows:

	Software A	Software B	Software C	Software D
Prestige in the Field	.433	.238	.169	.161
Vendor Support	.250	.250	.250	.250
Financial Considerations	.357	.172	.235	.235
Meets Project Technical Requirements	.147	.548	.158	.147

Referring back to the overall weights, you can now determine an overall value for each alternative. This is called the synthesis step. For example, the overall value for Software A is calculated as

$$(.223)(.433) + (.096)(.250) + (.287)(.357) + (.394)(.147) = .281$$

Again, these weights should total 1. Based on the synthesis, Software B has the highest weight of .342, then Software A (.281), then Software C (.192), and finally Software D (.185). This suggests that Software B would be the best choice, based upon your judgments. The following figure is a screen shot of Expert Choice/AHP being used for IT project prioritization.

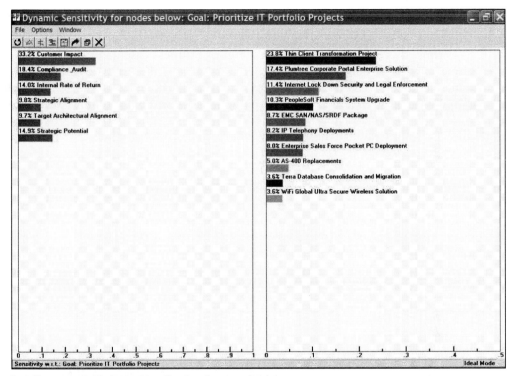

http://www.expertchoice.com/applications/itpmpreview.htm

A feasibility study can also be thought of as a business case analysis (BCA). According to Carole Meals at Mitretek, a BCA is input to the IT selection process and makes the business case for going forward with the project. It usually includes information concerning scope, alternatives considered, estimated costs and return on investment, schedule, risk, and acquisition and technology strategy. The BCA for IT projects usually includes[12]

> Part 1: Alignment
> > Section 1: Business Needs and Alignment with Strategic Business Goals
> > Section 2: Assumptions and Constraints
>
> Part 2: Gap Analysis
> > Section 3: Current State Assessment
> > Section 4: Future State Assessment
> > Section 5: Gap Analysis

Part 3: Alternatives Analysis
    Section 6: Analysis of Alternatives
    Section 7: High-Level Logical Design
    Section 8: Cost-Benefit Analysis
    Section 9: IT Architecture Compliance (especially for government agencies)
Part 4: Project Management
    Section 10: Risk Analysis
    Section 11: Acquisition Strategy
    Section 12: Project Life Cycle Schedule

There are other feasibility assessment or business case analysis approaches that are often used in addition to cost-benefit analysis and the Analytic Hierarchy Process. One technique is SWOT analysis (for Strengths-Weaknesses-Opportunities-Threats). Strengths and weaknesses refer to internal factors, and opportunities and threats are viewed as external factors. A sample SWOT analysis and marketing plan are shown here for determining on how an individual could best work in the IT field after graduating from college.[13]

Preview of a Stellar Career
A SWOT Analysis of Ken Erickson
[http://www.quintcareers.com/SWOT_sample.html]

By combining the top GPA in the business school with excellent work experience and campus involvement, I am poised to begin my career with a boom. Although the information technology field is highly competitive, with countless talented people holding a multitude of technical skills, the huge demand for skilled professionals allows a new college graduate to succeed.

Strengths

With a finance major and minors in information technology and economics, I hold the top GPA in the business school—4.00. I have been working part-time for two years as a systems consultant earning a respectable salary at a $36 billion (gross revenue) conglomerate, ABB. I have worked for several departments on campus, managed the *Stetson Reporter*, played in the wind ensemble, won numerous scholarships, and have been inducted into five honor societies at Stetson University. In addition to academic achievement and leadership skills, my computer skills include four hardware platforms, five operating systems, a programming language, and dozens of software applications. The above are just some of my strengths as a student and potential employee. However, being married for two years has taught me the value of effective communication and the power of teamwork.

Weaknesses

Even an unblemished academic record at the prestigious Stetson University cannot substitute for years of relevant work experience. In the information technology field, technical skills are the most important factor in job success, if not career success. Though I have abundant hardware and software experience for an undergraduate, a computer science major holds much more technical knowledge than an information systems minor. People working in the field for four or five years typically know many programming languages as well as enterprise-wide software, including Oracle, SAP, Novell, PeopleSoft, Informix, or others. Thus, lifelong learning and continuous improvement must be applied to my life for continued success.

Opportunities

Systems analyst and computer engineer are two of the fastest-growing job titles in the United States. According to the Bureau of Labor Statistics, both are expected to grow more than 90 percent by 2008. Salaries continue to be relatively high because of an imbalance in supply and demand for skilled professionals.

Threats

A great deal of publicity has surrounded the phenomenal growth in the information technology field, and more people are enrolling in training programs to take advantage of the trend. Many children have the technical skills in computer systems of entry-level analysts. Today's standard of technical competence will be tomorrow's level of incompetence. The technological landscape changes so quickly that being successful requires constant upgrading of skills and proficiencies.

Marketing Plan

1. Objective(s)
   Information technology specialist/systems analyst
2. Marketing Strategies
   Determine the top companies for IT professionals.
   Examine the potential of employment with dot-com companies.
   Find an employer with a corporate culture that aligns well with my values.
   Build and strengthen my network.
3. Action Programs
   Generate a list of the top fifty companies for IT professionals through a search of web sites and periodicals, as well as word-of-mouth.
   Research name and title of IT hiring managers.
   Join one or more tech-related discussion lists to determine the pros and cons of working for a dot-com. If more pros, develop a list of the best dot-coms to work for.
   Visit each potential company's web site and obtain other information as it relates to the company's corporate culture.
   Develop, nurture, and grow at least three network contacts per week.

The Balanced Scorecard approach is another a popular technique to use for feasibility assessment, as well as for strategic planning. According to the Balanced Scorecard Institute in Rockville, MD, the Balanced Scorecard enables organizations to clarify their vision and strategy and translate them into action.[14]

The Balanced Scorecard method was developed by Robert Kaplan and David Norton in the early 1990s. It views the organization using four perspectives: customer, financial, internal business processes, and learning and growth. For each perspective, objectives, measures, targets, and initiatives are determined. The customer perspective looks at "to achieve our vision, how should we appear to our customers?" The financial perspective is "to succeed financially, how should we appear to our shareholders?" The internal business processes perspective is "to satisfy our shareholders and customers, what business processes must we excel at?" The learning and growth perspective is "to achieve our vision, how will we sustain our ability to change and improve?"[15] Through the use of "strategy maps," as created by Kaplan and Norton, the balanced scorecard approach can link the processes (i.e., operations, customer relationships, innovation, and regulatory and social processes) to desired outcomes. A good example of the balanced scorecard and strategy map techniques, developed for The Vinfen Corporation, can be found at http://www.balancedscorecard.org/files/Vinfen_Newsletter.pdf.

SUMMARY ▮▮▮▮▮▮▮

Writing feasibility studies or other types of evaluations is a frequent activity of IT professionals. Testing the feasibility of an idea is often one of the first steps in the decision-making process. Whether designing a new information system, using an existing COTS (commercial off-the-shelf) tool, or starting an IT business, the feasibility study (or business case analysis) becomes a critical part of the process. This chapter provided some guidance on the importance of feasibility studies, how to write a feasibility study, and what feasibility assessment methodologies can be used.

EXERCISES ▮▮▮▮▮▮▮

1. Your boss has tasked you to develop a feasibility analysis on whether your company should use an e-learning software package, like Blackboard, for its internal employee training. Write a short feasibility analysis, citing any assumptions, to address this decision.
2. What is the difference between feasibility analyses and business plans? Do a literature search to explain the distinction, if any.
3. Perform a SWOT analysis on whether you should buy stock in Microsoft.
4. Use a Balanced Scorecard approach to determine whether your organization should offshore its IT development.
5. Do a 10-minute Powerpoint presentation for Exercises 3 and 4.

ENDNOTES ▮▮▮▮▮▮▮

1. *Guide to Centralized Foodservice Systems.* http://www.nfsmi.org/Information/cfs/cfsindex.html.
2. University of Massachusetts. http://www.unix.oit.umass.edu/~pwtc/tw/assign/feasibility.html.
3. Campbell, June. "A Feasibility Study and You: A Dynamic Duo." http://www.websitemarketingplan.com/Arts/Feasibility.htm.
4. http://www.ewebslu.edu/feasibility_studies. htm.
5. Greenwood Consulting Group. http://www.home.att.net/~g-jgreenwood/sbirt_proposal_writing_basics2.htm.
6. Whitten, J., Bentley, L., and Dittman, K. (2000). *Systems Analysis and Design Methods.* McGraw-Hill, New York.
7. Baccarini, D., Salm, G., and Love, P. (2004). "Management of Risks in Information Technology Projects." *Industrial Management and Data Systems Journal* 104 (no. 4), April.
8. Campbell, June. http://www.websitemarketingplan.com/Arts/Feasibility.htm.
9. Khoong, C., and Ku, Y. (1994). "A Holistic Feasibility Study Framework for Decision Systems. *IEEE Transactions on Systems, Man, and Cybernetics* 24 (no. 1), January.
10. Ibid.
11. Expert Choice, Inc., Pittsburgh, PA. http://www.expertchoice.com.
12. Meals, C. (2003). "Business Case Analysis." Mitretek Systems, Fairfax, VA.
13. http://www.quintcareers.com/SWOT_sample.html.
14. Balanced Scorecard Institute, Rockville, MD. http://www.balancedscorecard.org.
15. Ibid.

CHAPTER 5

Cross-Cultural Communications

Learning Objectives

- To learn to appreciate the global society in which we live
- To become more cognizant of other cultures when communicating
- To appreciate the customs and nuances of international business protocol

We live in a global society. We must therefore be sensitive to and proficient in cross-cultural communications. For example, IT outsourcing to India, China, and Russia is becoming quite common. According to *Wall Street & Technology*, outsourcing software projects offshore is one of the hottest topics in management consulting.[1] Countries like China, India, and Russia offer high intellectual capital, lower wages, and large numbers of programmers. As a result, many U.S. IT corporations are outsourcing their work to these countries and others. According to the Information Technology Association of America (ITAA), more IT jobs will be created offshore than onshore over the next 5 years.[2] And, according to *The Economist*, Asian firms are also outsourcing IT and back-office operations to some U.S. companies.[3]

As "the world becomes a smaller place," multinational corporations demand that their employees understand other societies' cultures. Employees need to understand their own frames of reference and those of people from other countries.[4] Additionally, they need to understand the primary cultural, historical, and sociopolitical aspects of team members from other cultures. It is a mistake to assume that people from different cultures think, feel, and act in the same way.[5] Ignorance of cultural differences could have serious consequences in business and personal settings.

People must be willing to learn to work with international diversity. To do that they must learn five key competencies:[6]

1. Cultural awareness: understanding the differences
2. Communicative competence: communicating across the differences
3. Cognitive competence: acknowledging stereotypes
4. Valuing differences
5. Gaining synergy from the differences

The need to understand these differences is made clear by the fact that the meanings of important possessions differ across cultures, which must be taken into account when designing marketing communications for foreign markets.[7] Even international dining etiquette is essential to know. In the United States, we typically have a "get down to business" attitude, but this will run counter to Asian practices.[8] For example, when dining in Pacific Rim countries, U.S. businesspeople should be careful not to refuse food, as this may insult the host. Additionally, they should not help themselves, but wait until the food is offered. Spouses should not be included unless specifically invited. And gifts should be carefully selected.

WARM-UP EXERCISE

Select a specific country and research the business and communications customs of that country. Then select a business deal to negotiate with a firm in that country. Prepare a cross-cultural negotiation to conduct in front of the class.[9]

▪▪▪ Cultural Differences

There are various differences in cross-cultural communications related to time orientation, personal space, eye contact, uncertainty, speaking, and gender issues. For example, Americans conduct business negotiations faster than people in most other countries. In Asian cultures, investing time in a negotiation signifies building a relationship. This relationship will then determine the value and merit of the eventual business agreement. Comfort zones—that is, the personal space maintained between people while communicating—also vary by cultures.[10] North Americans connect space to equality (first-come, first-served). North Europeans conduct face-to-face business at a distance of about 5 feet. Latin Americans, Southern Europeans, and Middle Easterners use about a foot or so between speakers for conversations. With respect to eye contact, North Americans look people in the eyes when speaking to them, whereas Asian and African cultures consider a direct gaze rude or aggressive (especially if the gazer is younger or lower in status). Handshakes also vary in firmness. For example, in North America, most people will use a firm handshake; however, in the Pacific Rim, a light touch is often used so not to show aggression. Some cultures and society have a high tolerance for uncertainty. This is partly based on whether a culture is high-context or low-context.[11] A high-context culture is one in which much of a message may be communicated indirectly (collectivistic cultures). A low-context culture is one in which communicators place the burden of communication on the words themselves rather than on other kinds of cues (individualistic cultures). In some cultures, women do not participate in business or their positions and responsibilities are subordinate to those of men (e.g., Asia, the Middle East). In terms of conversation, North Americans are "linear" thinkers and talk in a straight line, one step or idea at a time. Conversations in Latin American or the Middle East tend to loop.

Hofstede's Power Distance Index (PDI) is a useful tool for analyzing various cultures.[12] It measures the extent to which less powerful members of the group accept an unequal distribution of power. Examples of low and high cultural PDIs drawn from Hofstede's research are as follows:

LOW PDI	HIGH PDI
Inequalities between people should be minimized	Inequalities between people are expected and desired
Parents and children treat one another as equals	Children respect parents and parents expect obedience
Organizations are relatively decentralized	Organizations are relatively centralized
Narrow salary range between top and bottom	Wide salary range between top and bottom
Subordinates expect to be consulted	Subordinates expect to be told what to do
Boss should be a resourceful democrat	Boss should be a benevolent autocrat
Privileges and status symbols are frowned upon	Privileges and status symbols are expected

Those countries with a high PDI include the Philippines, Arab countries, Thailand, Brazil, France, Japan, and Korea; those with a low PDI include Israel, the United States, and Australia.

Cross-cultural training is clearly warranted in order to conduct business negotiations with those from other cultures. It should include information about gender issues and taboos relating to religion, culture, and sexual harassment. The training should also focus on conversational taboos, protocol as it relates to hierarchy, general behavior, and acceptable gestures and expressions.[13] According to Roger Axtell, a well-known expert on business protocol, proper protocol—or the understanding of cultural nuances—can often be the key to negotiating contracts and getting deals done. Educating executives on protocol has become a growing practice. A number of protocol specialists, such as like Gloria Petersen & Associates, the Lett Group, Protocol International, and even international lawyers, conduct training seminars to help people engage in business abroad. The Lett Group, for example, has worked with over 200 organizations on subjects ranging from handshaking and business card usage to presence, awareness and body language, and gift giving.[14]

A number of handbooks and texts include such information, but it often is rather laborious and tedious to get through the material. Hence, the Business Protocol Advisor was developed (Jay Liebowitz and colleagues) as an interactive aid to help businesspersons, students, educators, and government representatives become better acclimated to cultural differences in business protocol. (See the following screen shots to get an idea of how the Business Protocol Advisor works.) Developed over several years, the Business Protocol Advisor started as a proof-of-concept prototype, using expert systems technology, concentrating on the Pacific Rim. Multimedia was later integrated with the expert system to show short video clips of, for example, exchanging business cards to supplement the text description. The Business Protocol Advisor focuses on such areas as greetings, exchanging business cards, time orientation, business negotiating, business entertaining, visiting homes, conversational do's and don'ts,

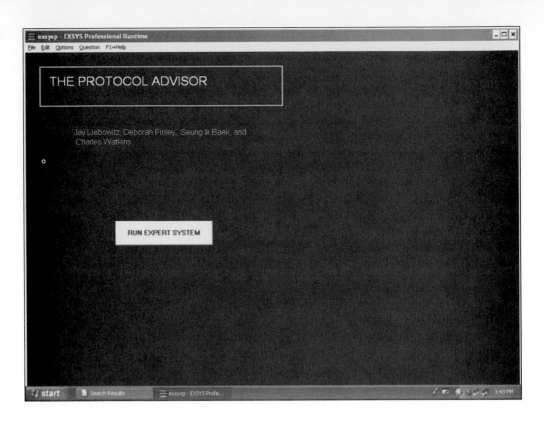

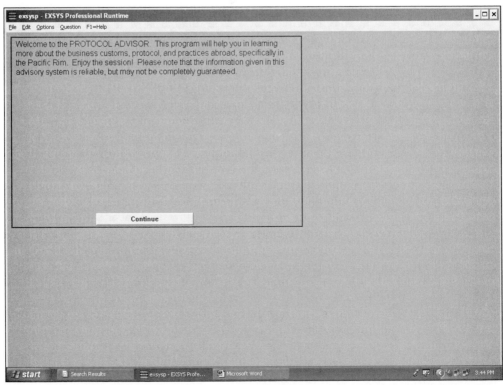

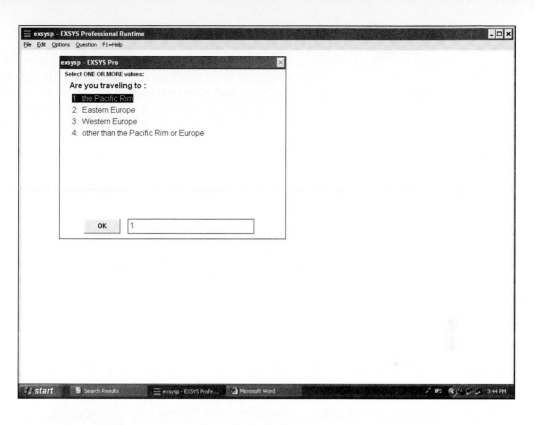

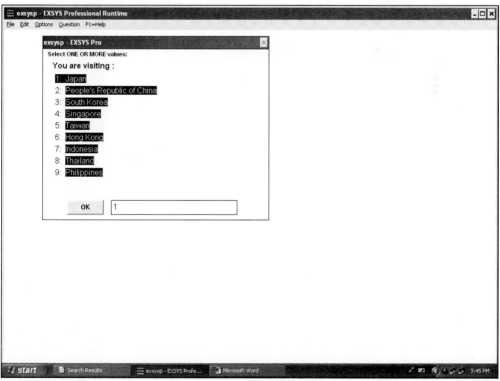

and general tips. Much of the information it contains came from knowledge acquisition sessions and materials from the Overseas Briefing Bureau at the State Department, World Trade Center officials, consultants working in the protocol area, and various handbooks and manuals. The current version of the Advisor has fully fleshed out the sections of the Pacific Rim to include protocol relating to Japan, the People's Republic of China, South Korea, Singapore, Taiwan, Hong Kong, Indonesia, Thailand, and the Philippines. Additionally, hypertext links have been created to include background and brief historical information on these countries. (See the following screen shot.) In addition, the Advisor now includes selected Western European countries (France and Italy) and other countries outside of the Pacific Rim or Europe (namely, Canada, Mexico, South Africa, and Colombia).

The next few sections of this chapter are descriptions from the Business Protocol Advisor, based upon information contained in the following sources: Roger Axtell, *The Do's and Taboos of Hosting International Visitors;* Roger Axtell, *Do's and Taboos Around the World;* discussions with Susan Keith, Culture to Culture, Inc.; Philip R. Harris and Robert T. Morgan, *Managing Cultural Differences;* and Larry M. Hynson, Jr., *Doing Business with South Korea.*

Japan

Business gifts are frequently given at first meetings, but do not embarrass your Japanese counterpart by being the only one to show up with a gift. Unless you have

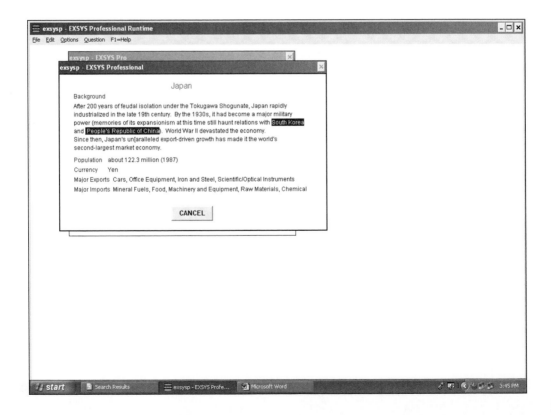

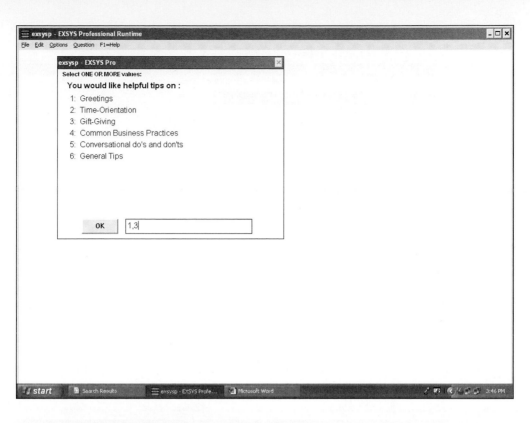

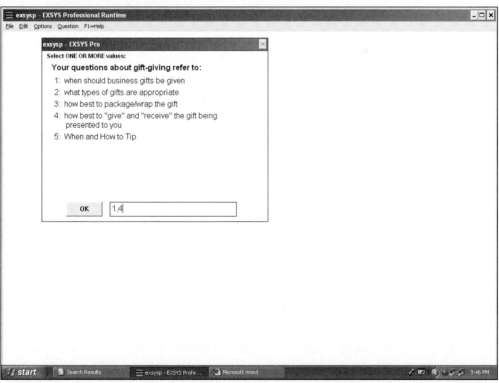

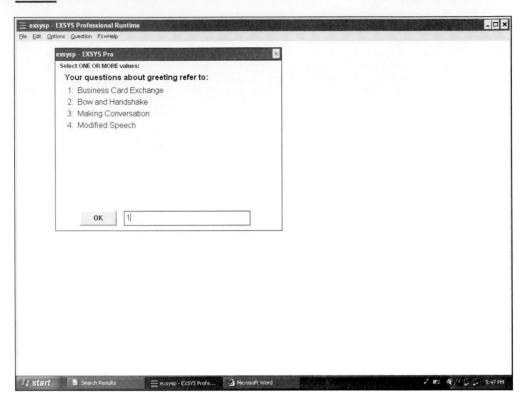

something for everyone present, give your gift while the recipient is alone. In any situation, it is better to allow the other person to initiate the giving. Do not expect him to open the gift in front of you, nor should you open yours unless he asks you to do so. Avoid outgiving the Japanese—and, by implication, placing an obligation on them. Avoid gifts in multiples of fours. The number four has morbid connotations.

Because the Japanese typically open their presents privately, never give the Japanese an unwrapped object. Remember that style is just as important as the gift itself. Perfunctory wrapping is almost worse than no wrapping at all. If you do not have the knack (or the materials), either wait and buy your gifts at a Japanese department store or arrange for someone who knows how it is done to wrap what you have brought. Never give tacky logo items such as imprinted matchbooks, T-shirts, caps, bumper stickers, cheap ballpoints, etc. Also, do not give anything with the company name printed tastelessly large.

You will rarely if ever be invited to a Japanese home, but if you are, flowers are appropriate. Be sure to check with the florist that you are not arriving with the 16-petal chrysanthemums reserved for the Imperial Family crest. Avoid giving white flowers as these are traditionally for mourning. Other welcome gifts such as imported Scotch, cognac, and frozen steaks bought at tax-free airport shops are appropriate. If you give gold, make sure it is heavy in karats—the Japanese prefer white precious metals. In Japan, a gift depicting a fox would signify "fertility," while a badger signifies "cunning." It is redundant to give a Japanese colleague a gift that is readily available in his own country—give him something American. Typically, the Japanese will cherish a gift of

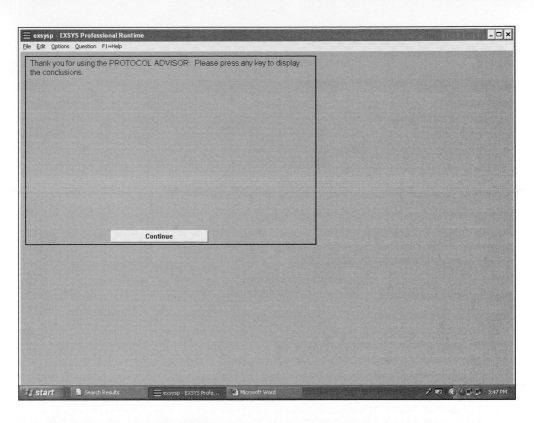

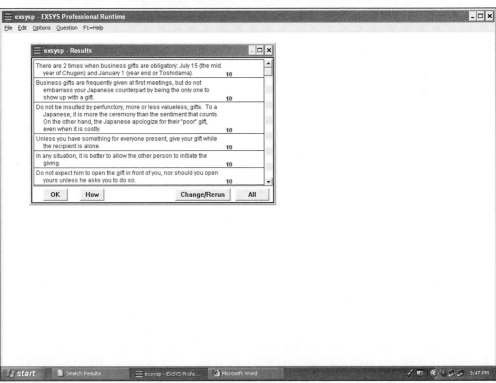

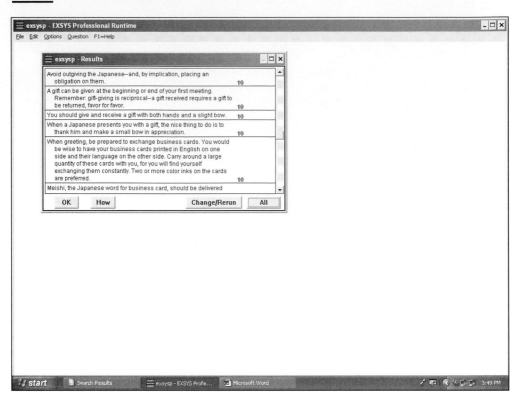

art—a painting, weaving, sculpture, or ceramic by an American artist. They also appreciate ties (somber colors), and scarves and handbags for the women, particularly if they have trendy designers' names attached. Whenever possible, give a gift that shows that you did your homework. Get to know the recipient's personal preferences if you can. Ribbons and bows are not necessary, and generally not recommended. The color and texture of the wrapping signify the type and value of the gift. Use boldly colored wrapping paper. Do not use bright red wrapping as it is considered inappropriate. Do not use black and white wrappings as they convey death overtones.

In the ancient tradition, a wrapped gift is presented in a silk scarf (a "furoshiki"), which is the final wrapping. A gift can be given at the beginning or end of your first meeting. Remember that gift-giving is reciprocal—a gift received requires a gift to be returned, favor for favor. You should give and receive a gift with both hands and a slight bow. When a Japanese presents you with a gift, the nice thing to do is to thank him and make a small bow in appreciation. The usual form of greeting is a bow and not a handshake. As a Westerner, you should learn to make at least a light bow (15 degrees) while nodding with your hands at your sides (not in your pockets). Count to three before finalizing the bow. A Japanese makes a lower bow for the more important individual, a lesser bow for his peer or a person of less importance. For a standing bow of respect, a Japanese bends forward at about a 30 degree angle, lowering his hands, palms down, down the sides of his body or down the front of his thighs almost to his knees. After a short pause, he lifts his head.

When greeting, be prepared to exchange business cards. You would be wise to do as the Japanese do and have your business cards printed in English on one side and Japanese on the other side. Carry around a large quantity of these cards with you, for you will find yourself exchanging them constantly. Two or more color inks on the cards are preferred. Never address a Japanese by his first name. Only his family and very close friends use the first name. To say "Mister (last name)," simply say the last name and add the word "san." When leaving a Japanese wedding reception, never say "sayonara" as it signifies parting and is bad luck for the occasion of a wedding. Otherwise, you can say sayonara when you are departing from your meeting. When you are visiting a Japanese home, remove your shoes right inside the door and place them neatly facing the door (a Japanese custom, so as to make the departure of the guest more efficient). If you are given slippers to wear, upon your departure be sure to place them neatly together on the floor, facing inside the house this time, to be ready for the next guests. Sake is the traditional, well-known drink in Japan. The Japanese believe that you cannot truly get to know someone unless you drink—seriously—with them. That's why it is called the "water business." Punctuality is advisable for both business and social engagements. Avoid the following topics: World War II, the bombings at Hiroshima and Nagasaki, Japan's military budget, the economic rivalry and competition between the U.S. and Japan, and seppuku (suicide). Avoid anything that will cause embarrassment. Good topics to discuss are culture, history, and art.

In general, the Japanese prefer a respectful and unhurried approach to business. Their goal is a long-lasting relationship. Don't attempt to rush into business dealings. It is preferable to send a team of 3 or 4 people to negotiate rather than just one person. A team commands more respect and shows seriousness of purpose. Avoid the use of slang. Do not assume that the Japanese person who speaks English best is the most important member of the team. If you direct comments to this person, you risk insulting more senior members. Be formal throughout the negotiations. Do not use first names and do not appear in shirt sleeves. The "white envelope" can appear in business transactions in Japan as elsewhere. It is viewed as a commission, not bribery, and found at all levels.

Silence during discussions may mean only that the Japanese are seriously considering your point. Try not to let it make you uncomfortable, or to compel you to fill the void with sounds. Speak slowly. Use fairly simple words, and repeat what you say, rephrasing your message. Avoid excessive praise of yourself, your product, or service. Japanese negotiators dislike power plays and individualism. The Japanese make decisions by consensus. This is referred to as the "ringi seido" and takes time. Observe protocol scrupulously as the negotiations proceed. This involves such issues as who sits where and what gift is to be presented to whom. Even though bowing is used extensively, handshaking is becoming more common. The Japanese handshake may seem like a weak grip so as not to show aggressiveness. Remember that patience, politeness, and humility are great virtues. Phrase questions so they can be answered with "yes." Harmony is important, so the word "no" is shunned.

Your Japanese hosts will entertain you extensively. You should accept an invitation to dine and not place limits on your time. You will most likely dine at a hotel or traditional Japanese restaurant. The Japanese normally drink sake (a rice wine) before a meal. It is polite to fill each other's cup, and to acknowledge with a thank you. The cup is held in your right hand and supported with the left hand. When visiting a Japanese restaurant, remove your shoes and sit on the tatami, or straw mats, on the floor. Sometimes you will find yourself in front of the tokonoma (alcove), which is the seat of honor; your host and hostess will sit together at the opposite end of the table. Remember if you are the host, you should place your honored guests in the tokonoma. It is considered polite to let the oldest or most senior person begin eating. Do not leave chopsticks in a crossed position on your plate or stand them up straight. Place them on the chopstick holder found on the table at the tip of your plate. Place your hand under the chopsticks to keep food from falling. It is polite to try every dish, but you need not finish everything on your plate. Soup is sipped holding the cup in two hands with the chopsticks in your cup. Use a quick dip gesture to dip food in sauces. The slurping of noodles is considered a sign of appreciation.

You will probably be served five entrees and rice and soup at a first-class dinner. When paying a restaurant bill, there will probably be a service charge of 10 percent added to your bill, and you do not tip more. Tipping openly is demeaning to the recipient. When you are in Japan, you will very likely be entertained by your host at a banquet. In reciprocation, you will be advised to have a banquet also, which can be arranged with a Japanese restaurant. Be extremely careful that your dinner does not in the slightest exceed the cost of the banquet given for you. This will cause your Japanese host to "lose face." Don't be insulted if the female representative(s) of your firm's negotiating team are not invited to the social function. Japanese entertaining generally does not include women. Sit in a kneeling position on a tatami mat. Women are supposed to keep their knees close together; a man keeps his knees 3 to 4 inches apart. A man sits with his hands on his thighs, while a woman's are clasped lightly in front of her. If you are offered a twisted moist towel, use it for your hands. After using the towel, refold it neatly and replace it in its container. Stay only for 30–45 minutes if you are a guest in a Japanese home. You will probably be served tea and cakes during your visit. When you leave, you will be urged to stay longer, but you should say that you really "must leave" (your hosts will be relieved). Be sure to pay your respects first to the older or more senior people in the room when you leave.

Some general tips are the Japanese are avid golfers and rarely decline an invitation to play. "Face" is important; do not joke or embarrass someone in front of others. You may be asked your age, your salary, the cost of items, and religion—subjects that are not sensitive to the Japanese. Do not take offense. The Japanese are careful about cleanliness. Show the proper respect at shrines and temples and remove your shoes before entering. Make an effort to be formal. Avoid public displays of affection. Speak in a low voice. It is also best to keep laughter quiet and to cover your mouth with one hand when laughing. You will make a big hit if you are willing to sing a song in English in a karaoke bar. The numbers 4 and 9 are considered unlucky. Little or no tipping is customary in Japan.

China

You should refer to the country as the "People's Republic of China" or simply "China." A slight bow is appropriate when meeting someone. A handshake is also acceptable. The Chinese are quite formal and will use the full title of their guests during introductions. Foreign businesspersons usually find that their trip to China is highly organized and that punctuality is very important. Prior appointments are necessary. Be prepared to wait a long time for Chinese businessmen to reach a decision. A visit to a Chinese home is rare—unless the government has given prior approval. Guests should plan to arrive a little early and should leave shortly after the meal. During the meal, be prepared with toasts expressing thanks, pleasure, and friendship. The Chinese consider tipping anyone an insult, although exceptions are starting to appear. Gifts of any great value can cause embarrassment and usually are not accepted by the Chinese. Seniority and rank are both very important. Dual-language business cards are recommended. The Chinese usually have three names; the first one is the family name. The Chinese may ask very personal questions: income, value of your home, etc. The Chinese have difficulty saying "no." Any type of touching is uncommon in China, such as hugging and back-patting. Among businesspeople, personal relationships are very important. Avoid talking about Taiwan. Good topics include history, culture, family, progress in China, differences between China and the West, and the advances the Chinese have made. Bad topics are mentioning Taiwan, cultural revolution, sex, wealth, politics, and Chinese leadership.

The Chinese do not like dealing with lawyers and most feel that lawyers create more problems than they solve. The concept of "face" is extremely important to the Chinese. If, in the course of negotiations, your Chinese counterpart feels that he has "lost face"—not been accorded the proper respect—negotiations will go sour. The Chinese have no protocol for introduction or the exchange of business cards, except that: cards are not exchanged until after introductions are made and introductions are made first according to rank. The Chinese will usually hold a banquet on the arrival of a new business associate, at the close of a business negotiation, and at the departure of a business associate. They will expect that reciprocal banquets will be held. It is important not to refuse an invitation to a banquet without a very good reason. This reason must also be conveyed to the host or it could cause them to "lose face." The purpose of a banquet is not just to eat but to establish relationships, be prepared to talk and take your time. Take every opportunity to praise the quantity and quality of the host food. It is considered impolite to refuse a toast. A Chinese banquet is also considered a place to drink together. The presentation of gifts to government officials, capable of eliminating bureaucratic delays, is common practice. Only a gift given with the intention of procuring an illegal action is considered a bribe. It is important to maintain an attitude of modesty and sincerity when you do speak. Never joke about the possibility of an evil in front of the Chinese. This means that one must never mention the possibility of bankruptcy at the grand opening of a business. If the occasion should come true, the Chinese might view it as a self-fulfilling prophecy of your origination. This is a possible source of creating business enemies.

South Korea

South Korean men greet each other by bowing slightly and shaking hands with both hands or with the right hand. Women usually do not shake hands. Family names come first. It is difficult to distinguish male from female names in Korea. Prior appointments are necessary and Westerners are usually expected to arrive on time. Shoes are always removed before entering a Korean home or Korean restaurant. Business entertainment is considered very important and is usually limited to restaurants and bars. Wives are rarely included. All courses of a meal are served at once.

If you are invited to a Korean home, it would be appropriate to take flowers or a small gift, to be offered with both hands. Gifts are not opened in front of the giver. The open mouth is considered rude; cover it when laughing. It's impolite to blow your nose in public. Women play secondary roles in Korean society. Patience, humility, and respect for age are important traits. Business entertainment is important and extensive. Solo or group singing is a tradition after dinner. Good topics are culture, history, and the successful Olympic Games. Bad topics include political unrest, secondary role of women, socialism, communism, internal politics, and criticism of the government.

Get the highest-status Korean to introduce you, for your initial status is no greater than that of the person who introduces you. Koreans prefer to communicate formally and intuitively. Vagueness is preferred over clarity, indirectness over directness, feelings over expressions, and silence over excessive talking. Be prepared to tell about yourself at the first meeting—about your family, your favorite sports, and your age. They want to know these things because age, position, and rank determine seniority. Your hosts will entertain you extensively. You should accept an invitation to dine and not place limits on your time. Koreans enjoy celebrations; they're quite hospitable. They frequently hold banquets for such reasons as welcoming newcomers, saying farewell to people leaving, the new year, and a contract signing. Remember that Koreans don't usually talk during the meal. It's only afterward that you can ask your questions. Before beginning to eat, the host will often make a formal welcome speech stating the purpose of the gathering and paying his respects to his guest. Korean food tends to be highly seasoned with red pepper, thus a careful sip of the soup is advisable before taking a large mouthful. To lay the chopsticks or spoon on the table is to indicate that you have finished eating. To put them on the top of a dish or bowl means that you are merely resting.

Singapore

Due to the influence of the British, Singapore is quite Westernized. However, the customs of the many ethnic groups are also followed, so greetings vary. The handshake is the most common greeting—with a slight bow to the Singaporeans. Western visitors are expected to be punctual. Prior appointments are advisable. Singapore is punctuality prized. Entertainment usually takes the form of a lunch or dinner. Do not use your left hand when eating with a Malay or an Indian. Should you be invited to a Singapore home for dinner, a box of chocolates or flowers would be appreciated.

Unlike the Japanese, gift-giving is uncommon in business. Business cards are presented respectfully with two hands. Take special care with name pronunciations. Streets and other places are kept wonderfully clean due to harsh penalties against littering. All Singaporeans speak English, even though the heritage is Chinese. Pride is taken in being practical, straight, and to the point. Business lunches can be long and informal. Unlike other Asian countries, power breakfasts are common. Shoes are removed when entering a mosque and sometimes before one enters a home. Singapore is virtually a nonsmoking society. Blunt questions may be asked, such as "How much do you earn?" American negotiating methods are considered pushy. Women are treated as equals in business. Good topics are clean, economically healthy country, travel experiences, news of countries visited, and economic advances of Singapore. Bad topics are being disrespectful over the country's size, religion, and politics.

Italy

The guest will be introduced first. Shake hands with everyone present. At large gatherings, if no one is introducing anyone, it is important that you introduce yourself and shake hands. Handshakes may include grasping the arm with the other hand. Very close friends and male relatives often slap each other on the back. In the north, punctuality is often conducted with American pressure and efficiency. Business gifts are sometimes given at a senior management level. They need to be small and made with craftsmanship and prestige. Liquors or crafts from one country may be appropriate. Do not give gifts with the company's logo. A small gift could be given to a staff member that is extremely helpful. Travel alarms, pens, and calculators are good gifts as long as they are name brands. Flowers and chocolates are acceptable for a secretary. If you are invited to someone's house, then bring gift-wrapped chocolates, pastries, and flowers. Never give an even number of flowers. Do not give chrysanthemums since they are used for funerals. Do not give a handkerchief or knife because they symbolize sadness. Italian businesspeople tend to prefer people that they know. Before doing business in Italy, it would be wise to have a strong contact person to help make appropriate introductions and appointments.

Negotiating in Italy is usually slower than in the United States. At social occasions, Italians do not exchange business cards, but it is normal at business functions. Business cards are often white with black print. The more important the person, the less is on the business card. The conversational subjects at social occasions deal with Italian culture, art, food, wine, sports, such as soccer, family, and films. Avoid talking religion, politics, and World War II. Italians do not tell off-color jokes and are uncomfortable when other people do. Never ask someone that you have just met about his or her profession. It is very insulting. Do not use the first name unless you are invited to do so. It is good to use a title for a doctor. Dressing is important. In the business world, good clothes are a badge of success. Women dress in expensive and elegant attire. Men dress in ties and suits that are fashionable and well cut. Casual clothes are smart and chic. Women wear pants in the city and hardly ever wear shorts.

Business dinners are important and refusing an invitation to a dinner will offend Italians. When dining with Italians keep both hands above the table; never put them resting on your lap. Use your knife to pick up cheese and do not eat anything with your fingers except grapes or cherries. Italians consider wine to be sipped with a meal and to drink a lot would be considered offensive. Business dinners involve only a small, important group. Dining is a serious business and an account may be lost or gained at the table depending on how the dinner goes. Italians like to pay the bill and may even slip the waiter an extra tip to make sure that they will receive the bill. Women executives find it very hard to pay the bill because the waiter always brings the bill to the gentleman.

Colombia

Introductions to Colombians are extremely important. When greeting a man or a woman who you do not know, always shake hands. Women generally grasp each others' forearms. When greeting workers who are known to be of lower status, it is common to just shake the hands of those closest to the newcomers. Colombian women are not permitted by culture to extend their hand for greeting when meeting men. Women are to wait at all times for the men to initiate the greeting.

It's important that the foreigner should always be on time. It is customary to send or bring some type of gift to the home. Typical gifts are roses, chocolates, or some imported wine. When gifts are given in Colombia, they are never opened in front of guests. The presents may never be acknowledged, which means that you may never hear a thank you. When arranging a meeting, it is always best to have an acquaintance or someone from an embassy make an introduction. At the beginning of every meeting, it can be expected that one of the nation's largest exports, coffee, will be served. Never decline a cup of the hot, warming beverage. Even if you do not like coffee, it is best to take a cup and just take a small sip. Business issues will never be discussed first.

The need to become personal with clients supersedes the business, and attendance of both parties at dinners and social functions beforehand is not uncommon. Aggressive behavior is looked upon as a negative trait. Attorneys do not attend negotiations but always review agreements. Allow negotiations to remain open-ended, so that confrontations can be avoided and talks can be allowed to fade away if an agreement cannot be reached. Try not to respond with a definite "no" to even the most minor of terms. Whether negotiations and meetings go well or not, there is a good chance that guests will be entertained and will dine very well while in Colombia. Be prepared to indulge in several drinks with your Colombian business client. Anything from whiskey to scotch to wine may be served or offered during a luncheon. Drinking and carousing may continue to later in the night if you choose to stay at the function.

Both men and women should wear dark, formal suits year-round. A suit is proper for a man; always include a jacket no matter how warm it is outside. Women always wear hosiery, extravagant jewelry, and formal makeup. Colombian women are very fashion-oriented and ahead of the United States. Colombians often extend invitations to reside in their homes while foreigners are doing business. When invited to stay at a home or even just to dinner, be prepared to dine well into 10 or 11 at night, even during the week. The Latin cultures do not eat their last meal of the day until later at night. The meal will usually be quite large, with wine served as the main drink. The attire is more formal than in America. Always bring your most personal items with you. These include soap, toothbrushes, toothpaste, washcloth or a hand towel. Always leave your room in the proper attire. It is not uncommon for Colombians to take two to three hours for the midday meal. When smoking in Colombia, always offer a cigarette to every person in the room even if you know the person does not smoke. It is not rude to refuse a cigarette if you do not smoke.

Mexico

There isn't as much of a sense of urgency or rush in Mexican business as there is in American business. There may be up to a half hour or even more tolerance for tardiness or lateness for a meeting. As much as three hours is spent in developing a relationship before actually conducting business. Networks of associations and recommendations are especially important in Mexican business and professional life. Getting to know your client by maintaining a regular exchange of visits will help secure future business dealings. Latin Americans like to drink a lot of coffee. Mexicans like to drink it black and very strong. One should not refuse coffee when it is offered, even if it is not to one's taste. Such a refusal can be interpreted as a social slight against a Mexican concept of hospitality. The etiquette of table setting for formal dinners is especially important in

Mexico. To mistake one utensil for another is a real faux pas. One must not slam knives or forks on the table, nor toss them carelessly onto a table. Mexicans are sensitive to such gestures. It is very important that one call a Mexican business colleague at the office to confirm an invitation, not at home.

When acting as a guest, one may find that toasts are common. It is better form to allow your host to give his toast before the guest gives his/her own. One should never criticize or even joke about the local food or wine. One should not automatically take offense or frown during the dinner conversation if one hears U.S. visitors or even oneself referred to as gringo. The term is not necessarily derogatory. The meaning depends on the tone of voice and the context. U.S. businesspeople are in the habit of asking a lot of questions early in a relationship about their conversation partners: how much they earn, their working hours, and the kind of neighborhood they live in. This type of "interrogation," often a part of habitual social behavior, can be interpreted as impolite and intrusive. Dealing with NAFTA regulations requires you to have personnel on staff who can speak Spanish. Mail service in Mexico is not as dependable as the United States mail service and it is generally a lot slower. One should not send invitations to social events by mail and expect them to get there on time. Mexicans are not generally as much in the habit of sending thank-you cards or gifts after a social invitation as Americans are. Sandals and/or shorts are not worn by adults except in tropical climates. Men should wear shirts and ties of a conservative character.

Canada

In Quebec, cater to the French culture. Try to speak French. This will greatly enhance your image. All presentation materials should be printed in both French and English. Assume that you will be conducting business in French. French Canadians are less reserved than English-speaking Canadians. The French Canadians tend to use more gesturing. Physical space is closer. Your French Canadian host may touch you while conversing. Use a reasonably firm handshake, and shake upon first meeting, greetings, and departures. Use last names until your host switches to first. He/she may go back and forth. Eat Continental style. Handshakes are firm. Use last names when introduced. First names will be used very soon thereafter.

English Canadians are not comfortable touching or speaking at close range. Privacy is important. Business meals are common. At dinner, wait for your host to bring up business. In business situations, maintain good posture. One can be more relaxed in social settings. Business gifts should be modest. Gifts are opened immediately. An invitation to a restaurant is considered a gift. Eat Continental style.

▪▪▪ Cross-Cultural Communication Situations

Visitors need to acclimate to the customs and culture of the countries they are visiting. For example, in Spain (especially during the summer), dinner is usually around 10 P.M. For the typical American who may eat dinner at 6 P.M., waiting the 4 extra hours may seem like an eternity. As another example, in Hong Kong, the guest of honor usually tries the food first as your hosts, out of respect for you, want you to sample the food. If you resist, this may put your hosts in an embarrassing position. In Brazil, and other South American countries, the "A-Okay" sign that you may make with your fingers in the United States has a very negative connotation and a much different interpretation. Gesturing, if not done appropriately, can certainly result in very awkward and uncomfortable situations.

Handling cross-cultural communications is important in the IT industry. The off-shoring of IT jobs is becoming more frequent, so much so that India's IT technology and services industry earned $12 billion in revenue in FY03, $9.5 billion of which came from exports. For FY04, India projected $15.5 billion in revenues with exports of $12 billion.[15] Global software outsourcing is a growing industry, and being able to manage cross-cultural issues resulting from global outsourcing is critical to the success of the outsourcing arrangement. As this chapter has pointed out, working across cultures when outsourcing software production is not a trouble-free process.[16] Different societies have various ways of operating and companies need to be sensitive to these customs and cultures. For example, according to Krishna et al., Indian companies have found that U.S. client companies normally work with extensive written agreements reinforced by frequent and informal telephone conversations and e-mail. However, Japanese clients prefer verbal communication, continuously negotiated agreements, and less frequent, but more formal, use of e-mail. Also, Indian programmers will typically not voice criticism in a face-to-face meeting, but prefer to send their opinions via e-mail after the meeting has ended.

Let's take a look at some embarrassing situations that IT professionals may find themselves in if not well versed in cross-cultural communications. The first scenario involves an individual giving an invited talk at an IT conference in South Korea. It was February, during the winter in Seoul, and the speaker, after a long flight from the United States, was picked up by his Korean host at the airport. As the host arrived, the invited speaker was blowing his nose, due to the dampness in the air, not realizing that this should not be done in public. The speaker then greeted his host, and the host drove him to the hotel to freshen up before dinner. The speaker asked whether he would be going to the host's home for dinner or would be eating in a restaurant near the hotel. Again, the speaker made another faux pas, as it is extremely unusual that a "stranger" would visit a Korean's home. Then, to make matters worse, the speaker asked if the host's wife would be joining them for dinner. Once again, mixing business and pleasure is taboo. The speaker was getting some negative nonverbal feedback from his host, and upon arriving at his hotel room, he pondered the events that had just transpired and then realized what a fool he had been. The speaker was then determined not to be an ugly American and to be a proud representative of his country.

Unbeknownst to the speaker, the "worst" hadn't yet occurred. Upon ordering his food in the restaurant, the speaker ordered shrimp since he thought shrimp would be plentiful in the Korean area. The speaker was surprised to learn that shrimp are a delicacy in Korea and are difficult to get (especially during the winter months). To stimulate dinner conversation, the speaker committed yet another mistake by asking about relations with North Korea and what they mean to the South Koreans. Finally, at the end of the evening, the invited speaker gave his host a gift, and the speaker was very proud of the lovely gift he had brought from the United States—an antique clock. Little did he know that a clock is a symbol of bad luck and death in Korea.

Well, you can imagine that the speaker wasn't invited back to Korea again after all these mishaps. Even the speech wasn't received well, as the speaker opened with a joke, used many clichés, and didn't properly thank and acknowledge his hosts. With proper cross-cultural preparation before taking the trip to Korea, all of these snafus could have been avoided!

Let's look at another sensitive situation regarding cross-cultural communications. A United States-based IT company was setting up operations in a developing country. The "white envelope" was the normal way of conducting business in this country whereby some "cash under the table" was expected. The US company had strict social responsibility and ethics policies in place and felt uncomfortable providing any type of kickback. The IT company was told that if it wanted to have a phone, it would have to wait a year; alternatively, it could provide a $10,000 "white envelope" and the phone system could be installed the next day. This situation involved an ethics question as to whether the same ethical standards should be applied and followed in foreign countries as in the United States. Chapter 6, on ethics, provides some additional insight into these types of situations.

SUMMARY ▪▪▪▪▪▪▪

Whether conducting overseas business, giving a presentation, writing a letter, or developing an IT marketing campaign, understanding other cultures is a critical part of being successful. Disney learned this lesson the hard way when developing EuroDisney in Paris. It tried to impose American customs and norms, which often ran counter to French and European business and family practices. This chapter tried to shed light on the importance of cross-cultural communications and what to expect in various countries. With this knowledge, IT professionals will become more adept and successful in adjusting to the global society.

EXERCISES ▪▪▪▪▪▪▪

1. Your company is deciding whether to outsource its IT operations to India, China, or Russia. Analyze the differences among these cultures as they relate to IT work habits and the customs of your American company. Prepare a 15-minute presentation on your findings.
2. Evaluate the gift-giving customs in Japan versus China. Write a brief report on what you learned.
3. Due to recent episodes of viruses (from overseas) infiltrating computer systems in your organization, the CIO has asked you to develop an IT security strategy for dealing with these attacks from abroad. Research this area, and prepare a Powerpoint presentation on the IT security strategy that you recommend for dealing with these attacks.
4. You have been asked by your CEO to research the customs of doing business negotiations in Singapore and Colombia. Write an executive summary that highlights the major points in negotiating business deals in Singapore and Colombia.
5. South Korea is becoming a major player in the electronics field. Your CIO thought it may be a good idea to visit South Korea and learn from their experiences in this area. The CIO has asked you to fill her in on the important South Korean customs that she should know. Prepare a 15 minute presentation on your findings.

ENDNOTES ▪▪▪▪▪▪▪

1. Gilerson, Eugene. (June 2004). "(misAlignment of IT Offshoring.)" *Wall Street & Technology.*
2. Information Technology Association of America. (April 2004).
3. *The Economist* (May 29, 2004).
4. Demers, Julie. (September 2002). "Crossing the Cultural Divide." *CMA Management.*
5. El Kahal, Sonia. (2001). *Culture and Business in Asia Pacific.* Oxford University Press, New York.
6. Ides, Paul. (August 1995). "Learning to Work with Differences." *Personnel Review* 24 (no. 6).
7. Watson, John, et al. (2002). "Cultural Values and Important Possessions: A Cross-Cultural Analysis." *Journal of Business Research* 55.
8. McShulskis, Elaine. (December 1997). "Dining Don'ts When Overseas." *HR Magazine.*
9. Adapted from El Kahal, Sonia. (2001). *Culture and Business in Asia Pacific.* Oxford University Press, New York.
10. Kramer, Melinda. (2001). *Business Communication in Context.* Prentice Hall, Upper Saddle River, NJ.
11. Ibid.
12. Hofstede, Geert. (1980). *Culture's Consequences: International Differences in Work-Related Values.* Sage Publications.
13. Nixon, Judy, and Dawson, Gail. (2002). "Reason for Cross-Cultural Training." *Corporate Communications* 7 (no. 3), Bradford Press.
14. Sisken, J. (October 21, 1997). "Protocol on Those Trips Abroad." CNN Financial Network. http://www.europe.cnnfn.con/fntraveler.
15. "News Track." (April 2004). *Communications of the ACM* 47 (no. 4).
16. Krishna, S., Dahay, Sundeep, and Walsham, Geoff. (April 2004). "Managing Cross-Cultural Issues in Global Software Outsourcing". *Communications of the ACM* 47 (no. 4).

6

Ethics for the
IT Professional

Learning Objectives

■ To understand the many ways that IT can influence the ethical analysis of situations

■ To learn traditional ethical approaches and how they can be applicable in IT ethics

■ To recognize when situations present ethical issues so that ethical principles can be applied

▦ Introduction

For the IT professional, ethical issues abound. They may appear in very public discussions, such as those surrounding the plans for massive federated databases to thwart terrorism, or as very private matters, your hand pausing over the "enter" key: Do you really want to read that personnel data? You have the access, why not? But, honestly, is there any business reason for doing it? Other ethical dilemmas do not even reach the conscious awareness of the IT professional. In fact, a theme of this chapter is to present a realistic way to deal with ethical issues, a method that places a premium on fine-tuning the "ethics radar" that will help to signal when an ethics issue exists.

To help understand the involvement of ethics in various situations and decisions, take the following quiz as a warm-up exercise. It is designed to probe your perceptions of whether there are ethical issues involved in the situations. Completing it will serve to baseline your ethics radar for the discussions to follow.

WARM-UP EXERCISE

The warm-up exercise focuses on establishing a baseline for your sensing when an ethical issue is present in a given IT-related situation. In the following five scenarios, assess the perceived importance of the ethical issue.[1] The scenarios are adapted from those in Kreie and Cronan, 2000.

(Continued)

(*Continued*)

For each scenario, answer three questions using the answer sheet in Figure 6-1:

1. If you had to make a choice between the protagonist's behavior being either acceptable or unacceptable, which would you choose?
2. On a 5-point scale from "very unimportant" to "very important," assess the importance of the ethical issue involved.
3. On a 5-point scale from "very improbable" to "very probable," assess how likely is it that you would act in the same way as the protagonist.

Scenario 1. Bob works at a bank where he also has an account. His account is overdrawn and he knows that an overdraft charge is scheduled to be applied. Bob makes an adjustment that hides his overdrawn account to avoid the overdraft charge. When he is later able to make a deposit, Bob undoes the modification he had made.

Scenario 2. Mary has just received by mail the software she ordered. In the package, she also finds another software package (that is clearly not a freebie). The invoice shows that she is not being charged for the second package. Mary decides to keep the second software package and not say or do anything about it.

Scenario 3. Kevin likes to help his friends by writing programs for them using his company's computers. He does this on weekends on his own time so as not to interfere with his work responsibilities. Kevin doesn't charge his friends for the programs he writes.

Scenario 4. Jenny was surfing the Internet looking into commercial software packages to find one that met her needs and her pocketbook. On the web site for one product, she was surprised that she was given full access to the software online without ever being asked to purchase it. Jenny assumed that this wasn't normal, but she went ahead and used the software without paying anything.

Scenario 5. Jake's company does work on a federal government contract at a government facility using its databases. He is working on an information system containing government demographic data on U.S. families. Jake's boss tells him to copy the data so it can be used by the company. Jake has access to the contract his company has with the government and examines it. He sees nothing explicitly forbidding the data copying, so he goes ahead and makes a copy for his company.

▪▪▪ Importance of the Ethical Issues

Compare your responses in the warm-up exercise to those who completed a similar survey. The respondents in Kreie and Cronan (2000) had fairly consistent results for Scenarios 1, 4, and 5, that is, Bob modifying the program, Jenny accessing software for free, and Jake copying the data.[2] In each case they thought that

- The behavior was unacceptable (85 percent, 75 percent, and 73 percent, respectively, for Scenarios 1, 4, and 5)

▐▐▐ FIGURE 6-1   **Perceived Importance of Ethical Issues**

Scenario 1: Bob's behavior is

Unacceptable	Acceptable

The ethical issues involved are

Very Unimportant	Unimportant	Undecided	Important	Very Important

I would act the same way as Bob

Very Improbable	Improbable	Undecided	Probable	Very Probable

Scenario 2: Mary's behavior is

Unacceptable	Acceptable

The ethical issues involved are

Very Unimportant	Unimportant	Undecided	Important	Very Important

I would act the same way as Mary

Very Improbable	Improbable	Undecided	Probable	Very Probable

Scenario 3: Kevin's behavior is

Unacceptable	Acceptable

The ethical issues involved are

Very Unimportant	Unimportant	Undecided	Important	Very Important

I would act the same way as Kevin

Very Improbable	Improbable	Undecided	Probable	Very Probable

Scenario 4: Jenny's behavior is

Unacceptable	Acceptable

The ethical issues involved are

Very Unimportant	Unimportant	Undecided	Important	Very Important

I would act the same way as Jenny

Very Improbable	Improbable	Undecided	Probable	Very Probable

Scenario 5: Jake's behavior is

Unacceptable	Acceptable

The ethical issues involved are

Very Unimportant	Unimportant	Undecided	Important	Very Important

I would act the same way as Jake

Very Improbable	Improbable	Undecided	Probable	Very Probable

- It was improbable that they would act the same way as the protagonist in the scenario (only 23 percent, 29 percent, and 28 percent, respectively, would act the same way, i.e., probable or very probable)
- The perceived importance of the ethical issue was high (63 percent, 62 percent, and 74 percent, respectively, thought it was important or very important)

Scenario 2, in which Mary keeps the second software package, was the most problematical for the respondents. The perceived importance of the ethical issue was most evenly distributed, with 39 percent saying it was important or very important, 40 percent answering unimportant or very unimportant, and 21 percent undecided. Although 60 percent thought that Mary's keeping the second software package was unacceptable, 56 percent said they would probably do the same thing. Respondents felt that the error was made by the software company; taking advantage of it was okay (Kreie and Cronan, 2000).

In Scenario 3, 78 percent of respondents thought it was acceptable for Kevin to write programs using company computers on weekends for his friends. The respondents in the survey would probably do the same thing (74 percent). Perhaps surprisingly, only 16 percent thought that the ethical issue was important. Although Kevin is doing this on his own time and not charging for it, he is using company resources. An additional dimension of the scenario is discussed in Kreie and Cronan (2000): If there were a company policy prohibiting personal use of company computers, only 16 percent then said they would still do it.

The Scenario 3 results were indicative of a broader trend observed in Kreie and Cronan (2000) after analyzing all the survey results (including more than are presented here). People rely extensively on their personal values when deciding how to act. Company policies come into play in people's decisions when the ethical issue is not as important.

Scenario 5 provides an IT version of a dilemma faced by other professionals who must consider instructions from supervisors in a broader context of their responsibilities as professionals. Contemporary technologies introduce new possibilities for IT professionals to be placed in these situations, for example, being instructed to write software for inserting spyware or adware on the computers of people who access your company's web pages.

How did your responses compare to those in the survey? It is important to note that the survey answers are not "correct." In fact, a theme of this chapter is to explore what is considered right conduct and on what basis would behavior be characterized as ethically sound or not. The warm-up exercise highlighted some of the most widely acknowledged concerns of ethics. Honesty and moral character are issues in Mary's keeping of the software package and Jenny's freely using online software. Bob's modifying the bank program highlights ethical issues of accountability and personal responsibility. When Kevin uses company computers for personal reasons, it raises questions of honesty and fairness. Jake's copying of data raises questions of privacy and accountability.

The scenarios also touch on many of the particular concerns of IT ethics:

- Access not equaling authority (Scenarios 1, 3, and 5)
- Rights in data and intellectual property (Scenario 3)
- Information privacy (Scenario 5)
- Accountability (all scenarios)
- Professional responsibility (all scenarios)
- Employer/employee relations (Scenarios 3 and 5)

These issues of ethics and, specifically, IT ethics will be explored in this chapter. The objective is to provide insight into moral standpoints and sources of guidance to assist the IT professional in dealing with scenarios such as those in the warm-up exercises.

▪▪▪ What Are Ethics?

Ethics refers to a person's individual beliefs about right and wrong behavior. Ethical concerns may be found in a wide range of behavior—fairness in dealing with other people, honesty in conducting financial transactions, and consideration for those who may be affected by actions. Ethics is at the center of one of the fundamental preoccupations of philosophy: the question of conduct. Understandably then, treatises and discourses on ethical behavior may be found throughout human history. James Rachels' *The Elements of Moral Philosophy* (2003)[3] is a good starting point for examining ethical considerations as they have evolved from antiquity to the present.

Every person "has" ethics, in the sense of personal beliefs about what is right and wrong. These beliefs are instilled in childhood through observation and guidance from influential figures like parents. There are several theories (e.g., Kohlberg, 1981) concerning the moral development of children and how they grow to acquire notions of right and wrong behavior.

Certain beliefs (e.g., killing and stealing are wrong) are fairly widely shared as people move into adulthood. Other notions of appropriate ethical behavior are not so clear-cut. As in the warm-up exercises, scenarios are often used to highlight differences in perceptions of what are considered ethical responses. Your natural response may be guided strongly by how you were raised to act in such situations:

- If the person in front of you drops a $20 bill, what do you do?
- Is telling a "white" lie in consideration of someone else's feelings acceptable?

A reasonable question, then, is the extent to which our notions of right and wrong behavior are immutable. Although the influence of one's upbringing is influential, one's ethics can evolve over time. Raising the visibility of situations and cases calling for ethical behavior can sensitize people to the need for revisiting, and possibly adapting, their personal philosophies for what constitutes acceptable action in such cases. So consideration of scenarios and case studies has proven to be a useful mechanism for sharpening people's notions of their own ethical beliefs.

▪▪▪ Ethical Perspectives: Virtue Ethics, Deontological Ethics, and Utilitarianism

Throughout history, life experiences and made-up scenarios have motivated very useful discussions about right and wrong conduct for each situation. Some of the world's great thinkers have offered broadly applicable philosophies, called *metatheories,* that aim for applicability in a wide range of circumstances experienced in people's daily lives. Three leading metatheories are summarized in this section. Notice in particular how they relate to the prevailing ethical themes uncovered in the warm-up exercises: honesty, moral character, and personal responsibility. Later discussion in this chapter will show how these centuries-old theories are applicable today in the most contemporary of IT-intensive situations.

Virtue Ethics

Virtue ethics provides a way of reasoning about appropriate behavior and action by asking the individual to consider "What would a person of good moral character do?" So virtue ethics does not have a set of rules or specific courses of action. Instead, it offers a perspective that depends on people already possessing a sense of what constitutes virtuous conduct. Virtue ethics has origins in Greek philosophy, which stressed the development of good character traits in the moral education of youth. So, in this sense, people's ability to find guidance from virtue ethics is tied to their moral development.[4]

Plato's cardinal virtues were courage, justice, temperance, and wisdom. Additional virtues have been proposed over the last two millennia in the spirit of trying to identify those attributes that define what a person of sound moral character would possess. For people operating in the world of business and IT, virtues often advanced (e.g., in Ferrell et al., 2002, and Reynolds, 2003)[5,6] as desirable character traits are

- Empathy
- Fairness
- Honesty
- Openness
- Self-control
- Trust
- Truthfulness

A list like this shows how a virtue can offer a basis for consideration of various actions or decisions but can fall short as a description of what to do. Seeking guidance from the virtue ethics approach means

- Envisioning how someone whose moral character you admire would act in such a situation
- Considering how various actions by you would reflect virtues like those listed

Aristotle believed that virtues might be envisioned as striking a balance (the Golden Mean) along each of the character dimensions. A person who entirely lacks empathy may be considered heartless, callous, or unfeeling—not to be admired on this count. Perhaps surprisingly, although empathy is an admirable trait, the Golden Mean invites people to consider that the other extreme may also be less than virtuous. A person with extraordinary empathy for others may be lacking self-respect and fail to give proper weight to his or her own feelings. In an organizational setting, this may render a person a less-effective contributor because of being consumed with effects and outcomes on others to the exclusion of other factors.

Given these caveats, virtue ethics does provide a resource for the IT professional by relating ethical behavior to virtues that society has associated with people possessing strong moral character.

Deontological Ethics

The ethical perspective based on deontology affirms behavior respecting the rights of the individual. It is the duty and obligation of individuals to act according to specific rules, regardless of the outcome of their actions. This ethical approach is referred to as duty ethics, or the ethics of obligation. The philosopher Immanuel Kant is most closely associated with deontology.[7] For the deontologist, ethics is focused on the actor and that person's duty to behave in a certain manner.

To follow a deontological approach when confronted with an ethical dilemma is to adhere to a rule absolutely. Consider the person who is living in a country that is being occupied by enemy forces during a war and is providing safe haven for a deposed government minister. The person answers the door to find enemy soldiers asking if the minister is inside. A person who is a strict "rule" deontologist would answer truthfully, no matter how certain that this action will result in the minister's death. Although such action in this situation may seem extreme, ethical behavior for this person means strictly adhering to the rule "Do not lie," without regard to consequences.

As such a dramatic example illustrates, this strict adherence may be difficult to characterize as right conduct to others who don't share the same ethical theory. In the practical application of deontological theories, it is more likely that an "act" deontological viewpoint will be found useful. Act deontology calls for knowing and respecting the rule but being willing to consider the particular circumstances of the act to determine if it should be applied in each instance. So the act deontologist knows that lying is wrong, but in the scenario above, that person would consider the specific circumstances outweigh following the rule.

In its focus on individual rights, deontological ethics dictates that each person deserves respect; no person shall be a means to someone else's end. Even the most mundane human encounters can illustrate the use of this ethical viewpoint. People who cut in front of others in line are thinking only of their own convenience and advancing their own desires by inconveniencing others. In a similar focus on the individual, deontology also embraces a widely familiar guideline for conduct, the golden rule. "Do unto others as you would have others do unto you" can be seen as variation on the same ends/means theme of deontology.

In offering guidance for ethical behavior, deontological theories include the notion of considering an individual's conduct to be ethical if that behavior were universally known and adopted. This is Kant's categorical imperative, "Act as if the maxim of thy action were to become by thy will a universal law of nature" (Ferrell, 2002). So, skirting the rules of a game "just this once" doesn't conform to ethical behavior on this attribute of universalizability. If everyone did it, the game would break down entirely.

Although deontological theories may appear extreme, absolute, and unrealistic, they can serve as useful standpoints for people to consider as they reason about various courses of action:

- What if everyone in this situation did what I am contemplating, would that be a good thing?
- In taking this action, am I respecting other people's rights? Or am I using them for my own gain?
- Would I like to be treated the way others will be treated if I go ahead with my plan?

Utilitarianism

A common-sense ethics would say that one way to tell if conduct is good or bad is to look at the effect it has on other people. Utilitarianism is the philosophical theory, formulated most notably by John Stuart Mill, that encompasses this viewpoint. In contrast to deontological ethics, which is oriented to the actor, utilitarianism focuses on the outcomes or consequences of the act. A person choosing from a set of alternative actions would select the one that does the best when figuring the gains and pains of all those affected by the action—in short, the action with the greatest utility for all. In this scoring of candidate actions, utilitarianism is an easy fit for those familiar with using cost-benefit analysis for business decision-making.

A person would more likely tell a white lie on utilitarian, rather than deontological, grounds, seeking to spare the feelings of the other person and also to feel better personally about not causing distress in others. Other examples span from the dramatic to the mundane. In a hostage-taking situation, if the negotiator were certain that killing one individual would spare the lives of 30 others, a classically utilitarian viewpoint would say that this single killing was justified because of the totality of gains and losses for all the people affected. In an IT policy dilemma, in which all but 10 of the 500 employees use a particular desktop operating system and the IT infrastructure unit cannot support both systems, the utilitarian-guided manager will decide to support the majority system. While those 10 employees will be faced with inconvenience, the net effect on all employees will be minimized by this action. With its ability to concentrate scarce resources on the support of one operating system, the IT department can provide higher-quality service. If it had the second operating system, the department would spend a disproportionate amount of effort providing connections to all of the interfacing systems.

Although utilitarianism enjoys an appeal of rationality, it also exacts a burden on the decision-maker. The choice of operating systems to support was fairly clear-cut (although in practice, even that decision is not always made the same way, owing to political realities or to the importance of the work being done with the minority operating system). More realistically, a person cannot know precisely all the consequences of decisions on all parties. To do so would require "standing in their shoes" to understand their hopes, dreams, and desires, which can only be guessed at. To compound the difficulty, an accurate accounting must have perfect knowledge of the future, including events and actions by others, to know fully the consequences of an action. So, anyone performing an ethical analysis based on utilitarianism needs to remain cognizant that integrating over the various pros and cons of each alternative for each affected party is likely to be an incomplete accounting.

These ethical theories—virtue ethics, deontological ethics, and utilitarianism—are three leading and influential ones, but there are others as well, owing to the thought that has been devoted to this fundamental philosophical question over the centuries. Rachels (2003) can provide further explanation of these and other ethical theories. The take-away from examining these theories is not to follow any of them blindly, but rather to use all of them as part of ethical analysis. They all have strong philosophical roots and can provide perspectives that can shed light on the wisdom of making decisions or taking actions.

■ ■ ■   Ethical Considerations for the IT Professional

It is natural for various professions to consider how ethics relates to them and how traditional ethical guidelines may help to deal with the special situations that arise in their professional practices. The most obvious example is the field of applied medical ethics. With advances in medical and biological sciences, physicians and bioscience researchers are faced with ethical dilemmas such as euthanasia, abortion, and human cloning. To an extent, practitioners can draw on the history of ethical theories, but medical ethicists also must deal with novel conditions brought about by scientific and technological progress.

IT Ethics

The ethical concerns of the IT professional constitute another subfield of applied ethics with parallels to medical ethics in terms of the need to consider new situations arising from technological advances. This applied ethics field is also known as computer ethics or information ethics, with the latter portrayed as more foundational than the former.[8] The IT professional must deal with a superset of concerns in IT ethics that encompass often complicated interactions of classical ethical issues with the most modern of information technologies.

IT professionals often like working in domains where there can be a "right answer." Some IT realms cooperate by being highly technical and mathematical. It can be very satisfying to apply scientific and engineering principles to determine the minimum bandwidth requirements for a network. Ethics isn't like that. That there is no algorithm for ethics can be disconcerting for IT professionals. You cannot dump in all the ingredients—the people involved, candidate decisions to be made or actions to be taken, emotions, points of view and positions of key players, relevant feelings and emotions about various eventualities, cultural sensitivities, context and setting—into a formula that will generate a magic number that will prescribe what you should do.

For guidance on each subject, the IT professional should look first to any laws and regulations that are applicable, then to any policies, procedures, or ethical codes of employers or professional societies. There is an abundant literature, both online and hardcopy, on each subject. You are encouraged to go beyond the summary here to consult the relevant references at the end of the chapter.

Ethics is a consideration in everyday life, but it is especially important in information technology. The context of IT heightens ethical concerns in two broad categories: the pervasiveness of IT and the responsibilities of IT professionals. The widespread use of computers and their extensive networking have created new arenas for human behavior and actions that call for the application of ethical principles. The emergence of IT as a profession raises questions about appropriately ethical behavior as these professionals render their expertise to the broader community.

IT issues are becoming inextricably tied to cases of business ethics. IT can be used as an instrument for ethical transgressions and crimes. IT policies and procedures for electronic content management, access control of corporate IT assets, and computer forensics become critically important for companies responding to charges of financial fraud[9]:

- The ENRON financial fraud case involved searching in excess of 400 computers and 10,000 backup tapes.

- For Boeing to comply with a legal discovery request, it had to search through 14,000 backup e-mail tapes to find the e-mail messages of interest.
- E-mail messages can now be considered business records if certain conditions are met, according to the Federal Rule of Evidence 803(b).
- Personal Digital Assistants are becoming acceptable as sources of evidence.

The warm-up exercises and examples throughout this chapter suggest the variety of topics related to ethical concerns and IT. Most of the issues can be grouped under one or more of the following subjects:

- Privacy
- Information security
- Intellectual property
- Professional responsibility
- Employment and work
- Freedom of expression
- Conflicts of interest

When Do Quantitative Improvements from IT Make a Qualitative Difference?

As computers are becoming more pervasive, more people have vastly expanded power and reach. A lone hacker has caused over a billion dollars in losses worldwide because of the impact of internetworked systems. To probe the power of IT is to discern, for various scenarios, whether the quantitative changes from IT are so extensive that they are rendering an ethical dilemma qualitatively different.

Consider the case of a male bank customer seriously flirting with a female bank teller, showing off as very wealthy. She decides to check out the balance in his bank account. She has no business reason to do so. Prior to computers, checking his balance may have involved physically going to a different part of the bank to find the appropriate file cabinet, locating his paper bank record, and examining it to determine the balance. The process would take time and, possibly, risk being challenged by a manager.

Does it matter that in the precomputer era she would have had more time in which to contemplate whether to go through with this action? Does it matter that she may get caught? Today, with instantaneous and interactive access to computer files, she simply conducts a search from her personal computer, easily finding the electronic record containing his bank balance. The same account balance information was accessible before the extensive computer-based automation of today but may have required a heroic effort: opening file cabinets and searching through paper records. Has the quantitative improvement in accessibility and speed altered the ethical issue at hand? If you believe that snooping into personal information without any legitimate reason for doing so is morally objectionable (access does not equal authority), then it holds true with or without computers. However, there is no doubt that the extraordinary ease of accessing information with computers means that people are faced with many more temptations to act unethically by not respecting the privacy of data.

Although the bank example is simply a quantitative improvement that did not alter the ethical analysis, many other uses of IT have no practical ethical counterpart prior to computers and networking.

What Is the "IT-ness" of Ethical Dilemmas?

In the face of rapid advances in IT and its innovative uses in virtually all aspects of life, it is understandable to think that IT ethics is brand new, dealing with dilemmas that have never occurred in the past. In fact, this is not at all the case. Although the IT element can render an ethical situation unique, many IT-intensive scenarios are, at their core, basic ethical questions that have been considered many times in many guises. In this sense, IT ethics is cumulative, because understanding the ethical conduct in IT-related situations may be guided by insights that are as new as the latest technology or as ancient as recorded history, and all points in between. It can be helpful to strip away some of the superficial trappings of situations to allow a focus on the ethical aspects.

This section discusses the "IT-ness" of situations and circumstances that are encountered in daily personal and professional life. Specifically, to what extent is the IT professional likely to find guidance only from the latest thinking about an IT-intensive situation. Or, does the situation rate lower on the IT-ness scale, and can the IT professional can gain valuable insights from the historical record?

Consider the coarse grouping of sources of ethical insight and guidance, roughly chronological:

1. Ancient Greek philosophy
2. Evolution of normative ethical models
3. Ethics of technology
4. Ethics of IT

The following situations are very contemporary, IT-related cases that raise ethical issues that draw on insights from each of the four sources.

1. Ancient Greek Philosophy

Plagiarism by copying material from the Internet is a serious problem in education. With the abundance of web-based material, highly effective search technology, high-speed connectivity, and very capable editing software, a student can prepare a term paper that plagiarizes from other peoples' published works in a way that is difficult to detect. Instructors are left to wonder at the true extent of understanding by the student.

The Internet and IT have made this a common occurrence today, but the ethical question for the student draws most powerfully on guidance from antiquity: Taking another person's goods is wrong. For Aristotle, ethical conduct followed from developing sound moral character in the formative years of personal development.[10] Modern-day Internet plagiarists may be using the latest technology, but their actions are unethical for reasons philosophers 2,000 years ago would understand.

2. Evolution of Normative Ethical Models

Computers enable extraordinary access and control. Reynolds (2003) discusses a case involving a visiting scholar at a computer science department of a university in the

United States. He had devised an ingenious way of very quickly grabbing identity information from an idle workstation so that later he could, if so inclined, assume that identity at his own workstation.

To the scientist, coming up with this method was a technical challenge to be overcome. He had no intention of actually using it to access information to which he was not entitled. However, as with any such computer procedure, it had to be tested to ensure its effectiveness. So he tried out his technique, swooping down on the idle PC of an officemate who just departed. Our scientist was delighted when, after only a few keystrokes, he successfully walked away with information encapsulating his officemate's network identity. The scientist's activity became known to the department chair, who was faced with trying to understand the ethical dimensions.

Although this case involves computers and clever programming, ethical guidance comes from a strong thread of normative ethics. The deontological view holds that no person shall be a means to another person's ends. This view is clearly applicable: The officemate was never given the opportunity to participate or not in this scheme. The decision was made for him by the perpetrator who was thinking solely of his own desires to test his method.

3. Ethics of Technology

IT has the potential to cause widespread destruction and death. Computer software controls power plants, vehicles, airplanes, medical devices, communications systems, water systems, and weapons systems. The potential impact of IT decisions is huge; society has had some experience mulling the ethical considerations of applying technology that can wield extensive impact. The most obvious example is the technology for nuclear weapons, which became feasible first in the 1940s. This development raised the stakes regarding the impact of decision-making. Earlier generations could scarcely imagine the potential devastation from a single decision. Kant said, "Do what is right though the world should perish" (Kant/Infield, 1981). Whether that outcome was ever envisioned as being a serious possibility in the eighteenth century, it was a realistic scenario in the twentieth. U.S. President Truman's decision to drop an atomic bomb on Japan in World War II was not straightforward ethically. A deontological view is that killing innocent noncombatants is wrong. A utilitarian standpoint would weigh those horrible losses against potential other extensive loss of life, a presumed consequence of a prolonged war if the bomb was not dropped.

4. Ethics of IT

The preceding IT examples can look outside of IT ethics for help, but there are circumstances calling for ethical behavior that arise solely out of IT. Sophisticated mining of multiple massive databases to uncover patterns in the data was simply not possible before the automated systems that are now in place. Retailers routinely mine across transaction, demographic, marketing, weather, traffic, geographic, and inventory databases to find relationships to predict customer purchases. In this case, IT has enabled new opportunities for privacy invasion by uncovering personal information through these cross-database relationships. One very public example of data mining in the United States was the proposal and early planning of the TIA program at the Defense Advanced Research Projects Agency. Significantly, TIA initially stood for Total

Information Awareness. After public outcry, it was called Terrorism Information Awareness to make it clear that its focus was terrorism.

The high IT quotient of such cases is due to the extraordinary capabilities of contemporary computer systems to store massive amounts of data electronically (in the range of 10^{15} bytes), establish relationships (often very subtle and intricate) among data items, and use creative data analysis and reduction (especially visualization) techniques to allow decision-makers to understand the patterns. These capabilities have been building over time. There was no single instant when they all came together. But clearly this ability, at this level of sophistication, to uncover relationships across disparate data sets was not achievable even 20 years earlier. This high-IT scenario touches on an ethical issues of age-old relevance—invasion of privacy—but does so in a way that challenges earlier ways of dealing with that issue. It is an example of quantitative change of such magnitude that it potentially causes a qualitative change in the way the ethical issue is discussed and dealt with.

▬▬ Continuous Ethics Improvement

IT professionals are challenged to keep ethical principles in the forefront of their everyday personal and professional lives. It is not uncommon for companies to schedule periodic ethics training, which can help remind employees of ethical issues and update them on current topics. In IT, it is especially important to maintain awareness of current events, as new technologies appear and new laws are passed to address computer crime, privacy, and e-mail communication (e.g., antispam legislation). Although training can be very useful, there can be a gap between assessing ethics scenarios in the classroom and identifying real-life situations calling for ethical behavior: "Oh, you mean I was supposed to use my ethics training *then*?" Ethical considerations need to be so ingrained in our behavior we naturally detect that they are relevant.

IT professionals have a great practical need to maintain ethics awareness and to work toward continuous improvement in their skills at dealing with ethically charged situations. A model having these features is the Continuous Ethics Enhancement for IT Professionals (CE2IT) framework.[11] CE2IT encourages IT professionals to "see-to-it" that they integrate ethics into their daily lives. CE2IT takes advantage of the fact that many computer software and systems professionals are familiar with the continuous improvement paradigm. It has been used successfully to improve software processes, especially through initiatives like the capability maturity models of the Software Engineering Institute. The rationale for continuous improvement for IT ethics is the recognition, as with the software process, that people will always play a critical role in the activities. Also, both the software process and ethical behavior are not static; both must evolve to reflect changes in technology and best practices.

The CE2IT model is based on the continuously evolving nature of the relationships among the following:

- The IT professional: the individual working in IT and striving to behave ethically
- Ethics enhancement resources: information that the IT professional can draw upon in the quest to improve ethical behavior
- World of action and reaction: ongoing environment in the life and work of the IT professional, presenting situations calling for ethical choices and behavior

In addition to the continuous improvement feature, CE2IT is distinctive also for high-lighting the following aspects of ethics:

- **Ethics Radar.** Cultivate an ethics radar to be better able to recognize when situations and circumstances call for ethical action. Study scenarios that raise ethical issues and learn the pros and cons of various responses and how they stress the ethical principles in effect in each case. The warm-up exercise earlier in the chapter is an example of a useful self-test aimed at improving ethics radar.

- **Ethical Analysis.** Look to minimize rash choices that may miss the mark ethically. Is an immediate response really needed? Or can you wait for your emotions to subside, to clear your mind and reassess the situation? Learn to identify circumstances when you may "buy time" in taking an action or making a decision. Accept that the pressure of IT and business may not permit thoughtful deliberation on every choice you make each day. But when the opportunity to "sleep on it" or otherwise defer a decision presents itself, consider doing so if only to give full reading to any ethical dilemmas that may be lurking just beneath the surface. Something needs to signal, "Wait a minute. Let me think about this."

- **Guidance.** Look broadly for sources of wisdom on appropriate behavior. Many current ethical "checklists" promote a single or very limited perspective on what is ethically admirable. Expand your sources to include guidance associated with other cultures and other philosophical themes. You don't need to tackle ethics improvement by yourself. There is a large community dedicated to understanding the ethical issues posed by contemporary society and offering guidance on ways to deal with them. CE2IT highlights the ongoing accessing of resources to get help in ethics enhancement.

- **Real-Time Ethics.** The press of work and daily life often does not afford the luxury of thoughtful ethical analysis, and people are left to their instincts. Acknowledge this fact and intentionally hone skills for on-the-spot ethical actions and reactions. From your efforts to heighten the sensitivity of your ethics radar and to seek guidance from ethics resources, you will contribute to enhancing your instinctive real-time ethics. In this way, your natural, unstudied responses will be consistent with your ethical principles. Test yourself by seeking out new scenarios to gauge your response with recommended ones that are deemed ethically responsible.

- **IT-ness Quotient.** Question whether the IT situation you face is really driven by the technology component or is it simply an age-old conundrum dressed up in modern clothes. The scenarios discussed in this chapter may provide a starting point. In your consideration and analysis of IT-related scenarios, pull apart the IT dimension, asking whether that indeed renders the situation essentially different from considering the question or decision without IT present.

- **Laws.** New laws related to IT ethics (e.g., data privacy) are being enacted regularly. Existing laws are being applied and modified. The applications and emerging case law help to build a body of knowledge about the practical effect of the law. While passing of new laws makes headlines, often less well known are subsequent actions and modifications—in some cases, a new law is thrown out entirely by the courts.

The CE2IT framework presented here may be thought of as a "metaprocedure" that provides a reference framework for continuous improvement of one's ethical sensitivity as an IT professional. Rather than prescribing precise actions to execute in sequence, the framework offers a foundation for enhancing awareness of ethical concerns and dealing with situations that may have ethical considerations.

▪▪▪ Practical Tactics for Handling Ethically Intensive Situations

IT professionals are familiar with having a set of software tools that help them in their work. Similarly, they can benefit from a set of ethics tools: strategies and tactics to help shed light on the ethical dimensions of a situation. This section discusses a simple tool set consisting of the following:

- Ethical analysis
- Systematic scenario modification
- Creating a third option
- Taking the viewpoints of others
- Documenting thoughts and feelings

Ethical Analysis

Ethical analysis is highlighted in the CE2IT framework. Professionals should have a structured way of addressing ethical situations for those cases when time permits such analysis. As a structured approach, Reynolds (2003) recommends the following steps:

1. Get the facts
2. Identify the stakeholders and their positions
3. Consider the consequences of your decision
4. Weigh various guidelines and principles
5. Develop and evaluate options
6. Review your decision
7. Evaluate the results of your decision

Although the individual steps may appear obvious, there are critical insights worth noting. The recommended starting point, to investigate the situation and obtain factual information, is a good example. Suppose you walk by an office and see a colleague using the desktop PC of your boss. What should you do? It's easy to jump to conclusions; after all, your boss has access to privileged information not available to you or your colleague. Before firing off an e-mail to your boss, consider that she may have called your colleague and asked that he use her computer to perform some action—perhaps something critical to a client presentation at the client's office where she now finds herself. The admonition to "get the facts" is designed to help ensure that you don't fret wondering about ethical conduct for a misperceived circumstance. Save your anxiety for real ethical dilemmas.

The recommended step to consider consequences of your decision should call to mind the utilitarian view of ethics. The next step, to weigh various guidelines and principles, encourages looking to other ethical theories as well: How would the situation be seen from the perspectives of virtue ethics or deontological ethics?

The final step, to evaluate the results of your decision, is aimed at self-improvement. How accurate was your earlier prediction of the consequences of the decision? What can be learned from examining the real outcomes of your decision? Should additional facts have been obtained? How will this experience contribute to making your next ethical analysis more effective?

Your behavior in ethically involved situations—every action and reaction, every move you make, statement you say or write—is playing a part in the continuous shaping of your ethical self. As a person, your behavior is the external manifestation of your ethical principles. Your colleagues will form opinions based on your external behavior and communications. If you are in a position of responsibility, such as the IT manager, you are defining the organizational ethics by your behavior.

Systematic Scenario Modification

Systematic scenario modification involves the orderly introduction of changes into the ethical situation under consideration. For example, change one factor or condition, then test to see if ethical issues have changed in important ways: Would the perceived ethical intensity of the situation be raised or lowered? How would your decision change, if at all? This tactic can be particularly revealing when you start at one end of the ethical/nonethical spectrum and gradually modify the circumstances to move slowly to the other end.

Consider the case of an employee who develops his own commercial product during work hours using company computers, in violation of company policy. He then markets the product, which competes with his own employer's products, and takes all the revenue for himself. Clearly at the extreme of unethical, this case involves at least accepting pay for not working on company business and the unauthorized use of company assets for personal purposes. Instead of sharing his good product ideas with his employer, he sought to capitalize on them himself. Regarding who has rights to the product and revenue from it, the company, through its IT assets, certainly contributed.

Now, take this clearly unethical action and successively relax some of the conditions that would seem to contribute to its being unethical. Suppose one condition is changed: He did all the work after normal working hours. Is this change sufficient to make the action ethical? No. He still used company assets in violation of policy. He still considered the company as a means-to-an-end, in the sense of deontological ethics, never consulting the company to understand if his goals could be met in some way that would be acceptable to the company. For example, perhaps in light of his product idea, the company would be willing to grant royalties to him. Perhaps he could arrange to resign and launch a start-up in partnership with his current company. He still is not acknowledging that the company has any rights to his product, although it was developed with company assets, albeit after working hours.

Other modifications may lead to similar critical examination to detect if the ethical issues have changed:

- The product does not compete with company products.
- Company policy holds that it is acceptable for employees to use their work computers for "reasonable" amounts of personal communication (e.g., communicating with family members via e-mail).
- It is not a commercial product, but rather a software system he is developing for a not-for-profit organization in which he is active (making it now similar to Kevin in Scenario 3 of the warm-up exercise).
- He decides to send money anonymously to the company amounting to half of the profits from sales of the product.
- He uses his personal laptop, which he has brought to work.

Systematic scenario modification can also serve to strengthen your original decision. Consider a case in which you are a nonmanagement IT staff person. When accessing data on the shared department server (something you do several times a day), you see a folder labeled "Staff Salaries." It has never been viewable by you before. You are thinking about clicking on it, but you pause to consider that action. In favor of not clicking, you think:

- Being able to see the folder is clearly a mistake. As a responsible IT professional, you know that access does not equal authority, and you have clearly not been authorized to read what is in that folder.
- You recall that any accesses can be traced, so you don't want it known later that you accessed it.

In favor of clicking:

- You are underpaid relative to others who hold the same job title, but you have no proof. You were previously thinking about making a case to your boss that you deserve a raise. Knowing other people's salaries would help a lot deciding whether or how to proceed.
- Morale is at an all-time low. The company has just completed its third downsizing in the past 12 months. People are nervous that they will be the next ones to get the axe.
- You have no loyalty to this place; you and your colleagues are treated poorly. The company is the worst you've worked for: low salaries, poor benefits, and lousy offices. You would quit if the economy weren't so bad.
- It's your last week of work. You have given notice and are thinking about your next job but dutifully finishing up and transitioning your work to colleagues. You've always been curious about salaries of your fellow workers, especially some well-known slackers. You are leaving; what's the harm?
- You are incensed because you suspect the new hire in your department was given a starting salary higher than you—and you have 2 years of experience!

With considerations like these, it can sharpen your awareness of where you go for ethical guidance and how strongly felt are your principles. From the viewpoint of virtue ethics, none of these considerations makes the action acceptable. It doesn't matter that your access may be traceable. All the surrounding conditions cited in favor of clicking don't change the ethical essence. The action is ethically wrong. In summary, this tactic aims to clarify the ethics issues by selectively modifying the situation and calling on you to analyze the impact of the changes.

Creating a Third Option

In terms of formulating possible decisions and actions, this tactic encourages you to think creatively and imaginatively about alternative courses of action. What may seem at first glance to be forcing you to choose either Option 1 or Option 2 may not be that way upon further reflection. Perhaps you can develop a variation, "Option 1a," that is more consistent with your ethical principles.

Badaracco (1997) describes a dilemma faced by a young financial analyst who used this tactic by looking beyond what appeared to be an either-or decision.[12] The analyst was invited to accompany a senior manager on an important client visit out of town. The invitation was quite unexpected because the analyst was a number cruncher at the investment banking firm and was not involved in any dealings with the client in question. A little digging provided the explanation: The client was African-American. Having the African-American analyst tag along would put a good face on the company's pitch.

The analyst faced a dilemma. He had deeply rooted beliefs, punctuated by incidents his parents had endured, about people of his race behaving with dignity and pride. But, purely as a practical matter, the presentation would expose him to the critical client side of the business while giving him valuable face time with an influential manager. It seemed possible that he may be doing more for his race by taking advantage of an opportunity to get visibility and advance in the firm, regardless of the propriety of the situation.

With only about a day to decide, he thought deeply about his feelings and his alternatives. Ultimately, he answered the invitation by saying that he would go, but only if he had a role in the presentation, and that he would be willing to work additional hours to get up to speed on the client proposal. The day leading up to the trip required a lot of time to gain the background and prepare his part of the presentation. The trip was a success and brought in new business. The analyst was pleased that he had modified the either-or situation he was faced with to create an option in which he was not a tag-along. He was using the tactic of creating a third option.

As with many such dilemmas, it is not easy to declare this outcome a slam-dunk victory. Was he completely true to his ingrained beliefs, or had he taken an expedient route? Would more have been gained by declining the invitation and pointing out how the situation appeared to him so it could be better understood by management the next time around? Conversely, should he simply accept the invitation, immediately signaling that he is a team player? After all, the economy is tough and he needs this job, with all its potential for career growth. If the client had been a female Princeton graduate, might his firm just as cavalierly looked in its ranks to trot out its own Princeton alumnae? Was his race just another affinity group and was he making too much of it? All these questions are perfectly reasonable to ask. In fact, if such questions do not come quickly to mind, it is probably not an ethical dilemma at all.

Taking the Viewpoints of Others

When faced with an ethical dilemma, stop to ask yourself: How are others seeing the situation? A potentially helpful tactic is taking the position of other principals in the current situation. Is it an ethical issue for any of them? How will others perceive any actions you may take? Is there a sense of timing? Many times people agonize over some course of action, only to find out that the situation was not as they thought it was and their actions would have been completely out of line. "Standing in the shoes of others" may give you a more well-rounded view of a situation.

Is there the possibility that you are making the ethical choice larger than it is? When there are complicated forces and interests at work, it can be preferable to make your best decision or take your best action and then see how others react, so the entire ethical enterprise can take shape. In this way, others can react and demonstrate the depth of their convictions about the situation. You may imagine that others—your colleagues, customers, and friends—are waiting for a dramatic and bold action that addresses all aspects of the situation. Perhaps that is indeed what is called for. But when many parties are anticipating your behavior, it is wise to consider what they are expecting. This is not to advise against taking appropriate action, only to submit that you may be seeing the picture differently; it may not call for as monumental an action as you may feel is necessary.

Badaracco (1997) discusses a complicated ethical case about the actions that a French pharmaceutical company should take after a new drug, RU-486, was shown to be effective in causing miscarriages and, therefore, becoming, in essence, an abortion pill. After much introspection, the company's chairman came to a decision that intentionally did not attempt to answer all of the ethical, political, social, medical, and business issues. By taking a single action, he stepped up to his responsibility while allowing the many other significant entities to react and then take steps of their own. In this way, the ethical concerns were dealt with through a series of actions and reactions, involving affected parties. He recognized that there were many other entities involved. Considering the perspectives and positions of others can help to shed light on action appropriate for you to take.

Documenting Thoughts and Feelings

A simple additional recommendation for dealing with a difficult ethical situation is to write down what you are thinking and feeling as you try these other tactics. Are there actions, incidents, or words from parents or mentors that will shed light on why you feel anguish about the decision you must make? Consider critically your own feelings—who are you?—that bear on the decision or situation. It is natural that your own sense of what is right includes feelings on both sides of the current dilemma, but this current circumstance is forcing you to explore how strongly are these feelings felt, how closely the ethical dimensions of responsibility and fairness really are defining who you have been to this point and who you want to be in the future. Aristotle saw critical personal decisions as connected to your past, part of a personal history. Your decision will be another step in shaping your ethical being. The simple act of documenting these thoughts and feelings can enable you to consider them more completely.

These five tactics—ethical analysis, systematic scenario modification, creating a third option, taking others' viewpoints, and documenting your thoughts and feelings—are aimed at helping you to articulate as sharply as possible what it is about the current dilemma that is causing such anguish.

■■■ IT Ethics and Communication

Instantaneous ethical behavior is even more important when we focus on communication. How easy it is to hit the "enter" key in the fast pace of life, only to have second thoughts about what you wrote. CE2IT emphasizes training the instincts of the IT professional to recognize when ethical issues are in play and to act and react in ways that are consistent with ethical ideals.

Much of communication is real-time, and increasingly so. There may be no time for careful ethical analysis, no time for thoughtful reflection on how the current situation bears on the ideals and moral fiber of your being. You need to say something or write something now. If you have honed your ethical instincts before that instant, it is more likely that your communications will be consistent with your ethics.

There are a host of issues surrounding IT ethics and communications. Every day brings new IT product ideas and creative uses of existing technologies. Examples of IT ethics-communication issues include privacy of information, freedom of expression, and the monitoring of computer use and e-mail traffic.

Privacy of Information

Justice Brandeis said simply and clearly that privacy is "the right to be left alone — the most comprehensive of rights, and the right most valued by a free people."[13] The privacy rights of every individual must be understood by IT professionals because they may be involved in developing or implementing policies that affect privacy, such as employee electronic surveillance, monitoring of employee e-mail, or biometrics for identification. In addition to respecting the privacy rights of people, IT professionals must understand the privacy provisions of information about people. Although people have a right to control what information about them is shared, they also must realize how routinely they give up that right when completing forms or providing personal data.

Laws and ethics are related. Both are influenced by socially acceptable behavior. However, laws carry sanctions from a governing authority.[14] Several laws aimed at information privacy are summarized in the Appendix to this chapter, which also provides Internet references. The Privacy Journal (http://www.privacyjournal.net) and the Electronic Privacy Information Center (http://www.epic.org) provide coverage and discussion of these laws.

Consider some of the issues that arise when laws are enacted to deal with circumstances that have ethical dimensions. The Gramm-Leach-Bliley Act of 1999 required financial services companies to tell their customers about their data privacy policies and allow them some choice about the extent to which information about them was shared. This act also illustrated that, by itself, passing a law does not ensure that it will have the desired effect. The passage of the act caused financial companies to send informational brochures that were often densely worded and used a small font: in short, difficult to read for customers. If customers discarded the brochure, as many did, they were "opting-in" on the data-sharing practices of the company, which meant it could sell their information to other companies. To "opt-out" of this data sharing required the customer to take explicit action to complete a form and mail it back (Reynolds, 2003). The lesson is that it cannot be assumed from the passage of a law that it will have the beneficial effects it may imply.

Freedom of Expression

In the United States, the First Amendment to the Constitution provides for an individual's freedom of speech. IT enables an individual's speech to reach a vast audience instantaneously. One particular case has been a prominent example of the intersection of freedom of speech with the Internet. An engineer for Intel was fired in 1996 in a dispute over a disability claim. He launched a web site to promote what he claimed was Intel's mistreatment of workers. As an ex-employee, he sent e-mail messages on several occasions to 30,000 current Intel employees to publicize his case and his new web site. Intel brought legal action, charging that he had trespassed onto Intel's property (its computer system) by sending e-mail messages. Here the individual's freedom of expression had bumped up against the company's right not to have its property violated by an outsider trespassing on it. Lawyers for the engineer claimed that he was simply exercising his right to free speech. The company said it had a right to control its own property, namely its computer system, by not allowing e-mail messages from the engineer. Two lower courts ruled in favor of Intel. In June 2003, the California Supreme Court overturned the lower courts by a 4–3 margin. The court ruled that Intel did not prove that its computer system had been damaged by the e-mails.

This series of legal decisions illustrates the difficulty of reconciling the issues being considered. The extended time period (recalling the original incident occurred seven years earlier) introduces another dimension to the case. Spam was a much more reviled practice in 2003 than it was in 1996. As evidence, the U.S. Congress passed the CAN-SPAM Act of 2003. So, sending 30,000 e-mails multiple times will be perceived differently at different times.

Other examples in which freedom of expression can exceed its legal protection include defamation, either orally (slander) or written (libel). Communications may also cause laws to be violated, for example, when the content is found to include obscenity, pornography, hate speech, or a death threat.

Electronic Surveillance

The extensive and growing use of surveillance and monitoring technology is a threat to a person's anonymity.

- There are an estimated 400 surveillance cameras per square mile on the island of Manhattan in New York City.[15]
- The Online Privacy Alliance found that 98 of the top 100 web sites collected personal information about visitors to their sites.[16]
- At Superbowl XXXV in Tampa Bay, Florida, in 2001, face recognition cameras were used to scan attendees as they walked through the turnstiles, finding 19 people with criminal records in the 100,000 people attending the game.[17]
- The USA Patriot Act of 2001 (see Appendix) was passed into law in record time on October 26, 2001, in response to the terrorist attacks in the United States. It expanded the powers of government to conduct surveillance of personal communications as part of counterterrorism investigations.

Employee monitoring is widespread, as reported in a 2001 American Management Association study[18]:

- 78 percent of U.S. companies monitor their employees in some way; it may be employees' Internet use (63 percent), e-mail messages (47 percent), video (15 percent), or phone messages (12 percent).
- Software is now available commercially to allow employers to monitor every keystroke of employees.

If there is a perceived need to monitor employees in the workplace, consider adopting guidelines for its implementation. It is critical to document clearly the objectives and expected benefits. For example, is the reason to improve quality, improve performance, ensure appropriate use of the organization's electronic resources, or detect unethical or illegal activity? To the extent possible, based on the objectives of the monitoring, it should be explained to employees when they are hired, along with the rationale and the expected benefits to the organization.[19] Consistent with monitoring being used for specific purposes, if problems are detected through monitoring, first occurrences should be the basis for discussion with the employee, not termination of employment (except for egregious or criminal behavior). Wherever feasible, the entire monitoring activity should be oriented to employee and organizational improvement.

▪▪▪ Communications About IT Products and Services

A distinguishing feature of a professional is that the person possesses specialized knowledge and needs to communicate it to the general public. IT professionals are called on to communicate about computer-based products and services. In a world in which salespeople are routinely chided for being overly enthusiastic about the products they are selling, professionals are expected to uphold a principle of honesty in the representations they make. A comparison to physicians who deal with life-and-death decisions may seem far-fetched. However, with software controlling X-ray machines, heart pacemakers, planes, cars, and many other systems that can cause death and destruction, an appeal to professional ethics in IT is entirely appropriate.

Highly ethical IT professionals are particularly needed because software is invisible and its properties are difficult to detect. It is a grave matter for a software engineer to misrepresent the fault tolerance or reliability of a product. The customer is at a distinct disadvantage because demonstrating the software in all its various failure modes is unreasonable. To do so would require other systems to be used and configured in particular ways to elicit the intended behavior. Customers must rely on the statements made or written about computer-controlled systems. Ethical behavior for the IT professional means communicating honestly in all instances.

Figure 6-2 provides a survey addressing the ethical attitudes of information systems professionals. The Centre for Computing and Social Responsibility at DeMontfort University in the UK developed the survey. It probes some of the key aspects of behaving as a professional. The survey can be especially effective if everyone in a class or training session completes it. Then they can compare their responses to those of the group as a whole, presenting a wonderful opportunity for a group discussion of different viewpoints on the ethical treatment of the situations.

▪▪▪ FIGURE 6-2 2002 ETHICOMP® Survey of Ethical Attitudes*

Please circle the answer that represents the extent to which you agree or disagree with each statement:

1. It is acceptable for me to make unauthorized copies of commercial software to use at work.

strongly disagree	disagree	indifferent	agree	strongly agree

2. I would refuse to work on a project that I considered to be unethical.

strongly disagree	disagree	indifferent	agree	strongly agree

3. Ongoing consultation with representatives of all those affected should occur throughout the information systems development life cycle.

strongly disagree	disagree	indifferent	agree	strongly agree

4. It is acceptable to use my employer's computing facilities for my own *non-profit-making* activities if this has no adverse affect on my employer.

strongly disagree	disagree	indifferent	agree	strongly agree

5. It is acceptable to use my employer's computing facilities for my own *profit-making* activities if this has no adverse affect on my employer.

strongly disagree	disagree	indifferent	agree	strongly agree

6. If an organization has purchased/developed software for use in the office, it is acceptable for employees to make unauthorized copies of this software for use at home.

strongly disagree	disagree	indifferent	agree	strongly agree

7. I think that all organizations should require all employees to abide by a code of professional ethics.

strongly disagree	disagree	indifferent	agree	strongly agree

8. If a project is significantly behind schedule or over budget, it is acceptable to cut down on testing effort.

strongly disagree	disagree	indifferent	agree	strongly agree

9. The level of data protection awareness amongst IS/IT staff should be high.

strongly disagree	disagree	indifferent	agree	strongly agree

10. The licensing of computer professionals should be introduced in my country.

strongly disagree	disagree	indifferent	agree	strongly agree

11. Employees should be allowed to re-create a product/program/design for another organization if they change jobs and are no longer employed by the organization who paid them to create it.

strongly disagree	disagree	indifferent	agree	strongly agree

12. When disagreements arise between development personnel and those affected by the system, it is the project manager who should have the final say.

strongly disagree	disagree	indifferent	agree	strongly agree

13. Most people can be trusted.

strongly disagree	disagree	indifferent	agree	strongly agree

14. Providing a systems development project provides me with an interesting challenge; I do not care about its overall objectives or purpose.

strongly disagree	disagree	indifferent	agree	strongly agree

15. It is acceptable for me to use other employees' access codes *with* their permission to access data I am not authorized to see.

strongly disagree	disagree	indifferent	agree	strongly agree

16. It is acceptable for me to use other employees' access codes *without* their permission to access data I am not authorized to see.

strongly disagree	disagree	indifferent	agree	strongly agree

17. It is acceptable for me to make unauthorized copies of commercial software for my own private use.

strongly disagree	disagree	indifferent	agree	strongly agree

(Continued)

18. My organization's security arrangements are sufficient to ensure that information held on its computer systems is safe from unauthorized access from *internal* sources.

strongly disagree	disagree	indifferent	agree	strongly agree

19. My organization's security arrangements are sufficient to ensure that information held on its computer systems is safe from unauthorized access from *external* sources.

strongly disagree	disagree	indifferent	agree	strongly agree

20. Organizations should develop and administer an ethics awareness programme for all employees.

strongly disagree	disagree	indifferent	agree	strongly agree

21. It is acceptable for a software contractor, provided with a brief specification, to go ahead and develop the system knowing that in the future rework under another contract will be essential.

strongly disagree	disagree	indifferent	agree	strongly agree

22. The level of data protection awareness amongst IS/IT staff is high.

strongly disagree	disagree	indifferent	agree	strongly agree

23. Consideration of the overall working environment is not part of the IS professional's responsibility.

strongly disagree	disagree	indifferent	agree	strongly agree

24. It is reasonable to take advantage of global economic differences to produce cheaper software.

strongly disagree	disagree	indifferent	agree	strongly agree

25. It is reasonable to take advantage of global time zones to produce software more quickly.

strongly disagree	disagree	indifferent	agree	strongly agree

26. IS/IT staff should design privacy and data protection compliance into information systems.

strongly disagree	disagree	indifferent	agree	strongly agree

27. Consultation with all stakeholders in an information systems development project is not always possible; to keep stakeholders informed is sufficient.

strongly disagree	disagree	indifferent	agree	strongly agree

28. I think that all organizations should require IS/IT employees to abide by a code of professional ethics.

strongly disagree	disagree	indifferent	agree	strongly agree

29. When people have failed in life it is often their own fault.

strongly disagree	disagree	indifferent	agree	strongly agree

30. Employers are entitled to use electronic surveillance to monitor employees' performance:
    (a) *with* their consent & *with* their knowledge
    (b) *without* their consent & *with* their knowledge
    (c) *with* their consent & *without* their knowledge
    (d) *without* their consent & *without* their knowledge.

(a)	strongly disagree	disagree	indifferent	agree	strongly agree
(b)	strongly disagree	disagree	indifferent	agree	strongly agree
(c)	strongly disagree	disagree	indifferent	agree	strongly agree
(d)	strongly disagree	disagree	indifferent	agree	strongly agree

31. To what extent do you feel able to refuse to work on a given project?

I have a free choice of projects to work on	I can some-times choose not to work on a project	I have no choice about the projects I work on

32. Does your employing organization have a policy concerning the use of computing facilities by employees for non-work-related purposes?
    (a) Software (e.g, game playing)
    (b) Printers and other peripherals
    (c) E-mail
    (d) Internet
    (e) Other (please specify)

(a)	Formal, written policy	Informal policy	No policy	Don't know
(b)	Formal, written policy	Informal policy	No policy	Don't know
(c)	Formal, written policy	Informal policy	No policy	Don't know
(d)	Formal, written policy	Informal policy	No policy	Don't know
(e)	Formal, written policy	Informal policy	No policy	Don't know

In choosing an *ideal* job (disregard your present job, if you have one) how important would it be to you to:

33. Work with people who cooperate well with one another.

of utmost importance	very important	of moderate importance	of little importance	of very little importance

34. Have an opportunity for advancement to higher-level jobs.

of utmost importance	very important	of moderate importance	of little importance	of very little importance

*Reprinted by permission of the Centre for Computing and Social Responsibility, DeMontfort University (UK).

▪▪▪ Professional Codes of Ethics

Published codes of ethics can be useful sources of guidance on the scope of responsibilities and behavior expected of the IT professional. Professional organizations have contributed to many of the codes, for example:

- Software Engineering Code of Ethics and Professional Practice, adopted by the IEEE Computer Society and the Association for Computing Machinery, http://www.computer.org/certification/ethics.htm
- Code of Ethics of the Association of IT Professionals (AITP) http://www.aitp.org/organization/about/ethics/ethics.jsp
- Code of Ethics of the International Information Systems Security Certification Consortium (ISC^2), http://www.isc2.org

Codes vary considerably in terms of the extent of guidance they provide. Certain codes are very concisely written, expressing idealized behavior. Some organizations consider it a success to draft and promulgate a code; others go further and enforce it. Some codes are backed up by details describing how various actions are consistent with the code or violate it.

Some organizations go beyond developing a code of ethics to preparing additional guidance. For example, ISC^2 also describes procedures for its members to file ethical complaints (https://www.isc2.org/cgi-bin/content.cgi?page=176). AITP has standards of conduct that provide more detailed statements of behavior in support of the code (http://www.aitp.org/organization/about/conduct/conduct.jsp). These standards of conduct are built around obligations of AITP members to

- Society
- Employers
- Fellow members of the profession
- Management

Similar to an ethics code, the Ten Commandments of Computer Ethics (Figure 6-3) are yet another set of succinct rules of conduct. Notice how these commandments would have been directly applicable by the principals in our five scenarios at the start of the chapter.

▪▪▪ **FIGURE 6-3   Ten Commandments of Computer Ethics***

1. Thou Shalt Not Use a Computer to Harm Other People.
2. Thou Shalt Not Interfere with Other People's Computer Work.
3. Thou Shalt Not Snoop Around in Other People's Computer Files.
4. Thou Shalt Not Use a Computer to Steal.
5. Thou Shalt Not Use a Computer to Bear False Witness.
6. Thou Shalt Not Copy or Use Proprietary Software for Which You Have Not Paid.
7. Thou Shalt Not Use Other People's Computer Resources Without Authorization or Proper Compensation.
8. Thou Shalt Not Appropriate Other People's Intellectual Output.
9. Thou Shalt Think About the Social Consequences of the Program You Are Writing or the System You Are Designing.
10. Thou Shalt Always Use a Computer in Ways That Insure Consideration and Respect for Your Fellow Humans.

**Source:* Computer Ethics Institute, The Brookings Institution, downloaded from http://www.brook.edu/its/cei/cei_hp.htm.

Codes of ethics represent another potential source of guidance or, at a minimum, a source of goals to which people can aspire. IT professionals should pay particular attention to ethics codes from employers and professional societies to which they belong. To make company codes of ethics effective, organizations will back them with periodic training and enforce them by their management practices.

SUMMARY

The pervasive effects of information technology on society require that IT professionals keep ethics in the forefront of their practice. This chapter discussed sources of ethics support:

- Understanding historical perspectives on ethics, such as virtue ethics, deontological ethics, and utilitarianism
- Distilling the true IT essence of an ethical situation, whether IT is changing a situation in a fundamental way or merely providing the context for a core issue that is not IT-related
- Pursuing a continuous improvement model for personal ethics based on cultivating an ethics radar and real-time ethics
- Using scenarios, discussions, self-tests, and other ethics resources for self-improvement
- Sharpening and applying practical tactics (e.g., ethical analysis, systematic scenario modification, creating a third option, taking the viewpoints of others, and documenting thoughts and feelings) for dealing with ethical situations
- Maintaining awareness of constantly evolving IT ethics dilemmas, such as those surrounding information privacy, freedom of expression, and electronic surveillance
- Ensuring that oral and written communications reflect personal ethical attitudes
- Taking advantage of guidance from codes of ethics both from employing organizations and the IT profession

EXERCISES

1. Should radio frequency identification tags be incorporated into driver's licenses? Does such a proposal raise ethical considerations? If you are part of a class or learning community, practice the oral communications recommendations in this book by having pairs of participants debate the pros and cons of this proposal.
2. Compare and contrast provisions of the AITP code of ethics with those for architects, librarians, and physicians, with respect to enforcement provisions and practices. Have any IT professionals been disciplined for ethics violations?
3. For Scenario 2 in which Mary keeps the second software package, describe the guidance that Mary would get from each of the moral standpoints of virtue ethics, deontological ethics, and utilitarianism.
4. Apply the ethical analysis framework of this chapter to the question of participating in peer-to-peer network for sharing files of recently released music.
5. You are working on a team to build a new order processing system. The objective is to make the company more competitive by introducing automation to reduce the labor hours needed in order entry and fulfillment. It is common knowledge in the company that staff will be laid off when the new system is deployed. You are concerned about working on this project, knowing it will cause lay-offs. However, you are not sure whether to raise this concern and

ask to be transferred to another project. After all, you really like your new boss and don't want to appear to be a troublemaker. And if you complain, the company may just decide to start the lay-offs early—with you! Should you ask to be taken off the project? What ethical issues, if any, are present in this case?

Endnotes ▪▪▪▪▪▪▪

1. Robin, D. P., Reidenbach, R. E., and Forrest, P. J. (1996). "The Perceived Importance of an Ethical Issue as an Influence on the Ethical Decision-making of Ad Managers." *J. Business Research* 35, 17–28.

2. Kreie, J., and Cronan, T. (December 2000). "Making Ethical Decisions." *Communications of the ACM 43,* 66–71.

3. Rachels, James. (2003). *The Elements of Moral Philosophy,* 4th ed. McGraw-Hill, New York.

4. Kohlberg, Lawrence. (1981). *The Philosophy of Moral Development: Moral Stages and the Idea of Justice.* Harper & Row, San Francisco.

5. Ferrell, O. C., Fraedrich, John, and Ferrell, Linda. (2002). *Business Ethics: Ethical Decision Making and Cases.* Houghton Mifflin, Boston.

6. Reynolds, George. (2003). *Ethics in Information Technology.* CourseTechnology, Boston.

7. Kant, Immanuel. (1981). *Lectures on Ethics,* translated by Louis Infield. Hackett Publishing Company, Indianapolis.

8. Floridi, Luciano. "Information Ethics: On the Philosophical Foundation of Computer Ethics," version 2.0, 1998, downloaded from www.wolfson.ox.ac.uk/~floridi/ie.htm on April 7, 2003.

9. Volonino, Linda, and Robinson, Stephen R. (2004). *Principles and Practice of Information Security.* Pearson Prentice-Hall, Upper Saddle River, NJ, 138–141.

10. Aristotle. (2000). *Nichomachean Ethics,* translated by Terence Irwin. 2nd ed. Hackett Publishing Co., Indianapolis.

11. Agresti, William W. (July–August 2004). "CE2IT: Continuous Ethics Enhancement for IT Professionals." *IT Professional* 6, 61–64.

12. Badaracco, Joseph. (1997). *Defining Moments: When Managers Must Choose Between Right and Right,* Harvard Business School Publishing, Boston.

13. Brandeis, Louis. *Olmstead vs. U.S.,* 1928, Electronic Privacy Information Center, downloaded from www.epic.org on Jan. 27, 2004.

14. Whitman, Michael E., and Mattord, Herbert J. (2003). *Principles of Information Security.* CourseTechnology, Boston.

15. DiJusto, Patrick. (December 2003). "You're Being Watched." *Wired,* 62.

16. Dickson, G. W., and DeSanctis, G. (2001). *Information Technology and the Future Enterprise.* Prentice Hall, Upper Saddle River, NJ.

17. Dotinga, Randy. (December 2002). "Biometrics Benched for Super Bowl." *Wired,* downloaded from http://www.wired.com/news/culture/0,1284,56878,00.html on Jan. 27, 2004.

18. Lane, Frederick S., III. (2003). *The Naked Employee: How Technology Is Compromising Workplace Privacy.* AMACOM, New York.

19. Baase, Sara. (2002). *A Gift of Fire: Social, Legal, and Ethical Issues in Computing,* 2nd ed. Prentice Hall, Upper Saddle River, NJ.

Selected References ▪▪▪▪▪▪▪

Beauchamp, Tom L., and Bowie, Norman E. (2003). *Ethical Theory and Business,* 7th ed. Prentice Hall, Upper Saddle River, NJ.

Johnson, Deborah G. (2000). *Computer Ethics,* 3rd ed. Prentice Hall, Englewood Cliffs, NJ.

Spinello, Richard. (2003). *CyberEthics: Morality and Law in Cyberspace,* 2nd ed. Jones and Bartlett, Boston.

Appendix

LAWS RELATING TO PRIVACY ISSUES (ADAPTED FROM WHITMAN AND MATTORD, 2003)

Law	Area of Focus	Reference
Freedom of Information Act of 1966	Individuals can access U.S. federal agency information	http://www.usdoj.gov/oip/ foia_updates/Vol_XVII_4/ page2.htm
Federal Privacy Act of 1974	Government agencies protect the privacy of the information they have on people and businesses	http://www.usdoj.gov/04foia/ privstat.htm
Electronics Communications Privacy Act of 1986	Interception of communications (including wire, electronic, and oral)	http://cio.doe.gov/Documents/ ECPA.HTM
Health Insurance Portability and Accountability Act of 1996 (HIPAA)	Requires organizations to protect health care information, including controlling access and distribution of personal information based on written consent	http://www.hhs.gov/ocr/hipaa/
Financial Services Modernization Act (Gramm-Leach-Bliley Act) of 1999	Financial institutions must disclose their policies on privacy and sharing of information	http://banking.senate.gov/conf/
USA Patriot Act of 2001	To combat terrorism, government law enforcement agencies were given significantly increased surveillance and investigative powers	http://www.epic.org/privacy/ terrorism/hr3162.html

CHAPTER 7

Effective IT Oral Communications

Learning Objectives

- To understand how oral communications can contribute to individual success in IT
- To discover ways to improve IT oral presentations
- To identify ways to shape oral communications for appropriateness to various IT contexts

Introduction

If you are effective in oral communications, you possess a valuable skill that can greatly enhance your success and that of your staff and your projects. One reason why oral communications is a worthwhile skill to master is the amount of time we spend doing it: Data show that 36 percent of programmers' time is spent talking or listening.[1] For other IT professionals, the percentage can be even higher because of their close interaction with users and customers.

If you do not now consider yourself adept at oral communications, you are not alone. One kind of oral communication, public speaking, is dreaded by a lot of people. According to a widely quoted entry from the Book of Lists, fear of speaking in public was the #1 fear of people, far ahead of dying, which was #7 on the list.[2]

Regardless of your starting point, the goal of this chapter is to improve your oral communications so that it becomes a personal strength that will benefit your professional development. This chapter explores the breadth of contexts for oral communications and offers strategies for preparing and delivering successful IT presentations.

WARM-UP EXERCISE

Prepare and deliver an elevator speech. If you are in a classroom setting, everyone should prepare one and deliver it in front of the class. If you are pursuing professional development on your own, deliver it to family and friends, asking for their comments and reaction.

The elevator speech owes its name to the scenario of the professional who walks into his or her multistory office building and gets in the elevator whose only other occupant is the CEO. With the prospects for conversation quite well defined, the CEO uses the opportunity of the brief ride up to get to know one of the hard-working souls who make this company what it is. "So, tell me," she says, "who are you and what do you do here?" With the average elevator ride reported to be 16 seconds,[3] you can't waste time stammering aimlessly.

This is your chance. You have a captive audience. A good performance here can mean instant promotion, perhaps a raise. At least doing well can mean that you won't kick yourself later for not being prepared. So, the warm-up exercise is to figure out what you would say in such an encounter, and then say it. Although it may seem trivial or unlikely, every professional is well advised to have an elevator speech handy for just such eventualities. You never know when the opportunity will arise—will you be ready?

Your topic can be anything that encapsulates who you are in the organization, your responsibilities, and your current work assignments. Ideally, you would like to give an articulate, concise summary that conveys to the CEO that you are an intelligent professional, you are involved in your work, and you can express yourself well to others.

Target your elevator speech to be approximately 30 seconds. How did you do? Did you come across as an asset to the company? Did you feel rushed or anxious? Did you express yourself clearly and forcefully? Try this warm-up exercise again after reading this chapter. Did the guidance of this chapter improve your elevator speech?

▪▪▪ Why Oral Communications for IT?

Being skillful at speaking and presenting may appear to be an obvious goal, but it can be instructive to consider more thoughtfully what effective oral communications can mean for the IT professional. Preparing and delivering oral presentations are frequent events in IT—from presenting proposals to delivering project status reports. Oral communications are also prominent features in the work of teams, a familiar working unit in IT. As professionals, we have responsibilities to speak up when ethical issues arise and alert customers to the consequences of using information systems (see codes of ethics in Chapter 6). Many IT professionals also see part of their role as serving as mentors to help junior IT staff members. All of these activities will be enhanced if you are skillful at oral communications.

Some perceive IT professionals as generally not effective at oral presentations. This is partly due to a misunderstanding of IT, that it is equivalent to programming. Studies of programmers have shown that many think of the opportunity to work alone as one of the desirable features of the job. But programming is not all of IT by any measure. IT also includes systems analysts, user interface specialists, domain specialists, project coordinators, program managers, requirements analysts, IT policy and standards specialists, infrastructure support specialists, and information systems architects. The activities of these IT professionals typically call for extensive use of oral communications.

The positive view to take with regard to oral communications and the IT professional is that this can be a skill at which you can excel, to the possible surprise of those in your organization! Developing your oral communication skills can contribute to advancing your career. IT career growth often means responsibilities that require greater communication, such as leadership of others on a project team and more contact with upper management and with customers.

The need for IT professionals to be effective at oral communications will only increase. Trends in system development (e.g., agile methods, cross-functional teams) encourage more oral communications, not less. With IT consuming enterprise resources that could be allocated elsewhere, IT investments must be explained and justified at the highest levels of organizations. This vetting process calls for IT leaders who are effective and skillful at oral communications. IT is called upon to reduce its costs to free up scarce resources, while simultaneously delivering strategic advantage to the enterprise by capitalizing on new information technologies. Business trends aimed at smoother and more efficient operations, such as Customer Relationship Management (CRM) and Supply Chain Management (SCM), demand more interaction with customers and partner organizations. And interaction means communications. These collaborations and partnering relationships don't happen magically by themselves. Although these trends relate to the networking of computer systems among organizations, they also will require human communications to establish and sustain the personal relationships necessary for CRM and SCM to run smoothly.

Another business strategy of the past decade is the identification by organizations of their core competencies. These become the organization's defining core of knowledge and capability and its foundation for developing products and services. A natural consequence of identifying core competencies is more focused organizational units, which is accomplished by selling off units that are not consistent with the core competencies and outsourcing to others. Outsourcing leads to a pattern of external partnerships. Organizations today rely for their effectiveness on essential contributions from other partner organizations. All these outsourcing and strategic partnering relationships place oral communications in a critical role. For example, often a significant element of outsourcing is offshoring, establishing partnering relationships with companies in different countries. Some organizations that had a track record of providing products and services to other companies are being caught off-guard by their customers' breaking off these long-standing relationships to go offshore in search of lower costs. So, sustaining those relationships places a new urgency on building strong personal ties, a key role of effective oral communications.

At the personal level of the individual IT professional, offshoring can be a threat to one's livelihood. IT workers in positions that are narrowly defined, such as help-desk support or coding, can be especially vulnerable to having their jobs lost to lower-cost competitors. A smart strategy to becoming less susceptible to offshoring is for the IT professional to take on positions that call for broader knowledge or to transform a current assignment into one with greater interaction with customers or suppliers. By possessing technical skills and also the knowledge of products, clients, and application domains—which calls for more oral communications—the IT professional can be more valuable to the organization and more difficult to replace.

Through effective oral communications, you can strengthen your interactions with others in the organization. You can build personal relationships that can move your job satisfaction higher up the scale, ranging from tolerable to downright enjoyable at times. With increased confidence in giving oral presentations, you will not shy away from opportunities, and perhaps even seek out chances to talk about your work and that of your team. These opportunities for oral communications provide visibility for yourself and your work, which can translate into greater recognition and reward.

In IT these days it's all about collaboration. The word *joint* is used more and more to emphasize the need for involving all the relevant parties in IT activities. The reasons for this are clear. Especially in systems development, experience and empirical results show the consequences of having to fix things later. When requirements changes are made further along in the development process, the costs go up exponentially.[4] By involving all the relevant parties early in the process, there is a better chance of eliminating costly surprises later. In addition to the clear objective of reducing costs, involving stakeholders serves the purpose of building a strong team. IT projects engage people both within the organization and outside it who will be relying on the future system to get their work done. Joint requirements planning and joint applications design are ways to integrate the contributions of others in the critical early activities that so often determine the success or failure of new systems. The trend to joint activities extends also to joint project planning. Within the U.S. Department of Defense, a major acquirer and user of large IT systems, the trend is to "purple" systems that must work across the Army, Navy, and Air Force.

Certainly, the skills needed by IT professionals are similar to those required in business and technology in general. After all, a hallmark of IT is the breadth of activities that comprise it. We have noted that IT professionals must deal with the factors of both business and technology. But there also are distinctive aspects of IT that place additional demands on the oral communications skills of its practitioners.

IT professionals must fulfill both commercial and scientific requirements in their communications. Some in IT must be as persuasive in their presentations as any salesperson in business. Others make technical presentations that are more like those heard in scientific conferences and colloquia. Often, the IT communicator must deal with both commercial and highly technical material in the same presentation, requiring a skillful touch to be effective. Because of the high cost and criticality of IT systems to organizations, IT professionals often will need to make oral presentations to widely varying audiences and to senior executives. The stakes are high; senior leadership will need assurances that IT projects are on track, which translates into more frequent oral communications than if the systems were not so critical and expensive. Because IT fulfills a strategic role in organizations—they want IT to make a difference—its representatives need to persuade others to provide resources. And the pervasiveness of IT in organizations means that the presentations will need to be crafted for a variety of audiences—stakeholders who vary widely in their technical backgrounds. From a single audience, an IT presenter may get the most basic question from one person ("How do I access this system?") and a very challenging technical question from another ("How can you be sure that the T3 line can handle the additional bandwidth requirements?").

Moreover, IT projects are known for having a poor track record of delivering usable systems. Overruns of budget and schedule are widely publicized. The Standish Group reports that 53 percent of software projects exceed their budget by more than 50 percent.[5] Awareness of this poor performance in the industry has implications for oral communications. Senior leadership is wary of IT projects that may be showing signs of getting out of control, consuming cost and schedule while not meeting functional and quality objectives. So, it wants more frequent status reports, often orally, possibly on a weekly basis, to keep close watch for potential problems. As a result, the starting point for some oral presentations may be a climate of distrust, with an audience that already suspects the project is in trouble and the presenter is using technical mumbo-jumbo to obscure that fact. The IT presenter starts off with something to prove to a skeptical crowd, thereby placing more importance on skillful delivery.

With these pressing needs for collaboration, stakeholder involvement, joint activities, and accountability to senior management, oral communications skills become even more important.

▪▪▪ Listening

Oral communication requires more than one person talking; someone needs to be listening. Listening has been incorrectly equated with hearing. Listening encompasses the physical process of hearing sounds plus the mental processing of what is heard. Active listening stresses the highly interactive nature of listening: reacting and responding to what is being said. The active listener is attentive, always working to incorporate the information being received. We have already noted how much of an IT professional's time involves oral communications. For managers, research shows that 45 percent of their time involves listening.[6] Now that attention has appropriately been focused on listening, researchers have recognized that it can be broken down into categories.

As an IT professional, you may often find yourself engaged in listening to learn,[7] for example, when you are interviewing users to understand their needs for a new system. The listening in this case involves focusing intensely on what is being said, because you must understand users' needs in order to take them into account in requirements and specifications documents. You will find yourself needing to ask questions to clarify what you are hearing. You also may practice critical listening, for example, when you are attending a product briefing by a prospective service provider. You are attentive to assessing what you are hearing for its credibility and validity.[8] When you are attending an IT research presentation, you may be practicing both critical listening and listening to learn.

Listening of all kinds is a critical skill for the IT professional who needs to interact with people, understand their needs, and interpret information coming from oral presentations.

▪▪▪ Oral Communications by IT Role

IT professionals fulfill many roles, and understanding these roles can help to identify the special skills needed for the oral communications required by each one.

The IT professional is often perceived (incorrectly, as we noted earlier) as an individual contributor who prefers to work alone. Certainly there are many in IT—such as some analysts and developers—who do spend a high percentage of their time working alone. But even in these circumstances, the individual contributions need to fit into a larger scheme—a team, a project—which implies the need to communicate orally. Our individual contributors will need to be effective in describing their work so others on the team can understand how it fits into larger project and systems contexts. It is especially critical for them to be clear about problems they are having; being effective in communicating those problems can make it easier for others to identify the right kind of assistance to provide. Our individual contributors may also need to be persuasive when they are being pressured to do more than is reasonable or when they need to persuade others why their approach or technique will work or should be adopted. In terms of performance reviews, all individual contributors need to have other people who understand their contribution. Being skilled at oral communications will enhance your ability to characterize your work and the contributions you are making to your supervisor and your customers. So, even IT professionals who are working as individual contributors have many occasions when they need to be good at oral communications.

A familiar term for a person with specialized technical knowledge is *subject-matter expert* (SME). As an IT SME, you are being contacted—perhaps by people throughout an international organization—because of your special expertise. Having expertise and being able to communicate effectively to varied audiences are two different things. Being skilled at oral communications can make an SME significantly more effective and valuable to the organization. Table 7-1 offers hints for effective oral communications for individual contributors, SMEs, and several other IT roles.

TABLE 7-1 Hints for Effective Oral Communications by IT Role

IT Role	Examples	Audience	Hints for Effective Oral Communications
Individual contributor	Developer, systems analyst	Fellow team members, supervisors	Be clear about what was accomplished or not, nature of problems or needs that inhibit progress.
			Characterize your contribution to larger entity (team, project): how does it fit?

(Continued)

TABLE 7-1 Continued

IT Role	Examples	Audience	Hints for Effective Oral Communications
Subject-matter expert (SME)	Lead architect, senior networking engineer, chief technology officer (CTO)	People from your project or other projects who need expert help, middle management and customers who need explanations of technical subjects	Do not talk down to the audience; recognize they may be experts in other areas. Your value to the organization depends on your ability to communicate your expertise so others can benefit from it. Consider visualizations, graphics, metaphors, and examples to explain concepts. Be truthful about the extent of your knowledge and the technical feasibility of the planned work. Use persuasive skills; as a technical leader, you will need to convince others that your approach will work and that your assessments of risks, technology trends, and technological maturity are accurate.
User interaction specialist	Human-computer interface (HCI) designer; requirements analyst; systems analyst	People outside your project who will be depending on the resulting system as users	Understand the position of the audience; take an interest in their needs and functional areas. Minimize jargon; translate technical topics into concepts people can easily grasp. Demonstrate rather than talk about a system feature; use oral communications to explain why the demonstrated features are being presented as they are and to ask for reaction and suggestions. Use persuasive skills to gain participation in determining an effective interface.
IT auditor	IT audit and compliance team leader	Senior management, chief information officers, chief security officers, CEOs, boards of trustees	Demonstrate solid understanding of the relevant compliance issues and laws. Seek opportunities for effective ways to organize summary content into tables or charts to deliver bottom-line messages (e.g., line charts to show trends over time in achieving compliance levels).

TABLE 7-1 Continued

IT Role	Examples	Audience	Hints for Effective Oral Communications
			Exercise caution so that your statements and conclusions are fair and accurate, out of respect for your organization and for the legal and regulatory foundations of the compliance standards.
Leader	Project leader, thought leader, team leader	Potential followers, people whose approval or resources you need	Use inspirational skills that make listeners want to follow you. Create visions and use imagery to give listeners a glimpse of the possible future state you envision. Create a sense of excitement about the prospects for the future. Demonstrate clear thinking and accuracy so that your inspirational message is reinforced.
Manager	Department manager, IT operations manager	People you manage, higher-level management, customers	Build confidence and trust; use words and persuasive communications styles that convey a sense of being in charge and having a clear understanding of all the relevant dimensions of the subject.
Customer	IT manager, chief financial officer, chief information officer	Potential service providers	Be forceful and clear in expressing needs. Ask questions that reveal key characteristics of potential providers, such as technical depth, relevant experience, flexibility, and customer orientation.
Partner	Program manager	Potential partners	Be clear about "rules of engagement" among partners. Be persuasive about capabilities and talents. Use graphics to illustrate potential relationships and interactions among partner organizations.
Teammate	Proposal team member, development team member	Team members	In your communications, express openness to new ideas. Ask questions to elicit the contributions of colleagues who may have good ideas but are shy about expressing them.

▮▮▮ Oral Communications by Meeting Context

Oral communications in IT come in many shapes and sizes; the great variety matches the diversity of activities and dimensions of IT itself. This section explores the various contexts for IT oral communications—from the most informal interactions to the most structured project reviews.

The communication strategies and styles you employ must be sensitive to the circumstances and expectations associated with the meeting context. Table 7-2 summarizes several familiar meeting contexts both for oral presentations and for informal oral communications. If a particular situation is not listed in the table, consider that it may easily be a variant of one of the table entries. For example, IT professionals frequently change jobs. Job interviews typically involve oral communications that will cover both technical and personal information. The hints in the table related to sales/capabilities and informal work group communications will be helpful for job interviews.

The process of acquiring IT products, systems, and services often calls for several interactions between the customer and prospective providers. The formats and ground rules for these sessions are defined quite specifically for legal reasons and may include capabilities briefings, best and final offer (BAFO) meetings, and "orals" for discussing details of a proposed system with a very few finalists. Even specific meetings like these share elements of the more generic meetings, such as sales/capabilities and technical presentations, found in Table 7-2.

TABLE 7-2 Hints for Effective Oral Communications by Meeting Context

Contexts for Oral Communications	Hints on Content	Hints on Tactics
Presentations		
Technical	Ensure technical accuracy. Provide flexibility, with back-up slides available to supply more technical details. Use graphics liberally to show technical relationships and provide perspective.	Know technical level of audience and develop slides accordingly. Do homework: Determine expectations of audience to see technical details. Use complementary handouts with technical details; refer questioners to handouts for explanations or to stem tangents.
Scientific research	Cover prior research fairly and effectively. Cite references on slides using smaller, still readable, font size. Be clear about claims of novelty for your work: What exactly is the contribution you are making? How does your work advance the field?	Refer to supporting written paper, if available, for details, so the presentation can hit major points. Determine expectations of audience; contact meeting organizers if needed to inquire about technical level of audience and presentation style expected.

TABLE 7-2 Continued

Contexts for Oral Communications	Hints on Content	Hints on Tactics
Proposals/Funding	Make the most persuasive case possible. What will happen if you *do not* receive resources? How will important activities be adversely affected? Use facts and supporting data wherever possible, so your case has objective foundations. Have you explored the pros and cons of viable alternatives? Why did you choose your approach?	Know who can make the decision you need to gain resources; is that person in the audience, or are you trying to influence people one level removed from the decision-maker? Be flexible in case the decision-maker or key attendee gets called away early; if there is a reasonable chance of it, make your request for resources at the start, then use the remaining time to explain why your proposal appears as it does.
Sales/Capabilities	When faced with a hypothetical question about how to handle a situation, state any directly relevant points or experiences; if you have no particular response that answers the question, resist routinely "designing on the fly"; instead, recognize a few of the key issues raised by the question and be willing to say, "we'll look into your question and get back to you." Do not overstate the capabilities of your people, products, or services. Be honest when claiming "the next version" will address a questioner's needed capabilities.	Work into the presentation your technical credentials, educational background, and professional experiences. If time constraints and setting allow, ask the audience questions about what they need, leading to your products and services as answers. Be responsive to questions; clients, or potential clients, want to see with whom they want to work.
Project/program review (Also see Chapter 8, "Technical Reviews")	Work with the person who controls the review on the items to be covered; this is not the time for surprises or side agendas. Be candid about expressing the reality of the situation; "sugarcoating" or "spin" has no place in a project review. Use objective data where it makes sense, but recognize that IT activities have significant human elements.	Seek to understand causes of problems or reasons for poor performance, not to assign blame but to improve progress in the future. Be prepared to take issues "off-line" when their continued discussion is not adding value.

(Continued)

TABLE 7-2 Continued

Contexts for Oral Communications	Hints on Content	Hints on Tactics
Informal Interaction		
Team or work group	Reserve the face-to-face sessions for purposes that take advantage of that format; identify topics that are better handled by reading material individually and commenting via e-mail. If you are not sure whether your idea will be effective, offer it in the form of a question, to encourage the group as a whole to consider its merits.	Prepare for the meeting by considering what you can contribute for each agenda item. Express yourself forcefully, with confidence. Make eye contact to engage others in your ideas. Be sensitive to cues about timing; if the meeting is drawing to a close, this is not the time to bring up a topic that requires a lot of discussion; instead, consider mentioning it briefly and asking colleagues to think about it and discuss via e-mail until you meet again.
Brainstorming	Think about how the question or issue you are addressing may be similar to what is encountered in other application domains or fields of professional practice.	There are many flavors of brainstorming; establish at the start if yours will really follow the guideline of being nonjudgmental (there's no such thing as a bad idea) and nonattributing (cannot identify the source of contributions). Be ready to remind colleagues who violate guidelines. Offer brief supporting and positive words to encourage openness and outside-the-box ideas.
Focus groups with users	Ask questions liberally to learn why users work as they do and how they depend on information to do their jobs. Tell them that the system needs to be usable by them for it to have benefits to the organization; their contributions are key.	Show genuine interest as users describe how they work and what they do; by understanding them, you can better meet their needs with your system. Listen attentively; the users' descriptions may provide insights that improve your design and implementation.
"Elevator speech" (impromptu quick personal or project summary)	Rehearse it, so it will be ready when needed. Hit the high points; there is no time for extraneous details.	Connect yourself and your work to the rest of the organization. Say it with confidence; this is your time to shine!

There are a few additional observations and examples to supplement the hints in the table. At the beginning of this chapter, we introduced the elevator speech. Because of its slightly frivolous title, you may regard it as a curiosity. It isn't. In the larger context, every IT professional should have at the ready a summary presentation just waiting for anyone to request it. This may indeed be the executive at your organization who, as in the elevator scenario, meets you and wants to know who you are and what you do in the organization. Why be thrown off? Instead, keep some key points always at the ready so you can be impressive in your few moments in the spotlight. You never know where such a positive first impression can lead. That same executive may remember you when a key position needs to be filled or when your name is discussed for possible advancement. The elevator speech may be about you and your work in general or it may be about a specific project on which you are working. Have a brief summary of project status available to you. This is especially critical if you are one of the key people on the project or if it is a project vital to the organization. When an executive hears you are working on a key project, the focus often shifts quickly from you to the project, and the encounter becomes an opportunity for the executive to collect informal input from "one of the troops" on the project to get "the real story" of how things are going instead of only from the more polished presentations coming from the project leader. So, a wise IT professional will be able to talk concisely and effectively about current projects.

An overarching guideline for effectiveness at meetings is to know who "owns" the meeting; that is, who is in a position to set guidelines for content and timing? Who can cut the meeting short? Who can insist on different material being discussed or presented? Someone will own the meeting, whether it is an informal group meeting or a formal program review. This ownership most often arises from an individual's position in the organization or from his or her role in having convened the attendees. If these are different people, then seniority in the organization prevails. A key to being successful with oral communications at meetings is to recognize that this person does exist (even if it is not obvious), know who it is, and prepare accordingly. Ignore meeting ownership at your peril.

Meeting ownership is perhaps most obviously revealed during IT project or program reviews. Reviews are covered in a chapter on their own (Chapter 8), owing to their pervasiveness and importance in IT operations. Often the review is communicated orally. When preparing for an oral project or program review, it is especially critical to know who owns the meeting. If this review is at the request of a senior manager or your customer, they own it; that is, the review is for their benefit. You may be the presenter, but control of the meeting belongs to them. Your presentation needs to match their interests and concerns. You cannot insist on content or format because it isn't your meeting. You will need to be flexible, adept at shifting entirely from your planned presentation to address a topic of interest to the meeting owner. Some IT presentations, scheduled for 3 hours with a strict and previously followed agenda, end up spending the entire time on one aspect of the project—for example, to explore in depth a critical risk issue. Your presentation may have the familiar charts outlining progress and risks, comparing actual progress to planned progress. It doesn't matter. If you don't control the meeting, all that prepared content can be ignored.

One dramatic example of this I-didn't-realize-I-wasn't-the-owner phenomenon occurred during a corporate annual review of a software technology center that consisted of four departments and over 250 technical staff in a corporation of

3,000 employees. The company had a matrix organization, with technology centers like this one bringing special talents and capabilities to the project teams across the company. The technology center was matrixed into the most critical projects in the company, and as technology centers, they were also the focal point for their technologies, for example, the locus for discussion of industry trends and the extent to which newer technologies were being adopted.

The annual review to the company president was scheduled for 6 hours. Naturally, the center director came prepared with 6 hours' worth of presentation slides, ready to report on all the activities of his center staff. After the title slide, the president said that since the software center was the technological center for the company, and since software is used everywhere in the company, he wanted to hear about the use of software everywhere else in the company, that is, outside the software center: What technologies were being used by project teams that did not use the staff of the software center? Does the success of projects and systems differ if projects use the software center or not?

Well, as you can imagine, this caused a huge problem for the center director. He had not prepared at all for this emphasis. He made some general observations and tried to steer the discussion back to his prepared slides. It wasn't successful. The planned 6-hour briefing ended early. The lesson learned, the hard way, is never take for granted who is the owner of a meeting. Do not assume because previous reviews have followed a particular format that the next one will as well. As a leader, understand what your responsibilities are in a broad sense: What do senior executives expect me to know? Am I prepared to shift my presentation to a topic that they realistically may expect me to know? Being prepared in this way can make the difference between an embarrassing and career-damaging failure and a brilliant and career-enhancing success.

▮▮▮ Oral Communications and Development Processes

The oral communications involved in systems development vary extensively according to the process used.[9] Many large systems projects follow sequential or iterative development processes, so it is natural to conduct review presentations at successive stages in the process. These presentations are most often formal, stand-up briefings, so that all stakeholders can participate and know the project status. However, oral communications can be quite different when development follows the practices of extreme programming, which is highly interactive. In the early stages of a proposed system, you might find customers and developers together in a room. Customers write stories—something that the system must do—on note cards. When a bunch of cards/stories is completed several other activities can begin:

- Customers can assign priorities to the cards: must have, want to have, and nice to have.
- Quality-assurance folks write a test on the back of the card—a test that will demonstrate that the system capability (story) has been accomplished successfully.
- Developers estimate the effort to deliver each of the stories and create groups of cards to be implemented together in an iteration.

The communication that results from this situation is often strikingly different from more formal presentations and is a distinguishing feature of lightweight approaches like extreme programming: "The reason heavyweight approaches fail is simple. There is a lot of talking, and certainly a lot of paper, but there isn't much communication."[10]

Extreme programming places a premium on instantaneous and face-to-face communication. Programmers working in pairs are in constant communication with each other and with other pairs. Talking replaces most written documentation. Planning is more talking, this time between the developer and customer. By having frequent (often at least daily) stand-up meetings, developers stay in synch and are not left trying to figure things out on their own. There is no place for the all-too-familiar wasteful, drawn-out, sit-down meetings that take on a life of their own. Ideally, in 15 minutes or less, a stand-up meeting will connect people who need to know something with those who know it.[11] If you face a roadblock, don't wait till the next morning, ask for help immediately. Open workspaces are essential: "When emergencies happen, everybody needs to be within earshot."[12]

General Guidance for Oral Communications—with an IT Twist

There is no shortage of helpful hints on how to give speeches and other oral presentations, which reinforces the wide-ranging importance of this skill. We need to resist the temptation that sometimes occurs in IT to think that everything we do is so different that everything needs to be invented from scratch. IT has distinguishing features but, in oral communications, there is a lot of general guidance that is useful. In this section, we draw from these generic sources, then add our own twist to relate them and modify them for optimum effectiveness in IT. The context here is a planned presentation, rather than informal oral communications. The remainder of this section will discuss the following aspects of an oral presentation:

Preparation
Goals and objectives
Organizing your story
Storyline templates
Audiovisual aids
Delivery

Preparation

Although we may all acknowledge that preparation is key to successful presentations, it remains surprising how often we ignore thorough preparation. Certainly some lack of preparation is due to the frequently occurring time pressure of life in the world of IT—the need to do the rest of your job while also planning a briefing! But, just as certainly, paying attention to the suggestions here can make the difference between success and that other possible outcome. Table 7-3 at the end of this section summarizes guidelines for preparing for IT presentations, including the previous caution about knowing who the owner of the meeting is.

It is axiomatic that you must know your audience, but there are many dimensions to characterizing the people who will be listening to you. Given our focus on IT, one dimension is certainly the technical knowledge of your audience: What do you expect them to know about the subject of your presentation? Most often the depth of knowledge is uneven. It is your responsibility to ensure that the technical materials are presented in an interesting and accessible manner to the mixed audience. Define your materials based on its levels of understanding of the topic and interests in it. Acknowledge that some attendees may not have a strong genuine interest in the topic; they may be required to be there.

With regard to the technical expertise of the attendees, recognize that some of them may be specialists in the field, perhaps more of an authority than you are. For these people, being accurate is essential to win their endorsement of your message. You don't need to feel that you must compete to determine who knows more, but you do need to be correct. These highly knowledgeable attendees may have an agenda that includes showing you and other attendees how much they know. If possible, have similarly expert people at your dry runs ask you the kinds of questions they may ask. If the questions probe technical levels beyond your understanding, say so, then reiterate that your representations of the technology remain accurate and valid for your message. For less technically savvy attendees, you will need to deliver clear and concise explanations of technical concepts. You may find university web sites on the Internet to be helpful sources of material on how to introduce these concepts. You also may need to have back-up slides with more tutorial or background material, especially if these people are the key attendees whom you want to influence.

Even if your presentation is accurate, your efforts will be wasted if your audience is not in a position (e.g., because of limited technical background) to receive your message. Organize and structure your presentation for the convenience of your audience. People bring their own attitudes, opinions, emotions, and experiences—all of which influence their opinion about your message. Consider their perspectives and try to see things from their points of view.

Another dimension of an audience profile is the extent to which attendees are sympathetic or hostile to what you plan to say. If the purpose and objective of your presentation is advertised beforehand, certain individuals may show up drooling at the prospect of countering your message, having had time to prepare a case against it. Planning for such a hostile crowd can require careful thought and strategic considerations. If time permits, practice by having colleagues take on the role of the hostile faction and prepare a case so you can anticipate what you may hear. In this way, you will have the advantage of having taken time ahead of the presentation to fashion responses and thereby minimize the number of times that you will have to think on your feet about the best response.

The circumstances of your meeting may be such that you are proposing the company pursue a particular approach that you know runs counter to the preferences of attendees. For example, your analysis has shown that it is time to disengage from the plan to go with a particular Enterprise Resource Planning (ERP) package. Although the company has already started on the plan, you have concluded from early experiences that continuing with it is unwise. Attendees will likely include the managers who made the earlier decision, so you will need extensive preparation, with objective and convincing data wherever possible, to counter the expected challenges you will face. In fact, if the situation is leading to such a clear-cut consideration of alternative directions, you should consider whether a formal stand-up presentation is the smartest way to proceed. It is more likely that a small meeting with principals around a conference table is preferable. Even in the smaller setting, persuasive oral communications will be needed.

If your audience will include people with multiple organizational affiliations (e.g., customers, competitors, and strategic partners), you will want to understand what each group expects from the presentation and ensure that your message will satisfy them. Not all attendees are equally important in terms of satisfying their needs. Your primary audience may be customers, so concentrate on addressing their needs.

If you have access to your audience, talk to them beforehand to find out what they expect from your presentation. If the planned attendees are not available, ask others who may know the technical depth and expectations of the attendees. With the wealth of content on the Internet, it is easier than ever to engage in business intelligence to find out more about attendees and their organizations. This background checking can lead to attendees giving you high marks because your presentation and your answers to questions demonstrate an understanding of their organizations. Realistically, though, you may simply not have time to conduct an audience analysis. In this case, try your best to develop a mental picture of your audience and plan and prepare for the presentation accordingly. The more you know about the audience and its expectations, the greater the prospect for a successful presentation for you and them.

When you have done as much as possible to discover key characteristics of your audience, you are ready for an extremely important preparation activity: managing their expectations. In as specific terms as possible,

- Why are they attending?
- What do they intend to gain from the presentation?
- How are they planning to use the information?
- How does this presentation fit within the larger contexts of their projects and organizations?

For example, if attendees represent other projects, you should know how your presentation relates to them:

- Can the technologies you are presenting be used on their projects?
- If you had their position and responsibilities, what would you want to gain from attending this presentation?

In planning the presentation, give consideration to the use of supporting hard-copy materials. The expectation for a formal speech (e.g., at an industry conference) may be an oral presentation only, supported by slides or not. In other settings, it is common to give attendees hard-copy handouts of the slides. Not to do so can appear unusual, based on prevailing practices. Another alternative is to provide copies of the technical paper that is essentially being summarized in the presentation instead of the slides drawn from the technical paper. This system is common at scientific meetings for which a proceedings document (compilation of technical papers) is provided to attendees. However, in many IT settings, presentation slides become essential documentation of a system. The slides from design reviews are the design diagrams describing the system architecture. Slides from project reviews become the documentation describing stakeholders and their needs, major system functions, and relationships to other systems. When more detail is needed than is typical for a presentation slide, the Notes feature of PowerPoint can be used to create an annotated briefing. Notes can be used in two ways: for the presenter only, to provide cues for the oral presentation, or for the attendees, to provide additional documentation. In contractual environments, deliverable documents are sometimes defined as the annotated presentation slides instead of a separate (and often costly, duplicative, and unread) technical report.

By following the hints in Table 7-3, you will be doing as much as possible prior to the presentation to help ensure that it is successful.

TABLE 7-3 Guidelines for Preparing IT Presentations

Know who "owns" the meeting.	Know who it is, what they want.
	Be flexible—ground rules may change!
Know the audience.	What do they need?
	What do they expect from the presentation?
	What IT knowledge do they possess?
Know your stuff.	No one expects you to know everything about everything, but do your homework on what they reasonably expect you to know.
Know your specific message.	Write one sentence that encapsulates your message.
Plan your presentation materials.	Decide what is best regarding presentation materials: oral presentation only, take-away slides, making presentation available electronically later, use of annotated slides.
Know how to recognize a successful presentation.	Write down precisely what success in this presentation means, that is, what specific outcomes—events occurring, memo's written, funds released—mark success.
Know the setting and logistics.	Visit the site; try out the lights and audio/video system.
	Make sure these are no slipups on who is invited, time/place, location.
	Anticipate possible adverse factors—weather, traffic, power outage—and how you will recover.
Build an emergency kit.	Make back-up slides in multiple formats, on the Internet or accessible servers, and with other people.
Rehearse.	Dry-run your presentation at the same site and under the same conditions as you will encounter.
	Invite colleagues to critique and ask questions.
	Dry-run again to build confidence and work on fine points.
Visualize a successful presentation.	Close your eyes, relax, picture yourself presenting a winning presentation!

Goals and Objectives

From their project planning work, IT professionals know a key difference between goals and objectives—the latter must be measurable. You need to give the same attention to goals and objectives when planning a presentation. Informally, the goal of a design review may be to get through it relatively unscathed! More formally, it may be to demonstrate to the sponsors that you are making satisfactory progress according to plan and are well prepared to take on the next phase of the development process. Although this goal may effectively express what you want to achieve with the design review, it isn't measurable in its current form. But it does provide a starting point for crafting measurable objectives for the review, as shown in Table 7-4.

Notice that each of the objectives in Table 7-4 is measurable. After the review, you will know if these objectives were met or not. The measures proposed in the table are not comprehensive or complete in assessing all aspects of the objective. In fact, they are more properly indicators of what the project leadership has agreed will mark the successful completion of the objective. Certainly, for each objective, different or additional indicators could be defined to capture more completely the notion of successful attainment of the objectives.

Organizing Your Story

The goals and objectives are the starting points for organizing your presentation. You are crafting a message that your presentation must deliver effectively. Your presentation is a series of steps that take listeners from their (sometimes various) starting points and lead all of them along a path to the successful communication of your message.

For the range of presentations of interest to IT professionals, we can identify a few techniques for deciding on the most effective series of steps, based upon the objectives and the outcomes desired. We call the series of steps a *storyline*,

TABLE 7-4 Example of Measurable Objectives for a Design Review

Objective	*How to Measure Success?*
We don't want the project cancelled.	You will know it if the project is cancelled!
We want the review to be assessed by the sponsor as being complete.	No more than five action items or follow-up items are opened as a result of the review.
We want the sponsor to consider our team to be prepared to move ahead according to the project plan.	We are given approval to continue with the project, or we are not told to do anything that would represent a holding action, such as being required to conduct a second design review or to suspend work until higher-level management can be briefed.
We don't want overt manifestations of lack of confidence in our team.	The review does not lead to any introduction of additional oversight, such as appointing and launching a red team review.

a logical progression that moves your listeners along in their thinking. It is a variation on the following:

- Storytelling, which has been shown to be a very worthwhile practice for knowledge sharing in organizations[13]
- Storyboarding, which is familiar to IT professionals who have worked on proposals and had to lay out a proposal story that satisfies the Request for Proposal (RFP) and makes the strongest case that their company should be awarded the job

Developing a storyline also borrows from the crafting of plot lines in books and films. Only now you are the director! How will you shape this story so your objectives are met?

A starting point for an effective storyline is to take the approach of designing the presentation backward, focusing on what you want to be the state of affairs after the presentation is over. Most presenters want to feel relieved, of course! We want to look beyond this to characterize more broadly how things are to have changed because of the presentation. Designing the presentation backward recognizes three broad classes of outcomes. Attendees are to be informed by what is presented, persuaded in some way, or inclined to give the presenter what the presentation said was wanted. Consistent with IT being a complicated mix of technology, systems, processes, and people, many presentations cannot be neatly confined to exactly one of these three outcomes, but will have features of more than one class.

When the objective is to inform, you want attendees, when they depart the presentation, to have specific knowledge they didn't have when they walked in. This is a tall order! The indicator of success would literally be the successful completion of a quiz on the key points of the presentation. And the thought of a quiz leads naturally to the question of how much do you really expect attendees to gain in new knowledge from what you have presented: What is your message?

The message for an informative presentation is the essential "take-away" information that you want all attendees to know as they walk away. It is unrealistic to believe that they will remember everything. Knowing that fact in advance can focus your attention on deciding precisely what your message is. If the attendees are questioned about what they remember about your presentation, they should be able to recall four or five key points. Even with a handful of points, prioritize them so you know which ones are most important to reinforce during your presentation. The messages cannot be too long, or you will be disappointed if you ever conduct the hypothetical exit quiz. Based on what is known about how humans acquire information in oral presentations, expecting people to remember long messages is unrealistic. So the focus needs to be on developing a crisp, clear message that will drive the entire presentation and encapsulate what you want attendees to take with them. Following are some points to consider while preparing your presentation[14]

- Create the presentation around the key points of your message.
- Include one slide that lists all the key points.
- Use your message to organize the presentation, expanding on the points in future slides.
- Design the slides so the key points can be easily explained.
- Reinforce the key points of your message on more than one slide.

When your objective is to persuade listeners, a useful first step is to conduct a rough gap analysis. As a result of your presentation, do you want attendees to

- Agree with your point of view?
- Be inspired to take action?
- Be open to new ways of thinking or feeling?

The gap analysis would also stress the importance of knowing, to the extent possible, what the starting points are of the minds and hearts of the people who will be listening to you. It may seem dramatic to discuss feelings and emotions, but it is the inspirational and motivational speeches that take them into consideration that have been etched in our memory. Your objective in the persuasive presentation may be to impart a sense of urgency, for example, that your organization is at risk of losing its competitive position in a given market. What are the attitudes of the people who will be listening to this briefing? Will this be entirely a surprise to them, or has the deteriorating competitive position been discussed already among the attendees? In the former circumstance, you will need to structure your remarks to be sensitive to the novelty of the message you are bringing to the people who are hearing you. In the latter case, you may be presenting the results of careful analysis to persuade attendees to see the competitive situation as you do.

One kind of persuasive presentation is a request for funding. You may be seeking a higher budget for your department or project. A new business opportunity may be prompting you to give an informative presentation that transitions into a persuasive request for funding to pursue this lead. When funds are being requested, you will want to lay out the business case or other justification during the briefing. The ideal presentation will be so convincing that by the time you actually make the request, the audience is well prepared to grant it and commit the resources.

Every time IT professionals engage in oral communications they should regard this, at least in part, as persuasive communication. Even in what may appear to be an informative presentation, you are persuading the listener that you are a competent and ethical professional, with specialized knowledge, who is able to operate effectively for the success of the organization or project. Consider some examples of what may appear to be entirely informative presentations to discover the persuasive elements lurking close to the surface. Your CEO keeps reading about security threats to information systems posed by wireless devices and has asked for a briefing from the IT staff. The reply may seem to be a solely informative one, even tutorial in nature, but think again. The presentation is an opportunity to demonstrate technical knowledge of the staff and perhaps give visibility to an individual contributor with strong technical expertise. The presentation may build confidence to the point that the CEO thinks of offering the in-house expertise to clients to help them with their concerns about wireless security. Do you really think the CEO will listen alone? More likely some of the senior staff or senior managers will be brought along. Now this is an opportunity to persuade all attendees of the IT staff's talent. Perhaps this will simply reinforce an already held perception, or it may help to reverse the impression left by some recent unconvincing technical briefing by the IT staff. By means of the CEO's prominent position, the presentation may lead to follow-on briefings to the board of trustees or executive roundtables or prestigious conferences.

While reveling in the possibilities arising from this apparently innocuous request, don't get carried away. You may see this as an opportunity to seek additional funds from the CEO to enhance security to guard against wireless threats — combining all three classes of presentations. You must be very cautious about taking this route and rely on your insight into the CEO's working style. Although one CEO may admire the aggressive posture of an IT manager who uses this opportunity to seek more funding, another may see it as entirely inappropriate. But a natural topic to include in even an informative briefing, and one that will likely anticipate a question, would be a characterization of your company's vulnerability to wireless threats, which can impart a persuasive message that sets the stage for later IT budget discussions.

The message for your CEO briefing on wireless security might be the following:

1. Wireless poses a formidable and growing security threat.
2. Business and personal trends (e.g., telecommuting, cell phones, personal digital assistants) serve to increase wireless security concerns.
3. We must understand technology trends and standards issues in wireless and how they will they affect security.
4. We must know the exposure of the company to wireless security threats and, if vulnerable, take actions to improve its security posture.

Granted, this wireless security message is ambitious, but this is the reality of many IT presentations. Our technology is rapidly changing. It can be used by anyone. There are highly influential legal, ethical, social, policy, regulatory, and process issues that are intermixed with the technology. In the sense of our backward-design paradigm, you want attendees to have a basic level of understanding of each of the four parts of the message. You may reinforce your message with clear presentation graphics and handout materials that are also made accessible on a company intranet for later reference by attendees. But there is no substitute — even with the most complicated IT subject — for taking time to clarify the message and to plan its delivery so that it gets through.

Your company asks the IT staff to present at its "lunch and learn" brown bag series the topic of protecting online privacy. This clearly sounds like an informative briefing. But think about the attendees. Think about the importance of building effective working relationships with all parts of the company. Think about the ongoing (never-ending?) task forces busily trying to figure out how to implement the huge commercial Enterprise Resource Planning (ERP) package across the company. These teams include people from all the divisions and infrastructure units — the same units represented at the brown bag lunch. Perhaps your IT group should see this as an opportunity to persuade attendees that you are very competent professionals who can tailor your presentations to those who are not IT specialists. A desirable outcome may be to build up your image with the rest of the company that you can be effective team members and colleagues who will respect them for their functional knowledge and not disparage their lack of IT expertise.

The message for your tutorial on protecting online privacy might be the following:

1. Protecting online privacy is the responsibility of every individual — you cannot rely on others for protection.

2. Failure to protect your privacy can have disastrous consequences, as news stories on cases of identity theft illustrate.
3. There are simple things you can do to protect your privacy (e.g., controlling settings on web browsers, ensuring use of secure socket layers in transactions).
4. The IT staff will post guidance information on the company intranet so employees can use it for their work and home computer use.

Organizing your story can clarify your message and provide a framework for developing your presentation.

Storyline Templates

One report cites statistics from Microsoft® claiming that there are 30 million PowerPoint presentations each day in the world.[15] It is natural to try to sort so many and varied presentations into categories according to how they are organized. Many IT presentations—for example, project reviews and status reports—do have structures dictated by defined formats. When the format is not prescribed, the IT professional will find that many objectives can be met by using one of these organizing structures[16]:

- Analyze/Recommend
- Big Bang
- Personal Action Appeal

Analyze/Recommend

The Analyze/Recommend model is widely used throughout IT. The IT professional may be given an assignment to investigate options for broadband networking services. The resulting presentation will fit this Analyze/Recommend scheme:

1. What was the assignment or charge you were given?
   - Identify any constraints you were given
   - What limitations did you introduce?
     - Why did you do so; what was the justification for it (e.g., time pressure)?
     - What are the ramifications of these limitations on your analysis process and ultimate recommendation?
2. What analysis process did you establish to respond to the assignment?
   - What were the steps in your process?
     - Summarize each step in your analysis process
     - Alternatively, depending on time, interest of key audience members, and your judgment, keep these process steps as back-up slides and focus on recommendation
   - Pay special attention to the criteria you adopted to evaluate alternative service providers; the criteria should be established before examining individual providers
     - Did you introduce weightings for the criteria?
   - Did you recognize relevant stakeholders and their priorities?
   - Did you take advantage of available resources (e.g., company experts, recognized industry sources)?

3. State the results of your analysis.
  - Summarize pros and cons with a table
    - Did you apply your criteria faithfully?
    - Use back-up slides with details of providers and analyses
  - Was there a clear-cut choice?
  - If there were a few top candidates, did you conduct a more thorough follow-up analysis on these top few?

4. What is your recommendation?
  - How did you use the results to get to your recommendation?
  - How does your recommendation fare with projected future industry trends?
  - Is your recommendation feasible?

5. What are the risks?
  - How might industry trends not under your control adversely affect your recommendation?
  - Summarize risks, with details in back-up slides
  - Reinforce your recommendation in the face of these risks

6. Next steps
  - Summarize steps needed to implement your recommendation

With minor variations, the Analyze/Recommend template is also appropriate for problem/solution or opportunity/response cases. In these scenarios, an IT professional is assigned to look into a problem and recommend a solution or pursue an opportunity and recommend a response. The steps outlined essentially cover both cases: analysis of the problem or opportunity, identification of alternatives, comparison of alternatives according to criteria, and recommendation of a course of action.

Big Bang

The Big Bang approach to organizing a presentation is designed to grab the attention of listeners and never let go. It is rooted in the inverted pyramid style of newspapers, in which the lead paragraph captures the essentials and subsequent paragraphs expand on who-what-why-where-when-how from the lead. In a presentation, the Big Bang starts with a dramatic, and often surprising, headline. The remainder of the presentation provides the supporting material. Note one advantage of the Big Bang: If the senior manager needs to leave early, he or she will know the punch line after one slide.

Use the Big Bang if you need to gain attention and you think that more conventional organizations will not produce the necessary energizing effect on your audience. For example, consider a company that has been struggling for years to be profitable at its computer performance evaluation (CPE) service. The end-to-end performance of a computer system for various usage scenarios can involve several commercial products and networks as well as homegrown code. The company provides a service to evaluate performance bottlenecks and recommend improvements. It began this line of work to help a customer who was frustrated by commercial software providers accusing each other's products of being the performance bottleneck. But now, although most managers at your company acknowledge the mediocre success of the service, no one takes any action. You have investigated the business model and concluded that the company would be wise to get out of that line of business. You tell your boss, who wants you to present your case. Your Big-Bang-structured briefing may look like Table 7-5, which will serve as an example of structuring a presentation as a series of messages and themes.

In Table 7-5, you really need to have made your case by Step 4. You must make sure that you have not omitted a cost element nor misread an industry trend. You will want to have back-up slides showing that industry data and experts confirm your observations about industry trends. Backup slides should also summarize the risk analysis you did.

In IT, Big Bang can be a higher-risk option than more linear approaches to organization. In particular, if the audience punches holes in the support for your opening big-bang headline, you can appear to have given more attention to the dramatic elements than to building a sound technical argument. Big Bang places great importance on conducting dry runs and having colleagues review your case to see if you have missed anything.

Personal Action Appeal

The Personal Action Appeal[17] is, like Big Bang, a persuasive strategy that aims to move listeners to action. Its strength is its focus on a sequence of steps that can be matched to presentation slides. The steps are as follows:

Attention   This step echoes the Big Bang theme: the need to grab the attention of listeners. You can do this through the content (e.g., a challenging or provocative statement) and through the techniques you employ (e.g., voice tone and volume, slide with dramatic picture, or video clip).

Need   The audience really has a need or a problem; you are simply bringing it to their attention. At this step, you let them know about their need. The attention and need steps work together to create a sense of urgency in the audience that there is a pressing problem that requires a solution. Consider an IT variation on what has been associated with letting incoming students know of the difficult path until graduation:

- Look at the person to your right.
- Look at the person to your left.
- One of you will be the victim of identity theft in the next two years.

Identity theft has an ominous sound. Indeed, the consequences can be disastrous for people, sapping their time and money in an attempt to clear their name and restore their credit standing. In this step, you cite examples of people—who are just like those in the audience—who have been victims and how it adversely affected their lives. Your audience now knows it has a need to find out how it can guard against this happening to them.

Satisfaction   With the need firmly established, listeners are eager for you to tell them how to satisfy it. You first will need to artfully answer the questions that will likely emerge from your statement of need. In fact, an indicator of being successful at establishing the need is to see hands shoot into the air because the audience is deeply concerned. This satisfaction step is your chance to lay out a remedy or solution plan for the need they have.

TABLE 7-5 Example of a Big-Bang-Structured Presentation

Step	Message	Purpose	Intended Effect	Voice Track: Secondary Messages
1	We must abandon the CPE business now.	Big Bang	Grab attention of listeners.	We must decide now. There is a sense of urgency. Doing nothing is no longer an option.
2	We will see why this action is essential.	Set agenda for remainder of presentation.	Tell listeners what is coming.	The speaker has investigated this thoroughly. This is based on facts and insights.
3	Sustaining CPE costs more than is apparent.	Begin marshalling facts to support claim.	Status quo is unacceptable.	We all know the obvious data (revenues, etc.). What you may not know is that there are significant hidden costs (tying up talented staff who could be better used elsewhere, misalignment with corporate mission, promotion costs in face of stiff competition, need to maintain costly computer resources, etc.).
4	Industry trends will make it even more difficult for CPE to be successful in the future.	Provide convincing evidence that applying more resources to CPE is not an option.	You have considered alternatives. You see the bigger picture.	If you thought we could stumble along as we have been doing, you are wrong. There are industry trends at work that are beyond our control.
5	How this action can help the company.	Paint a picture of a more successful company if CPE is abandoned.	You are focused on overall company success.	Visualize the company without CPE; tighter focus on other business lines, reallocated resources yielding greater revenues and lower costs, etc.
6	As with any decision, this one has risks.	Demonstrate that you have considered and analyzed the risks.	You are prudent. You understand what must be considered in management decision-making.	Not everything is under our control. You have considered the range and potential impact of risks (available in back-up slides) and concluded that this action to cut off CPE is the best course. You have the company's best interests in mind.
7	This proposed action is feasible; here is a timetable for next steps.	Show that you have considered implementation and transition details.	You are committed to seeing this proposal through.	There are many options for implementation. The next steps are not yours to take, but you wanted to offer an initial timetable to show feasibility. You recognize this means change, but the company's success demands it.

Visualization   While the satisfaction step has described a way to deal with the problem or need, the visualization step paints a picture in the minds of the audience of a future without the problem. You are creating a vision of their world at a time when the need has been satisfied. You are engaging them to envision all the corresponding benefits (e.g., increased revenues, no downtime, confident and convenient online transactions) of this future state.

Action   The imagery you create must lead the audience to do something. If appropriate, the action may be for them to express interest in engaging your services to satisfy their need. It may be that you have motivated them to check with their CIO to see if they have the problem you described. At a minimum, success may be for the audience to leave the meeting with a new understanding of a problem and possible solution, so they are better prepared to deal with the problem when they return to their organizations.

These three approaches—Analyze/Recommend, Big Bang, and Personal Action Appeal—can be useful templates for building the message that will guide your presentation.

Audiovisual Aids

Oral communications occur in multiple modes these days: through the familiar in-person exchanges that have taken place since the dawn of humanity and through the use of various electronic communication devices. You may be giving a presentation to an audience that is in the same room, but you have the help of a stationary microphone or a small one that is handheld or attached to your clothing, allowing you to walk as you talk. Although it may seem obvious to say so, these details affect how you deliver your message. If you are situated behind a lectern, you are limited in the range of physical movements you can employ to contribute to the impact of your talk. With the sound amplification from any type of microphone, you need to modulate your voice so you don't sound as though you are yelling at your audience.

There are practical hints that can enhance the effectiveness of oral communications when participating in audio-only conference calls. Begin by having the participants introduce themselves, so distant listeners can become acquainted with the different individual voices they will be hearing. An additional benefit of introductions concerns the issue of fairness of all participants knowing all the parties involved. It is not fair to have unidentified listeners at a site. Be prepared to interrupt when you can't hear. This happens frequently for a person's initial volume may fade as the meeting gets longer. Also, an individual may be too far from the microphone pick-up device or turn away from it at precisely the instant of making a key point or stating critical words (or dollar amounts). It is important to keep in mind that the modest, often small, microphone in front of you is your gateway to reaching people on the other end. An acceptable, and considerate, "process interrupt" is to inquire if people at distant sites can hear well, given the fluctuations in quality that can occur in the transmission of signals. Obviously, as a speaker in an audio-only format, you are restricted to your voice alone as a way to express yourself. However, continuing to use hand gestures can enhance the power of your voice and the emotion you bring to the subject.

With the advances in technology, IT professionals increasingly are communicating with people in all parts of the world using videoconferencing facilities or the Internet. Including video is a step up from audio-only communicating, but it typically renders a head-and-shoulder image to your distant listeners, thereby limiting your use of gestures and your physical movement. Pay attention to the location of the camera. Most setups allow you to see yourself as others are seeing you; check frequently to ensure that you are satisfied with your image. One hint is based on an observation of several videoconferences that included 5 to 15 people at each of two sites. The presenters in each case were trying to influence people at both locations. The videoconference setting naturally suggested an "us versus them" appearance, and the presenters devoted all their time talking to the camera, without any attempt to reach out (e.g., by eye contact) to connect with the audience in the same room. Never lose sight of who your audience is; they may be closer than you think.

Presentation slides are widely used to enhance IT oral communications. The step-by-step examples of messages given earlier in the chapter can guide a slide-by-slide presentation. Slides provide a way to divide the presentation into logical chunks and to mark progress as your story unfolds. They certainly provide cues for you about the sequence of topics. There are many books that provide detailed guidance on construction of slides.[18, 19] However, our focus on IT suggests using your judgment rather than uncritical acceptance of all general guidelines. For example, most advice calls for limited textual content on each slide. As we discussed, it is the practice in some IT organizations to use presentation slides for the dual purpose as deliverable documentation. A skilled presenter can use slides that are more text-heavy than they should be and manage to navigate through an effective presentation. The key is to use graphics along with the text and not to feel obliged to read every word on the slides.

Slides can be used along with other effective graphics, maps, and diagrams to illustrate points that are difficult to communicate with words alone, and you can even organize entire presentations around a few well-designed graphics, without any bullet-point slides. The presentation is essentially you explaining and describing what you are showing graphically. As a side benefit, not using words can eliminate time-consuming "word-smithing" and audience complaints about word meanings or choices.

Exercise judgment in the use of multimedia. Integrating sound and video clips can be very effective. For example, movement on slides or corresponding web pages is very helpful in IT presentations to illustrate transaction processing or data movement. But elaborate graphics can also be a distraction that delights only the presenter. A September 2003 survey concluded that, "People find too much text or too much fancy graphics and multimedia a big turn off."[20] The presentation tools may provide sophisticated multimedia capabilities, but use them only when they truly contribute to your message. In your quest to use elaborate animations and sound effects, you may lose your audience.

You would be wise to focus on the basics when using graphics, something that is widely overlooked as speakers play with the newer features. Use contrasting colors and appropriate type font sizes so people in all parts of the meeting room can read the slides. The color wheel presents a wonderful spectrum of possibilities. But the wisteria-colored words on a purple background that look dandy on your laptop can be an unreadable mess when projected. Such guidelines are obvious, but they remain the most often violated, even by seasoned presenters. Speakers who draw the most complaints[21] are those who

- Read their slides to the audience (60 percent of survey respondents cited this item)
- Use text that is too small to be readable (51 percent)
- Use full sentences instead of bullet points (48 percent)

Delivery

The best way to enhance your chances of delivering a successful presentation is to prepare thoroughly, guided by the earlier hints. Now that you are ready to take center stage and actually give the presentation, there are many factors that can strengthen your performance. Some of these will reveal themselves if you give dry-run presentations to get feedback.

A variety of factors can influence the effectiveness of your presentation. Remember that the context may make some of these infeasible; for example, if the audio system requires that you stand at a lectern, you will not have the flexibility to use all the hints concerning the use of physical movement during your talk. But many of the factors will be relevant. These tricks-of-the-trade reflect suggestions from Joss (1999), Ruch and Crawford (1999), Sarnoff (1970), and Toogood (1996), all of which can be useful starting points for locating additional and more detailed guidance. One more advisory: This chapter has discussed the variety of IT meetings and individual circumstances. Use judgment about when to use these generic guidelines for your meeting and your audience.

What to Do First

A strong first impression can go a long way toward launching you on a successful presentation. Sarnoff's (1970) suggestions are especially relevant for IT professionals, for whom credibility is key. She recommends taking a moment at the start to look around the room at the individuals in the audience, making brief eye contact. Your message is that you are confident, you are glad you are here, and you are glad they are here.[22]

Posture

Your body language begins with your physical bearing. You want your posture to broadcast that you are confident as a person and, by extension, are confident about the messages you will soon communicate. Obviously, you should not be hunched over or leaning on the lectern. You should stand erect, but not at such pronounced military-style attention that it looks uncomfortable to the audience.

Voice

Practice with an audio recording device to ensure that you do not speak in a monotone. Varying tone, pitch, and volume are valuable tools that you can employ to add emphasis to your message and make it easier to hear.

Time and the 18-Minute Wall

As the speaker, take advantage of your ability to use time for your benefit. Toogood (1996) discusses the perception-of-time gap: You often (especially in times of stress, as in speaking) perceive the passage of time very differently from what actually transpires. If you are videotaped practicing your speech, you will likely be surprised that what you remember to have been an embarrassingly long silence came across in the taping as a very natural and welcome gap in time during your presentation.[23] Silence, particularly after a strong or provocative statement, can be very effective to allow the audience to mull the impact of what you said.

Toogood (1996) also reports on the Navy study that identified the 18-minute wall, which is the amount of time one person can listen to another and remember some of what was said. The data supported calling it a wall; attention and retention dropped precipitously after 18 minutes. What does this imply for longer speeches? Toogood recommends activities that break the speaker-listener mode[24]:

- Start a brief question-and-answer session while material is fresh in the minds of listeners.
- Tell a story or an anecdote that will break the lecture mode and regain attention.
- Switch to another speaker; this can be a viable option, especially for lengthy program reviews.
- Use multimedia—a sound or video clip, or an interactive exercise with the audience, or with you acting as a user interacting with software.

Audience Rapport

Success hinges on your message being understood by the audience. Learn to read the audience: What are their eyes and their body language telling you? During your presentation, continue to sweep the audience (not in a mechanistic and distracting way) to look for feedback that your ideas are being heard or not. If fidgeting and blank looks abound, consider breaking the flow with an example or one of the activities just mentioned.

Gestures and Mannerisms

In a videotape of a dry run of your presentation, focus on the visual elements, even perhaps viewing the tape once with the sound off. Be on the lookout for mannerisms—like fidgeting with a tie, pen, or glasses—that can distract your listeners.

Are you using gestures to support your words? A well-timed gesture can add emphasis to a strong verbal message. Some familiar interpretations of some often used gestures are[25]:

- Vertical slicing movement of hand to emphasize points
- Sweeping hand motion from side to side to convey breadth
- Palms up and away from the body to show openness and invite participation

Physical Movement

If you are not tethered to a lectern, take advantage of your freedom to move about as a way to enhance your verbal message. As with any such advice, don't follow it to the point of distraction, moving metronomically from side to side. If you are using presentation slides, obviously do not face the screen and read the slides. Accept that by using slides you are creating competition: The audience can look at you or the slides. If you have done a good job of creating graphical slides with compelling content, you may come in second! One tactic is to stop talking (again, the use of silence), giving a moment for people to absorb the slide's content before continuing. In this way, your important speaking points will not be lost. An effective tactic when using slides is to maintain a presence near the screen, which has a side benefit of eliminating the chance that you will block some audience member's view of the screen. From this location, you are well positioned, at strategic times in your presentation, to move closer to the audience to make a key point or engage them in questions and answers.

Openings and Closings

Openings and closings merit discussion on their own because of the strong role they play in determining a presentation's success or failure. This guidance is most applicable for IT presentations that are more like public speeches (e.g., to an industry conference) but are also appropriate for the Big Bang and Personal Action Appeal presentations discussed earlier.

Openings should pack a punch. Do not apologize. Minimize, or eliminate if possible in the context, the familiar beginnings in which you thank people and say how happy you are to be there. You may start with a dramatic and controversial statement, one that goes against accepted beliefs. A story or anecdote can be very effective, especially one that relates to the circumstances of the audience members. Showing a video clip can capture attention and be the springboard for your remarks to challenge the audience to see beyond the obvious elements of the clip. This technique is used with great effect in business leadership sessions; for example, a clip from a military film is shown and then used to discuss challenges and tactics of effective leadership that translate to business settings. Citing news stories in an opening will show that your presentation is topical and will engage an audience. The test of an effective opening is that it motivates the rest of the presentation and launches you on a path of success with your message.

Standard guidance for a closing is to summarize the main points you made. This guidance has a place in IT presentations, in which you are often making recommendations or persuading others to follow your lead. There are also other possibilities. Telling a brief anecdote can work well for a closing as it does for an opening. In a public speaking context, an effective closing can be one that loops back to the opening. For example, after what you presented, perhaps the current situation you described in your opening is not as bleak as it appeared. There are signs of hope for a better economy, improved quality, and so on. An effective closing is one that contributes to the audience's retaining your message.

Summary

The references cited at the end of this chapter and many others provide more detailed suggestions on all these topics, plus additional ones such as how to breathe, how to dress, how to engage an audience, handling stage fright, handling disagreeable audience members, designing presentation slides, presenting from a prepared speech, using speaker's notes, and fielding difficult questions.

In summary, oral communications will influence your career and your success as an IT professional. There is no substitute for good judgment when adapting guidance and hints given here to your IT meetings and circumstances. You are wise to take time to improve your effectiveness with all kinds of oral communications.

EXERCISES ▪▪▪▪▪▪▪

1. Choose three people to act out a role-playing scenario. One person is the department manager of the other two. The two department staff members are IT analysts for enterprise systems. Both analysts want the manager to choose them to be project leader for an upcoming project. The manager has called in the analysts separately to discuss why they should be selected. The people playing the roles of manager and analysts should prepare and act out the two meetings. The remainder of the group should practice listening. At the end of the two meetings, discuss the following:
   - How effectively did the manager communicate his or her needs, demonstrate good listening skills, and respond to the questions and comments of the analysts?
   - How effectively have the analysts made persuasive cases that they should be selected?
   - How much consensus exists among the observers about what occurred in both meetings and how effectively the three principals communicated?
2. Only 5 percent of eligible people donate blood. Prepare a 3–5 minute persuasive presentation that will change the prevailing mindset of listeners and move them to action so that they want to voluntarily donate. Or choose a similar topic (e.g., training in cardiopulmonary resuscitation) that requires you to use speech to persuade. Deliver the speech to classmates or colleagues. Apply the Personal Action Appeal strategy discussed in this chapter. Document part of your preparation by writing down your answers to the following questions. In this way, you and the audience can discuss how the actual delivered presentation compared to your intentions.
   - What goal are you trying to achieve?
   - What does your gap analysis tell you about the differences between the audience's beliefs, values, and attitudes and what you are persuading them to feel, think, or do?
   - What do your listeners tell you concerning how persuasive your speech really was?
3. Your vice president has been reading about the open source movement in software. If you are part of a class or other learning group, divide up into pairs. Each pair will consider whether open source development or proprietary development by a company is a better approach for producing defect-free software. One person in each pair advocates the open source position, and the other will take the proprietary company position. Each person will prepare a 5–7 minute presentation, following the Analyze/Recommend strategy. Participants in the class will discuss the strengths and weaknesses of the presentations, identifying the strongest points from both the open source and proprietary positions. If you are not part of a class, prepare and deliver to colleagues a 5–7 minute presentation that analyzes both positions and makes a recommendation based on the analysis.
4. Listen to speeches that have been widely regarded as exceptional by scholars of rhetoric. For example, listen via the Internet (American Rhetoric Online Speech Bank, http://www.Americanrhetoric.com/speechbank.htm, August 16, 2004) to the following speeches:
   - U.S. President Abraham Lincoln's Gettysburg Address
   - Rev. Dr. Martin Luther King's "I Have a Dream" speech
   - William Faulkner's speech accepting the Nobel Prize in Literature

   Practice your critical listening skills to identify elements discussed in this chapter, such as voice tone and modulation, use of silence, imagery and visualization, and phrasing. How do these elements contribute to the effectiveness of the speech? Why are these speeches deemed excellent? What effect did they have on you?

5. The shareholders' meeting is next week. You are the CEO of an Internet service provider with 500,000 customers. Your company's help desk has been besieged this week by customer complaints about malicious code being sent through your service, and the media has picked up on the complaints with several prominent, critical stories. You will be addressing the shareholders and expect a lot of hostility. Use the steps in this chapter to define a message and a storyline for your address.
6. As an audience member, list the attributes of a good presentation, that is, one you would want to hear.
7. As a presenter, identify the attributes of a dream presentation that you would want to give.
8. Suppose you are the CEO of your company and are preparing a presentation to the board of directors, who are friends as well.
   a. What kind of presentation (formal or informal) would you prepare?
   b. Would you use formal or informal words and phrases in your presentation?

ENDNOTES

1. Boehm, B. W. et al. (2000). *Software Cost Estimation with COCOMO II.* Prentice Hall, Upper Saddle River, NJ., 341.
2. Laskowski, Lenny. "Overcoming Speaking Anxiety in Meetings and Presentations," downloaded from http://www.hr-info.com/hrarticles/laskowski/anxiety.html, August 17, 2004.
3. Harper College. "Develop Your Elevator Speech," downloaded from http://www.harpercollege.edu/learninglife/features.shtml, August 21, 2004.
4. Boehm, Barry W. (1981). *Software Engineering Economics.* Englewood Cliffs, NJ, Prentice Hall.
5. Boehm (2000).
6. Ruch, William V., and Crawford, Maurice. (1995). *Effective Business Reports: Written and Oral,* 2nd ed. Collegiate Press, San Diego.
7. Angell, Pamela. (2004). *Business Communication Design.* McGraw Hill, New York.
8. Ruch and Crawford. (1995). 83.
9. Auer, Ken, and Miller, Roy. (2002). *Extreme Programming Explained.* Addison-Wesley, Boston.
10. Ibid., p. 90.
11. Ibid., p. 87.
12. Ibid., p. 90.
13. Denning, Steve. (2000). *The Springboard: How Storytelling Ignites Action in*
Knowledge-Era Organizations. Butterworth Heinemann, San Francisco.
14. Wilder, Claudyne. "Presentation Points," downloaded from http://www.wilderpresentations.com/points/aug02.html, February 15, 2004.
15. Paradi, Dave. "Summary of the Annoying PowerPoint® Survey," downloaded from http://www.communicateusingtechnology.com/pptresults.htm, August 16, 2004.
16. Simon, Alan R., and Simon, Jordan S. (1993). *The Computer Professional's Guide to Effective Communications.* McGraw Hill, New York.
17. Ibid.
18. Joss, Molly W. (1999). *Looking Good Presentations,* 3rd ed. The Coriolis Group, Scottsdale, AZ.
19. Ruch and Crawford. (1995).
20. Communicateusingtechnology.com. "Survey Shows Organizations Wasting Hundreds of Thousands of Dollars Due to Poor Presentations," downloaded from http://www.communicateusingtechnology.com/pptrelease.htm, August 16, 2004.
21. Ibid.
22. Sarnoff, Dorothy. (1970) *Speech Can Change Your Life.* Dell Publishing, New York.
23. Toogood, Granville N. (1996) *The Articulate Executive.* New York, McGraw Hill, 109.
24. Ibid., pp. 94–95.
25. Ruch and Crawford, (1995).

CHAPTER 8

Technical Reviews

Learning Objectives

■ To understand issues involved with being a technical reviewer in the IT community

■ To learn guidelines for being more effective in reviewing technical documents and literature

■ To improve your ability and skill at presenting IT-related reviews and in conducting reviews of IT project and technical presentations

Introduction

Technical reviews come in many shapes and sizes in the world of IT. One form is the review of written IT-related materials. Two other forms arise from the familiar practice in IT projects of conducting oral reviews at various points in the project to determine progress. This chapter covers both sides of these reviews, that is, delivering them and being a reviewer who is called on to evaluate or assess them. The chapter is organized around these three notions of IT technical review:

- How to conduct reviews of written technical reports
- How to prepare and present oral reviews of IT projects and products (note that more general guidance on oral presentations in Chapter 7 is relevant here as well)
- How to be a reviewer at a project or technical presentation

Each situation calls for technical knowledge, professional judgment, and the communication skills that are covered in this book. How you execute your assignment in these scenarios can go a long way toward establishing yourself as a competent IT professional.

WARM-UP EXERCISE

You are handed a document and told to write a review of it. The document contains the following library description:

"Consider a small library database with the following transactions:

1. Check out a copy of a book. Return a copy of a book.
2. Add a copy of a book to/remove a copy of a book from the library.
3. Get a list of books by a particular author or in a particular subject area.
4. Find out the list of books currently checked out by a particular borrower.
5. Find out what borrower last checked out a particular copy of a book.

There are two types of users: staff and ordinary borrowers. Transactions 1, 2, 4, and 5 are restricted to staff users, except that ordinary borrowers can perform transaction 4 to find out the list of books currently borrowed by themselves. The database must also satisfy the following constraints:

a. All copies in the library must be available for checkout or be checked out.
b. No copy of the book may be both available and checked out at the same time.
c. A borrower may not have more than a predefined number of books checked out at one time."[1]

Write down a one-page review of the description. Your review should be based on how the description would be satisfactory to serve as part of a software specification.

When you have completed your review, analyze it because it can serve as an excellent introduction to key points in this chapter. The library description you reviewed is a classic one in software engineering. It has served as the basis for comparing software tools for verifying specifications, so there is a lot of discussion of the ambiguities and inconsistencies in the description. The following discussion points are taken from Wing (1988) and Fickas and Nagarajan (1988).

In your review, how many of the identified ambiguities (from Wing, 1988) did you notice?

- What is a library? The description talks about both the library and the library database. The database will have records of books and users. The library is the real world of people, books, physical facilities, and environment.

An implied library system consists of the library database plus the transactions on it and everything else needed to model the library as an information system.

- What is a user? The description appears to be clear: There are staff and ordinary users. But a person who works at the library (i.e., a staff member) can also operate as an ordinary user, so what are denoted as user types are really roles. Also, note that since transaction 1 is restricted to staff, ordinary users cannot check out books! Did your review catch that?
- What does "small" mean? The first line says it is a small database. Does that mean there is a limit on users or on books? Is it implying "simple," so there are a limited number of transactions? How does this affect anything?[2]
- What is a book? The description talks about books sometimes and copies of books at other times. IT professionals will recognize this distinction as anticipating one in which the key identifier of the database will need to consider both *book* and *copy* in defining a unique entity to be managed.
- What does "available" mean? Are constraints "a" and "b" redundant? Do you want to consider other states as well, for example, lost, stolen, or unaccounted for?
- What does "last checked out" mean? Is it the same as "currently checked out"? To implement transaction 5, would a computer system identify the person who currently has the book checked out or the person who checked it out prior to the person who currently has it checked out?

It is natural for you to think that the extremely detailed analysis of this exercise is all out of proportion to its innocuous appearance. That observation is precisely the point. Unless you obtain guidance about what is expected (or make and state your assumptions), you don't know whether you are being excessively detailed in a review or simply being thorough and analytical. If you accept the starting position that the purpose of your review is to determine if this description could serve as part of a software specification, then the detailed comments are absolutely appropriate. If you don't catch such ambiguities now, they will become causes of confusion later on for designers or implementers. A competent designer would not know what to make of the description as written, in terms of the ambiguities cited, and would need to raise questions or make assumptions. It is far preferable to resolve ambiguities as early in the process as possible.

A thoughtful reviewer of the description would probe even further than was done here. When it lists the five kinds of transactions, the document seems very systematic and organized. Are the five transactions the only ones allowed? Based on your knowledge of the domain (libraries), you can think of other possible transactions (e.g., placing a copy of a book on reserve or adding/deleting borrowers). There is no mention of the critically important topic of error handling. There are many constraints not expressed; for example, presumably a user cannot check out more than one copy of the same book.

One result of trying the warm-up exercise should be an awareness of how difficult it can be to use natural language to express requirements unambiguously and to conduct a thorough technical review.

▪▪▪ Common Elements of Technical Reviews

Before considering in turn each of the three scenarios of technical reviews—that is, reviewing technical documents, presenting technical reviews, and reviewing technical presentations—we should discuss review elements that are shared by all three. The warm-up exercise reveals several common reviewing elements:

Purpose

Know the objective of the review. Whether you are conducting a review or presenting one, there is no substitute for understanding its purpose. It is often the case that IT professionals are given something to review, but what does that mean? Notice that the warm-up exercise only made sense when you were told that the objective of the review was for you to determine the extent to which the description could serve as a specification for software. Reviews always fit within a larger context. If you are ever given something and told, "Review this and let me know what you think," you would be wise to ask some questions in return:

- What am I looking for?
- Is there some aspect of it on which I should focus?
- How detailed a review is wanted—broad impressions or a detailed, line-by-line critique?
- Should my review include comments on editing and exposition or only on content?
- By when do you need this?

You should ask these questions because one of the purposes of having you conduct a review may be to see if you are savvy enough to ask them! As a busy IT professional, you want to make the best use of your time, for your benefit and that of your organization. By asking these questions, you are demonstrating that you want to do a job that is most helpful to your boss. For example, the document may be a 500-page technical report. The answers to the questions are essential to using your time according to what is important. For example, if your boss says he wants your review as a way to know whether the author of the document is an effective technical writer, then that purpose is quite different from wanting to know if third-party testing (the subject of the document) is a potentially good new business area for the company. You should try to know as much as possible about the purpose of the review so that your time is well spent. In fact, you can reasonably ask additional questions, such as inquiring about how much time you should spend on this and in what form your boss wants your results (e.g., written review or oral discussion).

Context

Technical reviews are not ends unto themselves. They are part of something larger, which defines the context for the review. Realize that this review fits into a larger context. For example, you may be presenting a milestone review that marks the end of the design stage for a system development project. Your plan for the review will be driven by the expectations of the sponsor of the development project to have reached this stage in the process. If you are told to conduct a review of candidate IT asset management products, the context of your organization—its size, physical facilities, IT infrastructure, and workforce profile—will influence the criteria you should use to decide among the products.

A different dimension of context is the set of constraints on your review. For example, you may be bounded by resources, such as a review needed in 2 hours or a limit on the number of hours that you can charge to the review even if it is not required immediately. In such cases, you will be pressed to make the best use of the time you have.

Review Criteria

The nature of reviewing means that you are assessing something, which raises the questions of assessing in what way and against what criteria. The criteria may be explicit and accepted by both presenter or author and reviewer. This is the case in most project reviews in relatively mature systems development organizations. In other cases, the criteria are not obvious. In these cases, you should develop criteria based on the purpose and context of the review, calling upon your personal and professional judgment. Expectations will influence your criteria. If you are reviewing entries in an eighth-grade science fair, your expectations are different than if you are reviewing a journal paper reporting on an experiment conducted by professional scientists.

Audience Awareness

Effective reviewing means placing yourself in the position of the intended audience for the reviewed material. If you are planning a review presentation, this means learning about the attendees and their interests in your presentation. If you are conducting the review, you are doing it for some audience, either explicitly or implicitly. Know that audience and what it wants to achieve by having you conduct the review.

The warm-up exercise clearly relied on the very general knowledge expected of an IT professional. However, other documents and reports are often written for specific readers. An astute writer will often state early in the document the characteristics of the target audience. As a reviewer, you should keep those characteristics in mind to determine if the content and style are indeed a good match for the intended audience. If the writer does not identify the prospective readership, your job as a reviewer is to comment on any minimum knowledge levels or other characteristics that a reader must possess to understand the document. For example, in the exercise, the descriptions of transactions are expressed in natural language. They could have been expressed using the first-order predicate logic,[3] which would have defined a different and much smaller readership.

Reviewing Ability

In general, the process of technical reviewing consists of both intellectual and technical activities that include both subjective and objective elements. Effective reviewing in IT relies upon the reviewer's technical knowledge, domain knowledge, and reviewing skill. The reviewer must be objective, which means eliminating any personal, methodological, and technical bias toward what is being reviewed or the associated subject matter. This means that the reviewer should evaluate the technical document or presentation in terms of his or her own experience, skills, expertise, and knowledge. If you are requesting a review, you will get the most benefit from it by ensuring that reviewers have the appropriate knowledge and reviewing ability.

In the exercise, you need to be technically knowledgeable in general terms about the concepts of database and transactions. The domain knowledge is widely known information about the operations of a library. However, in other review assignments, to be effective in your review may require very specific levels of technical and domain knowledge. Lacking that knowledge may make it impossible to conduct the kind of review (in terms of depth of analysis) that was intended when you were given the assignment. Matching reviewers to review assignments occurs all the time at IT conferences and in IT journals. The authors of technical papers claim to have done some novel work, so it takes people with appropriate technical and domain knowledge to review those papers.

These common elements of technical reviewing—purpose, context, review criteria, audience awareness, and reviewing ability—will show up in the discussion of the three scenarios of technical reviewing that follow.

Reviewing IT Technical Reports

Effective review of technical literature is important to progress in science and technology. IT professionals are expected to write accurate reviews of technical documents. The reviews contribute to decision-making, such as

- Accepting scientific papers for publication
- Purchasing products or services
- Adopting a technology for use on a project
- Awarding a grant or contract

The importance of reviewing is reflected by its role in major decisions like these. Procurement decisions can translate into billions of dollars of revenue and even the success or failure of companies. So, a lot is riding on reviews of documents.

There are a variety of considerations when preparing a review of a technical report or other IT-related document. A first set of issues arises from applying the common elements to a review of technical documents.

Purpose You must keep in mind the expressed purpose of the document in your review. A well-prepared document will include its purpose so that you don't need to guess. Your review should say what the purpose is and how you established it. If you had to infer the purpose, put that in your review. Whether the purpose is expressed or inferred, comment on the extent to which the purpose was achieved or not. For example, you may be reviewing a technical report that has the expressed purpose of comparing telecommunications broadband service providers for your company. This purpose immediately sets part of the agenda for your review. You may conclude that the purpose was satisfactorily met. If it was not met, your review should state in what ways the purpose was not achieved, such as

- Certain candidate service providers were omitted from consideration
- Criteria used for comparison were not complete or not applied correctly
- Comparison failed to consider certain important user requirements of the company
- Methodology used for comparison was inappropriate for the task

Context   Your review must be guided by the context of the review. Again, the document should state the context for the documented work. Perhaps the context is well known, such as when you are called upon to review a design document for an ongoing project with which you are familiar. Your review must consider whether the content of the document fits within the larger context. For example, you may conclude that the design document should have included an interface to another system.

Audience Awareness   Your review should comment on the extent to which the document is appropriate for its expressed or implied audience. For example, if the calculations and mathematical models used in the document are not accessible to the intended readers (e.g., customers), your review should state it. Your review also should comment on whether the document is written in a way that satisfies other characteristics of the audience (e.g., their domain knowledge, language preferences, or style preferences). By making these comments, you can contribute to improving the document before it is released to the intended audience. It is preferable to hear the comment from you, as an internal reviewer, than from an angry customer.

Review Criteria   Your review should clarify the source of the review criteria you use. For example, on a system development project, there often is a process standard that identifies the contents expected in the documents produced during the project. You should reference that standard so there is no doubt about the source of your criteria. If, instead, you have no obvious source of criteria, you must be clear about how you established them. For example, you may refer to criteria used in similar reviews done elsewhere. You may need to create the review criteria. If that is the case, state it. Rely on your common sense, technical knowledge experience, assistance from colleagues, and references to establish criteria that are appropriate for the purpose.

Reviewing Ability   It is reasonable to consider the reasons you were given a review assignment. It may be obvious because of your expertise or your position in the organization. If you are assigned to review a scientific paper for a journal or conference, it may be because others know of your expertise, perhaps established through publications of your own.

In addition to the common elements, there are several other considerations regarding the process of your review and the product of it.

Process of the Review   Clarify at the start the resources you have available for the review. Make sure that there is agreement between the expectations for your review and the resources you have to complete it. If you need access to individuals, administrative support, access to computers or other equipment, this is the time to ensure that you have all that you need. Establish clearly if you are required to use a particular methodology or tool as part of your review. Most important is to agree on the schedule for your review process. Disappointment will surely be the result if your supervisor expects a detailed review of the document, and you are not given the time to do it. Also reach closure on the scope of the review. Ensure that scope creep does not occur, so that you are not drawn into tangents or additional topics not part of the planned review. Dissatisfaction with reviews can be traced to lack of clarity about scope and resources.

Product of the Review   Clarify at the time of the assignment the expected product from your review. Perhaps you are asked to report orally to a manager on what you found in your review. More likely, you will prepare a review report. You should clarify the expected size, style, format, and content of that report. Again, often there is a tradition of conducting certain reviews and the expectations are obvious. But if they are not, ensure that the review instructions are understood at the outset. Your review report should include the following content:

- **Executive Summary.**   This is clearly optional, depending on the length of your report. However, it is very important even for a review report of five pages. People often will not or cannot invest the time to read your entire report. Provide a concise summary: what was reviewed and what were your major findings regarding the quality of the document and the extent to which it met its objectives.
- **Introduction.**   Include exactly what was reviewed and the purpose of the review. Briefly mention the context for the document you reviewed to help orient readers of your report. Tell readers how the remainder of your review report is structured.
- **Reviewed Material.**   This section does not include your subjective comments. Instead, it summarizes the content of the material you reviewed to provide perspective to your audience.
- **Review Procedure.**   This can vary in length. It may be obvious that you simply read the document and wrote your report. However, in this section, include any additional statements about the process you used if you believe it is relevant. For example, if you also interviewed the author of the document or other people, say so. Describe the review criteria and how they were determined.
- **Body of the Review.**   This is the essence of the review: your considered opinion of the reviewed document and the extent to which it meets its objectives. You should help your readers understand the points you make, which often requires citing passages from the reviewed document. Your comments can be thought of as addressing the content, presentation, and grammar of the document. What you say about content must be accurate and correct technically. Have statistics been used correctly? (See Girden, 1996, for guidance.) Are technical statements in the document correct? Can you introduce graphics or tables that will help explain your review points?

   With IT, it is certainly possible that professional judgment will come into play. The issue is not as simple as being correct or not. For example, your professional judgment may be that a technology being used in the proposed solution is very immature and introduces a significant risk to a project or system. On this matter, your opinion may be different from that of the author of the document. But this is precisely why you may have been chosen as a reviewer. State your opinion and back it up with references to industry experts or the actual experiences of others who have tried to implement the particular technology. Always look for ways to clarify what is objective fact and what is your professional judgment.

   In general, it is preferable to focus on content. Many times IT professionals are called upon to prepare a technical review and they spend too much time on grammatical errors in the document. There are skilled editors who can do that. You are a reviewer because of your IT knowledge and experience; focus on those aspects of the document. Regarding presentation, it is appropriate to comment on the style of the document: Is it logical in its flow? Will it be readable by its intended audience? Does it use unnecessary jargon?

- **Summary and Conclusions.** Summarize the main points in your review. Indicate the level of seriousness of the points: Are they minor ones that can be corrected? Are there major technical flaws? Your conclusion should loop back to the introduction to address any specific objectives of your review. For example, you may have been reviewing a document as the basis for obtaining your opinion on whether to accept the recommendation in the document. Your conclusion will need to state whether you agree or not with the recommendation or whether some additional action should be taken.
- **References.** Document any sources you use in your review, including references to people who have contributed.

Review of Widely Used IT Documents

Your review may be strongly guided in its process and product by reviewing documents that are widely used in IT, such as system specifications, design documents, and test plans. Your organization may have a standard that specifies the expected content and style of documents that have roles in the development process. In these cases, your review should obviously assess whether this prescribed content is present or not and whether the prescribed style is being followed.

Even if your organization does not have a documented standard, there are many public sources that describe recommended contents of documents used in software development. IT professionals who are conducting reviews of similar documents can base their reviews on these guidelines for recommended content. Two influential guidelines are MIL-STD-498 of the U.S. Department of Defense[4] and the *Manager's Handbook for Software Development*, developed by the Software Engineering Laboratory at NASA's Goddard Space Flight Center.[5] Both documents are available on the Internet (see endnotes for URLs). Table 8-1 identifies the documents for which templates are provided in MIL-STD-498, the SEL *Manager's Handbook*, and the Adaptable Process Model.[6]

Use the Table 8-1 documents as starting points for planning your review. The specific circumstances of your document review will often indicate that adjustments must be made on actual content.

This section provides some additional guidance on reviewing three of the most widely written and reviewed documents:

- System Specifications
- Design Documents
- Test Plans

System specification documents are often generated as a result of the requirements analysis activity. If you are reviewing a specification document, assess whether it will indeed satisfy the requirements of users. Look for completeness, that all the required functionalities are described clearly and correctly. Make sure that there are no inconsistencies or contradictory statements. The document should also describe all the needed data flows, interfaces to other systems, and the infrastructure platforms

TABLE 8-1   Document Templates Available on the Internet

Document templates associated with the Adaptable Process Model of R. S. Pressman & Associates, Inc. are available on the Internet (RSPA, 2004).[6]

System Specification	Software Configuration Management Plan
Software Project Plan	Software Requirements Specification
Software Quality Assurance Plan	Software Design Specification
Test Specification	Software Change Report

Military Standard 498 (MIL-STD-498) describes recommended content for the following documents (DOD, 2004).

Software Development Plan	Software Test Plan
Software Installation Plan	Software Test Description
Software Transition Plan	Software Test Report
Operational Concept Description	Software Product Specification
System/Subsystem Specification	Software Version Description
System/Subsystem Design Description	Software User Manual
Software Requirements Specification	Software Center Operator Manual
Interface Requirements Specification	Software Input/Output Manual
Software Design Description	Computer Operation Manual
Interface Design Description	Computer Programming Manual
Database Design Description	Firmware Support Manual

SEL Manager's Handbook describes recommended content for the following documents (NASA/GSFC, 2004).

Software Development/Management Plan	Detailed Design Document
Requirements and Functional Specifications	Test Plans
Operations Concept Document	User's Guide
Requirements Analysis Report	System Description
Preliminary Design Document	Software Development History

and networks required for the system. The size of specification documents obviously will vary by system. The complete specification for Excel® when it was shipped was 1,850 pages.[7]

Design documents are the developer's blueprints. These documents should provide precise directions to technical staff about how the components and subsystems should be structured and built. The documents should include a description of the overall design concept and a high-level summary of the design. Design documents should consist of tables, figures, and diagrams that translate the functional specification into a detailed design that is implementable by system developers. Components in the design should be traceable to functional specifications. The required inputs and outputs of all components should be defined. You should make sure that the documents provide an overall architecture of the system and describe the interactions among its subsystems. Also make sure that the design documents define all the standards and technologies used, including computer platforms, programming languages, software tools, and interfaces. All the technologies and standards defined in design documents should be appropriate for the environment and consistent with company standards.

Test plans should document the objectives, scope, procedures, and individual cases required to test the system. The set of tests must measure the integrity and quality of the system and demonstrate coverage of its operational modes. In reviewing test plans, you should make sure that the test procedures are described clearly without any potential ambiguity. The associated documents, especially the related functional requirements specifications, should be used to verify that all documented requirements are addressed in the test plan. This will ensure that the tested module performs the required functionalities. Within the test plan, the test cases should cover all possible test scenarios, including nominal and exceptional behavior. Comprehensive error-handling should be addressed by the test cases and their input parameters, test conditions, and expected results should be clearly defined. There should also be test scripts, which describe the specific steps (e.g. which input screen to use, which button to press, etc.) to execute each test case.

More detailed guidance for all three documents—system specifications, design documents, and test plans—is provided in DOD (2004) and NASA/GSFC (2004).

Ad Hoc Reviews

In contrast to a well-planned and anticipated specification or design review, your assignment may be to conduct an ad hoc review with very little time to prepare for the review and little guidance about how to conduct it. Your boss may ask you to

- Review a proposal received by a subcontractor who wants to take on a key role in a project
- Assess a technical report or published article that appears relevant to your work
- Conduct an unplanned review of a project, especially one that is in trouble
- Evaluate a report written by a colleague or a team from elsewhere in your organization

An effective ad hoc review is easier if the subject is familiar to you. In this way, you can still draw upon the general review approaches discussed in this chapter. However, if the subject is highly technical or domain-dependent and outside your expertise, it may be exceedingly challenging to conduct an effective review. In such cases, invite a colleague with the necessary expertise to participate in the review, if possible. Your review should be prefaced by remarks that characterize the extent of your knowledge of the subject. Often, ad hoc reviews are also needed quickly. This may still allow enough time for a phone call to a domain expert or a consultation or query via an online capability such as a corporate intranet, knowledge management system, library, or the public Internet.

Reviewing Development-Related Documents

Development practices vary considerably. During the past 20 years, software engineering has made great progress in identifying practices that are not cost-effective. Preparing large documents that are unreadable and difficult to maintain is near the top of anyone's list of ineffective activities. So, the references to document templates are merely examples that can serve as starting-point checklists of information that is reasonable to associate with specifications, designs, test plans, and so on.

Your organization may use development practices that have significant effects on the kinds of documents you may be called upon to review. Functionality for commercial products is defined often by a feature list. For example, at Microsoft, a product feature is typically described in a few pages within an outline specification, which also states the problem solved by the feature.[8] The features are grouped by major functional category and by being packaged together for implementation. The documents you review for companies developing commercial software may be very modest in size; the theme is "keep it simple and direct." At Microsoft, the monthly project status reports amount to two screens (which is a helpful reminder that most documents today are electronic and living, that is, undergoing configuration-controlled change over time). They have to be that concise, even for large systems like Word and Excel. When he was chairman, Bill Gates read all 100 or so of the status reports each month. Regarding what to look for when reviewing a status report, he particularly looked for "schedule slips, cutting too many product features, or the need to change a specification."[9]

The practices at Microsoft also highlight the importance of knowing the context and purpose of the review. With commercial products, status reports need to reflect the all-important competitive environment in which the products exist. Microsoft status reports include comment sections (again, in 3–4 concise sentences each) from development, program management, testing, and marketing. Reviewers are looking for consistency across the sections. If a new version of a competing product has just been announced, will Microsoft's specification stay as planned? If there are changes, are they reflected consistently across the four commentary sections?[10]

Extreme Programming (XP) is a lightweight method of development that acknowledges the reality of incomplete and constantly changing requirements. Managers, customers, and developers are all part of the same team. Managers and customers make decisions on the priority of the requirements, and technical people come up with timelines for delivering the requirements. When it comes to documentation, XP does not require a lot of written documents and reports. Documents are written on an as-needed basis. Also, unlike traditional software development, a formal sign-off is not required on any of these documents, and the documents are subject to changes at any time.

Presenting a Technical Review

The technical review session is a particular kind of meeting, so guidelines for effective meetings (e.g., Streibel, 2002) are very relevant. The first step in conducting a technical review is to define its objectives, because once you know its objectives you are ready to conduct it effectively. Technical review meetings are conducted to monitor or evaluate given products or projects. For many IT professionals, a technical review means a stand-up briefing. You are presenting a review. It may be a planned review, such as a design review, as part of a software development project. It may be an ad hoc review, for example, your presentation to report on the results of a "red team" review of a project in trouble. This section discusses preparing and presenting oral technical reviews. The guidance in Chapter 7 on oral presentations is applicable, with the focus here on particular kinds of presentations: those involving a technical review.

As emphasized in Chapter 7, your oral presentations should be organized around a clear and concise message. For an example of a design review, your storyline and message may be the following:

1. We have completed everything called for at this point in the project.
2. We have a few uncertainties related to near term activities, but we have solid plans to address them.
3. There are no other significant risks that we have failed to identify.
4. We are well prepared to move forward with the project.

This is the message you want to deliver. You want your presentation to persuade people that this is the state of affairs regarding your team and its performance on this project. You will communicate this message by actually stating it and by providing information (e.g., the online project database showing that all required review items are present) that will lead people to agree that the spoken message is indeed an accurate reflection of reality.

Project Review

In a management review for an ongoing project, you may be fulfilling several roles as a presenter, for example[11]:

- Project champion (a senior manager from the performing organization)
- Customer
- Project leader
- Activity manager
- Project staff member, especially senior technical leaders

Assuming you are a project leader preparing to present a review of your ongoing project, an example of your presentation might be

- Summary slide on overall health of the project
- Single-slide status of costs and schedule: actual versus planned, cost and schedule variances
- Single-slide summary of product quality; open defect reports
- Risk-management status showing current top 10 risks and their mitigation status
- More detailed information on cost, schedule, quality, and risk issues based on variances, as needed
- Changes since the last review regarding key personnel, subcontractor issues, changes in marketplace, results of technology studies, and so on
- Supporting material with more detailed reports by activity managers and senior technical staff, as needed
- Profile of current activities
- Readiness for next milestone; expectations regarding successful attainment
- Questions and discussion by all attendees
- Schedule for next review

In each review as the project leader, you identify critical issues; formulate, articulate, and frame those issues into management and technical perspectives; and propose actions to mitigate risks and resolve problems. Your presentation style should reflect honesty about project status and openness to ideas that may improve the project. Your communications must continually reinforce your determination to do anything possible to produce a system that is successful for all stakeholders. However, your judgment may be tested during a review presentation. In an effort to be up-front about difficulties in the project, you may start getting challenged on decisions you have made. Through your body language, tone of voice, and clarity of expression, you must exhibit confidence in yourself and your project team. As a project leader planning a review presentation, you will have many opportunities to use a variety of oral and written communication skills. You are responsible for scheduling the project review, ensuring that the review process is moving in the right direction, and ensuring that all items and issues are covered. Typically, you are also expected to take responsibility for the action items and their resolution.

You must coordinate the contributions of other activity leaders and technical staff who will be presenting at the review. These project team members are responsible for presenting more detailed review results. You will need several discussions with them in advance to examine and dry-run their presentations to ensure that they are effective in reporting on their work. You should help them with their messages and presentation style and make sure that they have a focused understanding of their objectives. Encourage them to use examples and interactive exercises to illustrate key points.

During the review process, some deficiencies in accomplishing the project's objectives may be revealed, and consequently some action items will be recommended to resolve the issues or problems. Therefore, you should follow up on action items by

- Going over comments with the appropriate staff members, seeking outside experts as needed
- Sending reminders about action items and making sure that appropriate steps are taken to resolve them
- Resolving pending issues promptly

An effective project review should promote the efficient and successful completion of a project. The review should result in

- Better understanding of project status from technical, schedule, and budgetary perspectives
- Recommendations for appropriate corrective actions to resolve any issue or problem
- Enhanced workflow practices or methods
- Ongoing documentation of lessons learned on the project
- Improved team building and customer relationships
- Dissemination of information so all parties are "on the same page" and better equipped to collaborate in the future

Product Review

A technical review is also conducted if the organization is looking to purchase a new product or to acquire a new technology. Occasionally, top management wants a summary of new technologies, their applications to a particular area of interest, or the solutions they offer to a given problem. Technical reviews include reviews of alternative products and services. At any given time in your career, you may need to evaluate products and services for your business or for your customers. Typically, your review is pointed at a decision. Your review involves comparing products, reviewing them with respect to evaluation criteria, and selecting the best alternative that meets the requirements and evaluation. There will be a subjective component in performing a product review, although based on professional experience.

In today's technologically advanced world, you must be qualified to be able to review a given complex product. During a product review process, find out what the product promises to do. Analyze the product specifications and seek to understand how well it achieves its goals. Take the time to read any other reviewers' reports, the user's manuals, and other documentation of the product. If the product has any built-in tutorials, run through them. By reading what other users and reviewers are saying about the product, you may pinpoint its strengths and weaknesses. Better than any of these is, of course, to execute the product. This alternative is often possible through downloadable, limited-capability versions of products accessible via the web.

There are a few standard types of product reviews[12]:

- **Stand-Alone Review.**   This review examines one item only, without taking into account the other products on the market. It examines how well that product solves the problem you have.
- **Comparative Review.**   This review answers the question, "Which of these products solves the problem best?" This type of review is common when several products offer the same basic functionality and features, but you are looking to purchase only one of them.
- **Technology Review.**   This review is very similar to a comparative review but is generally not as evaluative or as exhaustive. It describes different technological approaches to solving a given problem and the products as possible solutions. These are becoming more popular as some product categories increase in complexity.

To write an effective and accurate product review,[13] begin by writing an introduction that states the problem to be solved and possible constraints on the kinds of solutions that will be considered. Explain how the product would serve as a possible solution; describe its strengths and weaknesses in solving the problem or addressing the need. Use objective data (e.g., from performance evaluations) wherever possible to support your main points. Finally, summarize your opinion with a strong and relevant conclusion. A template for Software Product Evaluations is provided as Appendix D of MIL-STD-498 (DOD, 2004).

For the more specific case of reviewing outsourced products, check for the following items[14]:

1. Each piece of functionality provided by the outsourced product should be traceable back to a corresponding requirement in the specifications.
2. Custom changes to the product should be limited to only those required to make the systems work properly with the organization's infrastructure. Changes significantly increase the ongoing maintenance and upgrade costs to the system.

3. Products delivered by the vendor should make use of existing infrastructure components.
4. Applications from the vendor should have the ability to export data from the system in a nonproprietary format.
5. Vendors should provide system design and code documentation for the product.

Avoiding Disastrous Reviews

What presenters dread at a project review is an unmitigated disaster. This may occur because of aggressive questioning, unprepared presenters, or some combination thereof. The audience may be especially aggressive, picking on details or probing for weaknesses in the material presented or the presenters' knowledge. Attendees at a review sometimes bring up, or even focus on, topics that are of questionable relevance. But if the enthusiastic questioner is the highest-ranking person in the room, the review may continue toward disaster, no matter how unreasonable the questioning may seem.

Another primary reason for disastrous reviews is that the presenting team is unprepared. The team members may fail to demonstrate that they understand the critical issues and risks in the project. They may have failed to follow previous guidance from executives. This error is made frequently. The executive's role often is to point out related efforts going on elsewhere within the company or with partners. After all, the company wants to conserve resources and not duplicate work being done elsewhere. The executive's breadth of awareness of activities and projects usually exceeds that of any of the project team members. So, a familiar review comment is, "Make sure you check with division X to see if their work on project Y can help you." If, by the next review, the team has failed to check out this lead, problems await them in the review room.

When a project team realizes that a disaster is looming at the next scheduled review, it is imperative to take steps before the review to minimize the damage. This typically means leveling with the responsible manager about the true state of affairs. In this case, "communicating as an IT professional" means using common sense: What is in the best interests of the project to make it successful? The answer is not to proceed toward the scheduled review, hoping by some miracle that the weaknesses will be overlooked. That behavior will only delay critical steps to place the project back on a solid footing. Instead of accepting the pending disaster, the wise project manager will get advice from superiors on how to proceed. One possible outcome is to inform the reviewing executive of the problem. Although no one relishes bringing problems to light, this early notification is usually preferable to the alternative of waiting for a disaster to happen at the review. With early warning, the review may be postponed, thereby conserving the time of the reviewing executive. More important to the objective, steps can be taken to get the project back on track.

Most organizations recognize that an especially aggressive "ambush" review accomplishes nothing, except, perhaps, establishing the executive reviewer's reputation as a hard-nosed taskmaster. Even at Microsoft, which might be considered in the IT world a high-pressure development environment, ambush reviews are not the norm. Troubled projects are headed off by meetings with managers to address the problems and avoid surprises at the review.[15]

▪▪▪ Conducting Technical Reviews of Projects

As an IT professional, you may be called upon to participate as a reviewer at a technical presentation. Reviewers contribute by

- Actively listening to the presentation
- Identifying issues, problems, and risks
- Introducing new insights from their unique organizational and technical perspectives
- Suggesting new approaches or strategies
- Confirming the merit of ideas and decisions

These contributions can be significant. For example, at a preliminary system architecture review, an expert reviewer who notices that two systems will not interoperate as the project team thought will be performing a valuable service. Ultimately, these contributions translate into higher-quality systems with a better likelihood of being completed on time and within budget.

As noted earlier, planned reviews are frequently done in the context of a larger process, such as the software or product development process or the project management process. These processes specify various reviews at critical points that are quite clearly defined by the role they play in the larger process. Each review will have

- Entry criteria: the specific activities or products that must have been completed prior to conducting the review
- Exit criteria: the set of conditions that must be met for a successful review

The combination of entry and exit criteria helps to mark the review as a "progress gate" or "quality gate" in the encompassing process. In a systems development process, a familiar milestone is the design review. Often there are multiple design reviews, for example, to assess preliminary and detailed designs. In other cases, the design activities occur at several points in the process because an iterative or spiral development process is being used. Passing a design review signals the project is into the next phase of development because it has met the exit criteria associated with the review.

There are many sources of guidance on key issues on which to focus during a software development project review. The *Guidelines for Successful Acquisition and Management of Software-Intensive Systems*[16] has handy checklists on what to look for in reviews related to

- Software design
- System integration
- Software engineering processes
- Cost management
- Risk management
- Requirements engineering
- Planning
- Software life cycle
- Project management

Other guidelines are available on the Internet that are based on decades of experience with software development reviews, such as those at the NASA Goddard Space Flight Center (NASA/GSFC, 2004), and that provide guidance on what to look for during the following types of reviews:

- System requirements review
- Software specifications review
- Preliminary design review
- Critical design review
- Operational readiness review

For an IT professional, the most frequently occurring review is the project review, in which the project leader is reporting on the status, plans, progress, and risks to successful completion. If you have been assigned to be a reviewer at one of these project status presentations, the following questions will help you prepare[17]:

- What is the scope of the review? Is the entire development effort being examined or only some particular aspect of the project?
- What is the output of the review—a written report, a presentation, an informal oral report?
- To whom will the results of the review be presented?
- What is the timetable for providing output from the review?
- What administrative staff or other resources are available to support the review?
- Has the project team been informed that the review is occurring?
- Have specific individuals on the project been made available for follow-on questions if needed?
- What constraints exist on the review regarding access to documents or people?
- Where are the sources for documentation about the project (e.g., requirements statements, plans, etc.)
- Are there specific formats or guidelines that the review should follow?

During your actual participation in the project review, these are generally the key issues on which to focus[18]:

- Determine the current status of the project
  - According to the plan, where should the project be, in terms of progress against cost and schedule?
  - What is a realistic view of the current status, in terms of progress and the quality of the evolving system?
- Determine whether the development process is under control
  - How stable are the requirements and interfaces?
  - Is the plan being followed?
  - Is adequate leadership being provided?
  - How are external events (e.g., technology trends, economy, external product or service providers) affecting the project?
- Identify key items that are endangering successful completion
  - Are resources adequate?
  - Are risks being identified, mitigated, and managed effectively?

- Identify specific actions to put the project on a successful course
  - Based on the preceding answers, develop actionable steps for improvement

To take an example from the world of commercial software products, program reviews at Microsoft occur about every 3 months and take about 2 hours each time. As a reviewer, Bill Gates wants to know if the project is under control, if the people expect any major problems, and if they are adding something that might reduce the performance of the system being built. Often his comments reflect the broader context of the project, for example[19]:

- "Didn't we promise this thing to HP?"
- "What about the RISC version? You didn't mention that?"
- "I asked to get drag-and-drop into this thing, and I don't see it in the status report."

To prepare yourself as a reviewer, try to avoid what Karl Wiegers calls the "Seven Deadly Sins of Software Reviews,"[20] transformed in the following as positive recommendations:

1. **Understand the Review Process.** You may not understand the level of detail that is customary and want to explore all items in depth. Ask to attend a different and similar review as an observer to learn about the process before your review.
2. **Critique the Product, Not the Producer.** Check your egos at the door. The goal of the review is to improve the system being developed. Focus on the content, such as designs or work products. Phrase your questions that way. For example, say, "The architecture diagram shows an interface to the marketing system, is that necessary?" not "Why do you have an interface to the marketing system?"
3. **Plan the Review with Adequate Resources.** Project planning software helps encourage a view that milestones are zero-time events. But reviews take time, and that means money, for preparation, delivery, follow-up, and the participation of reviewers. Ensure that funds are in the budget to support reviews.
4. **Don't Use the Review for Problem Solving.** IT professionals are problem solvers, so it is natural to try to solve problems that arise in the course of the review. If it can't be solved in one minute, record it and move on. The value of having this collection of people in the review room is to identify the problem; solve it later.
5. **Prepare for the Review.** Your individual preparation for the review, not the review itself, is the best chance to find problems or defects. You should arrive at the review meeting with relevant presentation slides and documents heavily marked up with questions and notes. Perhaps take a lesson from code inspection meetings, in which the moderator, at the start of the session, asks reviewers how much time they spent preparing. If the times are inadequate, the session is rescheduled.
6. **Get the Right People to Participate.** Reviewers participate to add value. Ensure that the people reviewing have the knowledge and experience to detect problems in the project. Don't dilute the effect of capable reviewers with lots of hangers-on who waste the time of presenters.
7. **Focus on Substance, Not Style.** Style can be a defect or problem, for example, because lack of uniform style is wasting project members' time. However, when project reviews spend more energy identifying problems that are style issues, it can be a red flag that substantive issues are being ignored. Have capable IT professionals focus on their areas of expertise.

No discussion of reviews in IT would be complete without a few gems from the classic *Handbook of Walkthroughs, Inspections, and Technical Reviews,*[21] which was already in its third edition by 1982. Its review tactics never go out of style. Some are well known: By playing the Devil's advocate, a person is liberated from having to be reasonable and to defend a position and so may stumble on a brilliant observation or alternative while keeping the presenters sharp. To test the effectiveness of the review team, a manager may engage in error seeding: deliberately introducing flaws to see if they are detected in the review. Reviews have benefited from using a simple automatic kitchen timer to keep the agenda moving; it is impersonal and neutral, taking the pressure off a human timekeeper.

SUMMARY

Technical reviews provide important opportunities for IT professionals to contribute to their organizations. The guidelines in this chapter can make IT professionals more effective communicators as technical reviewers.

EXERCISES

1. How do you make sure that your key messages and important points will be well understood in a technical presentation?
2. Prepare and deliver a technical review comparing two competing products that claim to be intrusion prevention systems. Either use your organization for context or assume that you are an IT analyst for a specialty online bookseller with annual revenues of $50 million.
3. In reviewing a technical article that is composed of abstract, introduction, discussion, and conclusions sections, what sections do you think are more important to pay attention to?
4. Is using sophisticated technical jargon in technical presentations a good idea? Why or why not?
5. Why is it not a good idea to introduce a new fact or finding in the conclusion section of an article?
6. How do you define the success factors of becoming a good reviewer of technical articles?

ENDNOTES

1. Wing, Jeannette M. (July 1988). A Study of 12 Specifications of the Library Problem," *IEEE Software* 67.
2. Fickas, Stephen, and Nagarajan, P. (November 1988). "Critiquing Software Specifications," *IEEE Software* 37–47.
3. Wing (1988).
4. DOD, MIL-STD-498, Standard for System Development and Documentation, U.S. Department of Defense, downloaded from http://www.pogner.demon.co.uk/mil_ 498/, August 22, 2004.
5. NASA/GSFC, *Manager's Handbook for Software Development,* Software Engineering Laboratory, NASA Goddard Space Flight Center, downloaded from http://sel.gsfc.
nasa.gov/website/documents/online-doc/84–101.pdf, August 22, 2004.
6. RSPA, Roger S. Pressman & Associates, Inc., Adaptable Process Model—Document Templates, downloaded from http://www.rspa.com/docs/, December 3, 2004.
7. Cusumano, Michael, and Selby, Richard. (1995). *Microsoft Secrets.* The Free Press, New York, p. 218.
8. Ibid.
9. Ibid., p. 29.
10. Ibid.
11. Wysocki, Robert K., Beck, Robert, Jr., and Crane, David B. (2000). *Effective Project Management,* 2nd ed. John Wiley & Sons, New York, p. 290.

12. Schindler, Esther. "How to Write a Product Review," downloaded from http://www.west.net/~sbpcug/review.htm, February 15, 2004.

13. Ibid.

14. Cap Gemini Ernst & Young, Outsourcing, downloaded from http://www.cgey.com/outsourcing/faq.shtml#_Toc16389641, February 14, 2004.

15. Cusumano and Selby (1995), p. 30.

16. STSC, Software Technology Support Center, Hill AFB, *Guidelines for Successful Acquisition and Management of Software-Intensive Systems,* Condensed Version 4.0, downloaded from http://www.stsc.hill.af.mil/resources/tech_docs/gsam4/appendix.pdf, August 23, 2004.

17. NASA/GSFC (2004).

18. Ibid.

19. Cusumano and Selby (1995), p. 29.

20. Wiegers, Karl. "Seven Deadly Sins of Software Reviews," downloaded from http://www.processimpact.com/articles/revu_sins.html, August 23, 2004.

21. Freedman, Daniel P., and Weinberg, Gerald M. (1982). *Handbook of Walkthroughs, Inspections, and Technical Reviews*, 3rd ed. Little Brown and Co., Boston.

SELECTED REFERENCES ▪▪▪▪▪▪▪

Auer, Ken, and Miller, Roy. (2002). *Extreme Programming Explained*. Addison-Wesley, Boston.

Girden, Ellen R. (1996). *Evaluating Research Articles from Start to Finish*. Sage Publications, Thousand Oaks, CA.

Streibel, Barbara. (2002). *Manager's Guide to Effective Meetings*. McGraw Hill, New York.

Wilder, Claudyne. "Presentation Points," downloaded from http://www.wilderpresentations.com/points/aug02.html, February 15, 2004.

CHAPTER 9

IT Consulting

Learning Objectives

■ To understand how communications can enhance your success as an IT consultant

■ To learn effective ways to communicate with your customers

■ To become aware of the communications aspects of internal consulting and responding to Requests for Proposals (RFPs)

IT is big business throughout the world. Gartner Group reports a healthy annual growth of 6.2 percent in the IT services business to $569 billion worldwide in 2003.[1] Billions of dollars are spent each year on IT consulting services provided by IT consultants who range from multibillion dollar international companies to single individuals. Success in IT consulting depends on effective communications, because the essence of consulting is a business relationship between a customer with a need and a consultant providing support to fulfill that need. Whenever there is a relationship between people, communication plays a decisive role in the success of that relationship.

WARM-UP EXERCISE

Aban Computers, a large learning center, has experienced phenomenal growth in the past 10 years. Management would like to refine its decision-making process for purchasing a new set of computers. As currently practiced, managers submit requests to purchase new computers based on their subjective perceptions formed by listening to their customers (students learning how to use computers), attending trade shows, reading IT-related publications, and talking to vendors. Of course, managers' experiences with existing computers are factors also. These requests are then approved or denied by Larry Strong, their boss. This process worked well enough in the early days of the company but has become unwieldy now that the company has grown and spread out geographically. Aban has brought you in as a consultant, even though you have been warned that Larry has reservations about the benefits of hiring outside consultants because of his repeated bad experiences with them.

Larry is the first person you will interview. He travels all over the country. He keeps an office in Washington, DC, although he is there less than a quarter of the time. Even when you can catch Larry at his Washington office, he is busy

---

answering phone calls, attending meetings, and marketing their products and services. He cannot give you a lot of interview time, but his input is critical and, of course, he is the big boss at Aban.

1. How would you approach Larry to grant you some time for an interview?
2. Will you plan to give a presentation? If so, on what topics?
3. What types of interview questions would you ask Larry?
4. What will you tell Larry about your approach to developing a better decision-making process?
5. What should you do to gain Larry's confidence that you will be an effective consultant?

Your answers to the warm-up exercise suggest the complicated mix of technical topics and communications issues that the IT consultant experiences.

▐▐▐ Introduction

Technical consulting provides companies an objective view for diagnosing, analyzing, and resolving business and technology related problems. In providing these services, consultants make direct contributions to their customer's businesses. IT professionals take on the role of consultant in various ways. They may join companies that provide consulting services to other organizations. As employees of the company, they are serving as IT consultants by performing analyses and providing services to these outside customers of the company. An IT professional may also establish a consulting business as a single individual or with colleagues to offer services in the marketplace. Frequently, individuals decide to create consultancies because they have developed expertise that they perceive will be in sufficient demand to support them in business. They may have acquired or enhanced their expertise through some combination of education, training, and professional practice.

Consider an example of an IT database professional who has worked at steadily increasing levels of responsibility in a company for over 10 years, rising to be a senior database analyst. Over her career, she has encountered and resolved countless database performance issues. She prefers to work on the most technically challenging problems, but half of her current assignments are more routine and not as challenging. So, motivated by the chance to work more exclusively on highly technical performance problems, she starts a business and offers these services to other companies. As an IT professional, her sense of the marketplace is that her knowledge will be in high demand and she will be successful.

All of the other chapters in this book contain material potentially helpful to the IT consultant: writing and speaking clearly, behaving ethically, and understanding cross-cultural communications. This chapter highlights how the activities involved in IT consulting draw upon these other skills. This chapter covers three aspects of IT consulting and their reliance on effective communications:

1. Communicating with your customer
2. The role of internal consultants
3. Communications aspects of responding to Requests for Proposals (RFPs)

▪▪▪ Communicating with Your Customer

Management consultants must play a proactive role in establishing effective communications with their customers. You will want to avoid potential pitfalls, disappointments, and frustrations that can result in failure. The recommendation throughout this book, to know your audience and listeners, is extremely important for IT consultants. Know your customers to the extent that you can anticipate their concerns and be responsive and sensitive to their needs and expectations. This relationship can only be achieved through effective communications.

As an IT consultant, the main goal of your provided services is to guarantee customer satisfaction through out the life cycle of the engagement and interactions with the customer. The extent of that satisfaction is often contingent on the customer's expectations about your role and contributions. A major benefit of effective communications in IT consulting is to ensure that expectations are clear. In this way, you can minimize an outcome in which the customer is unhappy and therefore not inclined to give you additional work nor to be a reference as you seek other projects within the customer's organization or outside of it.

Your communications are influenced by the working relationship between you and the customer. In some IT consulting scenarios, you will be a single consultant embedded within a customer's IT organization. An example is the database performance expert mentioned earlier. She may have a two-week engagement to analyze performance problems and work with the customer organization to get the problems rectified. Because she works side-by-side with her customers, it is tempting to say that she is one of them, but she is not. The communications skills of this database consultant must reinforce the special nature of her consultant-customer relationship. To have a successful engagement, in which the performance problems are solved, she needs the help of database technical staff members of the customer's organization. Her chances of success will be enhanced if she can interact in a friendly and personable way with them. But she is ill-advised to allow her informal working interactions to lead to such familiarity that it undermines the job she is hired to do. She is an outside expert in her field. There will be occasions in which she may (gently, if possible) assert herself to make a point that reflects her expertise or that moves a process nearer to a solution. She will need to express herself with confidence, making eye contact and stating her position forcefully. Ideally, she will have paved the way for these successful and effective communications by her previous activities and interactions, in which her expertise and her clear willingness to work as part of a team contributed to the customer's staff having a positive feeling about her.

A different working relationship exists when an IT consultant works separately from the customer's employees. The interactions are more formal and staged. For example, you may have been retained to make recommendations for reorganizing the IT functions at a company. This is an example of a type of engagement that can spark fearful reactions among the customer's technical and management staff. *Reorganization* can be a code word for eliminating some positions. Your assignment will likely require you to meet with various groups of employees and their managers to understand the current functions and how they are performed.

In this more formal consultant-customer interaction, you may be working alone, talking and listening to people who are suspicious of you and anxious about what your eventual report could mean for their livelihood. In your approach, be open about the high-level charge you have been given: You have been retained for your expertise in organizing IT functions to make recommendations for improvement. (Consider working into the discussion informally some information that will help establish your expertise, such as having served as CIO at a company, if it can be done without seeming like you are boasting or trying too hard to impress them.) The overall objective is to make the organization operate more effectively and efficiently, which will improve the overall profitability of the company. You have no preconceived notions or hidden agendas. You want to understand the nature of the work, how the work gets done, and you would appreciate their assistance. If they have other concerns or questions, they will be better advised to ask their managers, who are aware of your assignment and can confirm what you are saying.

In the world of IT consulting assignments, these two examples represent points in a spectrum of possibilities for the relationship you may have with your customer. The duration and the closeness of the working relationships will also affect the communications patterns and styles that you will find to be most effective. Certain consulting engagements in IT extend over several years. In some cases, this is due to restrictions on adding full-time employees, but no restrictions on hiring consultants. Also, certain organizations prefer to get work accomplished via formal contractual instruments with external parties rather than through employees. These practices contribute to the extensive use of IT consultants. These scenarios also imply that some IT consultants are not necessarily subject-matter experts like the database performance analyst, but instead are competent professionals performing their work for organizations (and often at their facilities) under a professional services contract and not as an employee. Still other companies use temporary agencies to bring in IT staff with the intention of trying out people as potential full-time employees.

A more frequently occurring role for an IT consultant is to serve as an auditor. Organizations may retain IT audit consultants to provide additional assurance that they are effectively managing costly IT projects, such as major system conversions.[2] Increased IT auditing in the United States may also be attributed in part to the role of IT in functions that are subject to rules of legal and regulatory compliance. For example, provisions of the Sarbanes-Oxley Act that became effective in 2004 require auditable systems for recording transactions and archiving business communications. Because information technology is used for data storage, transaction processing, and electronic communications, IT professionals, in both internal and external consulting capacities, are being called upon in greater numbers to serve as auditors.[3] Significantly for its communications, IT auditors may have an audience that includes boards of directors and law enforcement. Their oral and written communications must thus reflect the highest ethical principles and present honest and forthright representations based on their analyses and auditing activities.

As an IT consultant, these scenarios can be complicated, calling upon your judgment to make the best use of various communications skills in writing, speaking, and listening. You will want to apply these skills in ways that respect the formal contractual relationship with customers (you know that you are not "one of them") while retaining an informal style that always is telling the customer that you are a team player and will work as diligently toward the success of the job as if you were an employee.

Establishing Rapport

Effective communication between two people can be enhanced when they have a natural rapport. Rapport is a human behavior that is usually more subconscious than conscious.[4] Historically, the traditional advice for establishing rapport is to mimic the other person's behavior as you are talking. In modern customer relationship management, it just means that you should be aware of establishing some kind of similarity and synergy. In the work environment as an IT consultant, you should develop an understanding of the customer's values and expectations. Through listening and observing, learn to anticipate how the customer thinks, behaves, and communicates under different circumstances. Armed with this knowledge, you can align and synchronize your responses to the customer's behaviors and communications styles. Maintain a keen awareness of a customer's words and behaviors that give you clues about their expectations. For example, if customers recount to you their experiences with other consultants, are their mannerisms telling you that they didn't value the output received? Perhaps their starting position with your consulting project is not to expect much of value from you. Your overall behavior, reaction, discourse, and communications styles should be always in sync with the customer environment. You should work toward developing, with your customer, modes of communication that are effective.[5]

General recommendations for establishing rapport include the following[6]:

- Look for opportunities to reinforce your working relationships with informal and friendly conversations with the customer about topics unrelated to the business at hand. The informal topics should preferably lean toward your customer's areas of interest.
- During business conversations, keep trying to improve your understanding of your customer's perspectives, needs, values, and expectations. Ask open-ended questions and listen attentively to the responses to understand customer priorities and assumptions about the assignment. This information will help you develop deliverables to satisfy your customer's expectations.
- Respect people's sociocultural values and styles of communication. Be flexible and open. Ensure that your communications will not be perceived as disrespectful, hurtful, or insensitive. Seek opportunities to learn more about diverse cultures.
- Try to establish informal communication styles as much as possible; they will be helpful in developing rapport. Reserve the use of more formal written memoranda to situations when they are needed.

Determining Customer Needs

Learn about your customers from multiple and diverse sources. It can save the time of customers if you can learn facts and figures from documented material rather than from interviewing them. Express a willingness to take different paths to acquire information. Show that you respect the time and talent of your customers.

If you interview staff, it can be an opportunity to win support for your project and build rapport. As you listen attentively, your respondent may give you hints about promising directions to explore in the future. Asking questions is a valuable way to show interest and build rapport. Ask smart questions that seek clarification, verification, acknowledgment, or specificity[7]:

- **Clarification.** Clarifying questions are important to avoid inconsistencies. It can easily happen that you review your notes from an interview and wonder if an answer you heard applied to all users of the system. You wish you had asked a clarifying question at the time. You know that there are three user classes and are fairly sure that the answer does not apply to all classes. Now you are faced with either making an assumption about the answer or contacting the person again. The former is risky because it could lead to a defective policy being designed and implemented in the software. The latter is not attractive because the person you interviewed is very busy. Asking the follow-up question will interrupt her day, and it will be obvious that you should have asked the question at the time of the interview. A compromise is to make the assumption and also enter it into an online log of items that must be checked. This will work if you really do check so that you obtain the correct information, and you are likely to see the interviewee again soon so you can confirm the user class question informally.
- **Verification.** Ask verifying questions to confirm critical information. These questions should not be a substitute for failing to listen. Repeatedly asking every question twice for verification is annoying, so reserve verification questions for times when the matter is important and the consequences of getting it wrong are significant.
- **Motivation.** Ask motivation questions when you need to understand the underlying reasons for an answer or statement. Motivation questions are important when you are interviewing stakeholders. If you record only answers to your questions, you may later wonder why the answers appear as they do. You are more than a voice recorder. To be effective, you need to understand what is behind the answers. This understanding may enable you to recommend alternative ways of addressing the underlying need. There are many occasions when IT consultants ask employees why they do something, only to cause employees to question it themselves. They may have always done something in a certain way without realizing that the underlying need has gone away. In one example at a manufacturing company, the administrative person said that he pulled off his copy of the receiving report and filed it by vendor name. The consultant asked why, and the clerk said that this allowed them to find the copies when asked for. He had a large stack of forms waiting to be filed. The consultant didn't stop there: "So, how often do you get requests to access copies by vendor name." He replied once or twice a month, because most of the requests were by order number; the requests by vendor name usually went to the purchasing department. The clerk was left wondering if the company could do away with this time-consuming filing activity. By understanding the motivations, you will be prepared to rethink truly needed services and ways to satisfy them.
- **Specificity.** Specific questions are asked to get detailed information and to gain specific knowledge about a matter. Often, a customer speaks in general about a project assuming that consultants have a good general understanding of it. As an outsider, you may need to ask specific questions to get detailed information and to improve your understanding of the background of the project.

Anticipating and Addressing Customer Concerns

Your familiarity with the customer organization and its associated technologies and application domains can be very influential in your ability to anticipate its concerns. You may be called upon to decide on the extent to which you want your consulting practice to be specialized to particular technologies or domains. It is quite common for IT consultants to spend their entire careers working with the IT issues within the aerospace business, air traffic control, medical informatics, or other domains. Many IT consultants have worked as full-time employees in the organization that is now their customer. Your experiences as an employee contribute toward building rapport with the customer and may have left you with good working relationships with key individuals in the organization. All of this familiarity can benefit your consulting efforts. If you decide to build your expertise along a domain area, you can often be more effective, and more quickly, in your successive consulting projects. You will have a reference context from other assignments and projects that will provide a baseline upon which to solve the latest problem or analyze the current issue.

Endeavor to look at issues from the customer's perspective. Strive to take on the value propositions of the customer as a way to help you detect where they will see value and benefit in your work products. Develop and present solutions based on your customer's requirements, expectations, standards, and terminology. Ideally, you should know what your customers want, when they want it, where they want it, and (if appropriate) at what price. This understanding will help you to anticipate the concerns of your customers and to prepare effective responses to them. You must remain vigilant that by anticipating concerns, you are not contributing to scope creep. One source of dissatisfaction with IT consultants is that they steer projects toward technologies or subjects that interest them rather than serve their customer. Ensure that any work you do is consistent with the statement of work associated with your consulting engagement.

Following-up with Your Customers

The consultant-customer relationship is extremely sensitive. There are several avenues for possible misunderstanding and failure. The success of a project and satisfaction of the customer depend on the project outcome as it compares to the customer's expectations. Therefore, as a rule conduct a follow-up after project closure. It is important to ensure that your project deliverables meet the customer requirements and project expectations. Any unfinished or incomplete activities can be addressed or completed in the follow-up activities. This follow-up activity will close out the engagement on a positive note.

Following up after the project deliverable will enable you not only to demonstrate your commitment to customer satisfaction but also to set the stage for capturing further business with this customer. Your experience with the customer should dictate whether your follow-up communication is by telephone, e-mail, postal mail, or in person. The follow-up will also lead naturally to your contacting the customer periodically to find out if your contribution helped, if the business environment has changed in any way, and if you can help with any current concerns or opportunities. Customers will also appreciate being kept well informed of any new developments, changes, opportunities, upgrades, or additional products and services. A way to keep in touch and also provide a potential benefit is to send the customer an article you have written or an industry study you have found. Make sure that anything you send truly will have a reasonable chance of being perceived as useful. Sending lots of unsolicited documents can quickly sour what had been a strong relationship.

Another kind of follow-up is a more formal, brief survey to gauge your performance and contribution. There are certain circumstances in which this can be useful. For example, the most senior executive at your consulting organization sends the survey (emphasis on concise) to the customer counterpart, who then has it distributed and completed by the individual customer contacts of the consultants used. The purpose is to improve the performance of the consulting organization. The survey approach provides an opportunity for feedback that can elicit candid comments that may not have been delivered before. The consulting organization may learn more about the effectiveness of its consultants through this survey vehicle. A survey sent directly by the consultant to the customer contact can often be ill advised; the response will just echo what was already expressed orally about performance and contribution and the survey will be seen as a time waster by the customer.

Working Together with Customers

One mistake commonly committed by consultants is that they point out everything that is wrong and create a negative mood among managers and employees as soon as they start on a project. Some consultants believe that this way of exhibiting their skills and knowledge will prove their competency to the customer. However, in most cases, such a negative approach makes the consultant unpopular with the customer. Look for opportunities to compliment the work of employees and show respect for them in front of their manager. However, do this sparingly and only when it is genuine. Otherwise, it will come across as a disingenuous attempt to ingratiate yourself with the employees. When you send positive messages, and they are genuine and appropriate, it will make employees feel that you respect them for their skills and talent and do not intend to make them look defensive and incompetent in front of their manager. If you work together with employees in their projects and tasks to solve problems and develop solutions, be certain to share the credit with the employees. This professional behavior will contribute to your being viewed, by both employees and managers, as a team player. This behavior will definitely build rapport, improve the level of synergy, and make your working environment healthier.

The management at the customer site expects you to work in a diligent and efficient manner based on the agreed-upon plans, schedule, and cost. Therefore, it is important to keep management updated on project progress and changes. The plans should have provided for a progress reporting process; if not, ask the relevant manager what reporting activity (including content, frequency, and style) he or she desires. Be aware if scope creep is occurring, that is, if your work is leading you to topics that are beyond the stated scope of the work. If this is happening, inform management immediately without making any excuses. Your prompt action will avoid any surprises and unpleasant events. Finally, to be successful, concentrate on the assigned task without getting involved in office politics and other issues not relevant to your assignment. Always conduct yourself in an ethical manner, consistent with codes of conduct for IT professionals (see Chapter 6). Respect all confidentiality and non-disclosure agreements and the privacy of customer information.

Customers' Issues and Their Resolution

In your role as an effective IT consultant, you should take the initiative and participate proactively in resolving your customer's problems. In fact, your position as external to the customer's organization may provide you an ideal perspective to see things differently from those who are insiders. As an outsider, you can sometimes get away with comments that are perhaps more candid than would be expressed by a customer's employee, and yet, when you express them, they are met with nodding heads of agreement.

Always show respect for your customer and be responsive to the issues or the problems that the customer is experiencing. Practice active listening. If customers are having trouble communicating their problems clearly, you can contribute by posing just the right question to get a clearer picture of the issues. Sometimes customers do not know how to state their problems correctly, because the technological issues are not well understood.[8] In these cases, you can contribute by gently educating the customer about the relevant information technologies to provide a common baseline for discussion of the problem and possible solutions.

The following recommendations provide guidelines for managing and resolving customers' issues[9]:

1. **Resolving Issues as Soon as Possible.**   An issue is an urgent concern that could threaten the success of the project. Often an issue has unknown elements, which is why it resists being addressed completely. Issues abound in IT consulting for just this reason of uncertainty. There may be an issue whether two systems can interoperate. It continues to be an issue until it is settled. It can be settled decisively by actually having the two systems interoperate, or you may be satisfied if there is sufficient reported experience of others who state that this interoperation occurred. Obviously, you want to resolve issues as quickly as possible. A defining characteristic of an issue is urgency to get it resolved, so if an issue lingers, it raises questions about whether it really is an issue. The interoperability is an issue because this lack of knowledge delays designers who cannot be confident about representing the system design with this uncertainty.

2. **Clarifying Issues vs. Action Items.**   The preceding discussion of issues may have suggested to you that you should log issues and monitor their resolution. But this reasoning is not consistent with issues being urgent concerns. Logging and tracking is appropriate for action items—steps that must be taken by a named party.

3. **Dealing with Large or Multiple Issues.**   Keep the definition of *issue* in mind. If an issue appears too difficult to resolve quickly, consider breaking it down into manageable pieces. If you encounter a barrage of issues in a short period of time, consider whether they may be related, so there is essentially a single underlying issue. For example, in an IT project, multiple disparate issues may have in common a single stakeholder with whom effective communication has not been established.

4. **Resolving Issues at the Root Cause and Not Just Treating Symptoms.**   When you look into an issue, ask a series of "why" questions until you get to its root cause. If your team identifies personnel turnover as an issue, don't simply attempt to resolve it by adding new staff. By asking "why," you may find out that people do not feel that their contributions are being appreciated. By continued probing, you may reach a root cause of a project leader who could benefit from some mentoring.

5. **Choosing Among Bad Alternatives.**   As an IT consultant, you may be supporting a customer project that is being paralyzed by its inability to resolve an issue that is delaying progress. The failure to resolve the issue may be due to not having a desirable alternative solution. This situation can arise especially with issues related to corporate politics and culture, in which delays will not improve the alternatives. You may need to step in to get the team to make its best choice among a set of unattractive alternatives as a way to get the project moving again.

In summary, your job as an IT consultant is to perform assigned tasks effectively and efficiently. Effectiveness requires the communication-related aspects of

- Sharing knowledge and skills with the customer staff members as appropriate
- Developing constructive working relationships with customer staff members
- Keeping customer management informed of progress and status
- Respecting the privacy and confidentiality of customer information
- Helping customers by anticipating their needs and helping them to resolve issues

⟋⟋⟋ Role of Internal Consultants

The working model thus far for the IT consultant has been an individual supporting a separate organization. In today's competitive market environment, organizations are reshaping the traditional roles into internal consulting positions in order to be more efficient. In this model, skilled professionals work within their own organizations, but they conduct all their interactions in the context of a consultant-customer model. With specialized IT skills often scarce, and IT spread throughout the company, the internal consulting model is used for IT services. IT internal consultants may provide services to support e-business, customer relationship management, supply chain integration, or other IT-intensive capabilities.

Internal consultants strive for high levels of customer service and satisfaction, just as if they were supporting external organizations. As consultants, they need to practice highly effective oral and written communications skills because they will prepare statements of work, proposals, plans, and capability briefings—only now they will be for potential internal customers. If an organization prides itself on having employees who are driven by customer satisfaction, then the organization itself will benefit from having these motivated professionals supporting its own goals and objectives. The organizational challenge lies in reevaluating the roles of the organization's managers, technical staff, and support staff so that they can be seen as internal consultants. An internal focus will leverage the customer service skills of a company. It can also lead to an increased level of efficiency and internal service. Internal consulting offers another opportunity for many skilled IT professionals to contribute if their capabilities and talents are currently underutilized within the company. This model also provides professional experience for the staff with a formal consultant-customer operating mode that is directly translatable to work for the organization's external customers.

There are additional advantages to internal consulting. For example, companies may prefer internal consultants when projects involve proprietary or sensitive information. Organizations can benefit from the internal consultants' tacit knowledge, which is based on their personal experience and is difficult to capture and share. For the internal consultant, there are specific professional rewards, such as the motivation to perform successfully because of having a stake in the company.

A concern with internal consulting is whether the organization possesses the required knowledge and skills to solve its own problems. Organizations sometimes need outside assistance. They want the skill sets, objectivity, flexibility, and new perspectives that can come from an external consultant. So, the decision to use internal consultants is not a clear-cut one for an organization.

To what extent is internal consulting merely a cosmetic, and not a substantive, change? Being a consultant demands that you see the working relationship from a consultant's point of view. If the IT professionals in the organization wanted to work as consultants, they would have pursued that line of employment. Perhaps their skill sets (in particular, communications skills) do not lend themselves to success as consultants. Therefore, declaring them internal consultants may be just an artful renaming. Effective internal consultants, like their external counterparts, need to challenge their customer's thinking and assumptions. An internal consultant may not feel free to make bold recommendations because he or she still works for the company/customer. The office politics of the customer take on a new importance when they are the same as yours. Wesselius (2004) continues on this theme, highlighting some of the differences between external and internal consultants, as shown in Table 9-1.[10]

TABLE 9-1   Examples of Differences Between Typical External and Internal Consultants (based on Wesselius, 2004)

Distinguishing Factor	*External Consultants*	*Internal Consultants*
Employment status with customer organization	Not an employee; selling their services to organizations not their own	Employed full-time by the organization
Duration of consulting engagement	Retained for a fixed period to work on a specific problem (typically)	Able to spread their knowledge, skills, and experience throughout the organization to other business units
Resource flexibility	Flexible resource—the organization is not committed to long-term costs; when the job is finished, the consultants leave	Employment relationship exists; when project ends, still shows up for work and needs to be paid
Expertise and skills	Specialized expertise and skills not present in the organization	Expertise and skills already part of the organization
Knowledge of organizational context	Often not familiar with customer's business environment, therefore the customer is paying for a learning curve in the initial stages of a project	Part of the organization— understand the overall business, goals, mission, and vision; no training or learning curve is required
Motivation for successful project	Want project to succeed, but typically have no vested interest in the customer organization	Able to identify with the organization and its success; motivated to contribute because their organization benefits; part of the organization
Objectivity and independence	As an outsider, can be objective, independent, and critical in analyzing and solving the problems	Potentially constrained in candidness because, after the project, will still be employees; likely to have perspectives

(Continued)

TABLE 9-1 *(Continued)*

Distinguishing Factor	External Consultants	Internal Consultants
		similar to other employees; not independent; susceptible to office politics and internal dynamics
Working relationships	Will establish working relationships, but for limited duration; typically need time to build relationships; no need to consider consequences of sustaining relationships beyond end date; not required to live with the consequences or end results of their work	Must redefine relationships with people in the organization from being colleagues to customers; needs and relationships must be communicated properly to avoid conflict and manage the expectations

Learning Internal Consulting Skills

Internal consultants must manage all aspects of the customer relationship effectively and efficiently, just as if they were external consultants selling their services. Their challenges involve the following:

- Acquiring customer service skills
- Learning to think of colleagues as customers
- Understanding what motivates and drives their internal customers' interests
- Building trust and teamwork
- Managing the customer's expectations throughout the project
- Handling political sensitivities of working within the organization

By developing an internal consulting capability, organizations can build on the knowledge and skills sets of their people. However, with the benefit of understanding the organizational context, internal consultants are sometimes held to a higher standard than external service providers. So, to be successful at internal consulting, the organization may need to invest in education and training, including sessions on technical communications and managing the consulting relationship. Once the internal consulting practice is running smoothly and efficiently, the focus may turn outward to seek revenues from the newly developed capability by effectively responding to requests for proposals from customers.

▪▪▪ Communications Aspects of Responding to Requests for Proposals (RFPs)

To make use of external providers of IT products and services, organizations prepare documents to describe their needs and to request other organizations to bid on the proposed job. One of these documents is a formal Request for Proposal (RFP) that invites potential providers to respond with a proposal describing how they would satisfy the needs.

Government entities in particular rely extensively on external providers in IT and have laws governing the solicitation of services. The RFP should give a summary description of the needed work and a timeline for respondents to follow. The IT work needed often is too extensive to describe within the RFP, so the RFP typically refers to another document, a Statement of Work (SOW), that provides the details of the needs that must be met by offerors. The RFP also describes the plan for the solicitation, often including references to web sites for current notifications related to the offering, announcements of open meetings, and frequently asked questions. With formal solicitations, there are defined "rules of engagement" for legal and fairness reasons. The rules specify the process for awarding the contract, acceptable ways to contact the organization that issued the RFP, and requirements for the size, content, and delivery date of the proposal.

As a potential offeror, you or your organization must decide if you want to respond. If you determine that the RFP is a possible opportunity because of the general subject matter involved, then the following are some important considerations to help you decide if you indeed want to put together a responding proposal[11,12]:

Assemble a team.   Form a team from within your organization. Identify key people who have the experience and knowledge to pull together this effort on what is typically a demanding schedule. Appoint one leader or proposal manager to oversee and coordinate the entire response. One of the first actions of the proposal manager is to build the remainder of the team and develop a realistic schedule to build and deliver the proposal on time.

Increasingly in IT, your team will extend beyond your organization, because performing the tasks called for in the SOW requires a combination of often diverse and specialized skills and expertise. For example, the RFP may be for an organization that is outsourcing its IT support. Clearly, this is as broad as it can get in requiring diverse IT-related knowledge and talents. In considering a response, you may determine that to provide the required information security capabilities, you want to use biometrics for access to facilities and networks. You consider identifying separate companies specializing in biometrics to join the emerging team because you do not have that expertise in house.

Focus on the right opportunities.   If there are many candidate RFPs, place priorities on them. Know your capacity to develop proposals, which can be very expensive to produce. Also, by working on proposals, some of your best people are not free to contribute in other ways to the organization. In setting priorities, understand your organization's own market position, strengths, weaknesses, and types of business opportunities that will help it advance in ways consistent with its strategic goals.

Analyze the RFP and learn as much as you can about the prospective customer. Study the RFP carefully, along with the SOW and any related documents. While adhering to rules about contact with the RFP-issuing agency, pursue any opportunities to meet with them to learn as much as possible about what is really desired in a performing organization. For example, you may learn that there is an incumbent company that is on site performing similar tasks and is highly regarded and expected to bid on this RFP. Any face-to-face meetings you have become excellent chances to practice skills from Chapter 7 on oral communications, especially speaking confidently about the talents of your team, asking thoughtful questions that you have rehearsed, and listening actively to responses for their direct messages and indirect implications.

Identify the true decision-makers and assess your customer's needs. There are typically a small number of key people in the RFP-issuing agency who are driving the solicitation and truly understand its key features. If possible, identify and learn all you can about those people and about the agency and its needs. Perhaps a colleague or a teammate has worked with the agency and can provide insights into its operations. You will want your eventual proposal to fit with the culture of the agency.

Respond to the RFP exactly as directed. This is not the time to be creative if it means deviating from page limits or omitting required sections. Use the prescribed format and structure. People in the agency will evaluate your proposal to ensure that it is compliant with the RFP. Unless there is an overwhelming reason not to do so, use headings that match the required content as specified in the RFP. Make it easy for evaluators to find the content that matches what they are looking for.

Focus on the customer. In your proposal, focus on the customer's needs and how your proposal satisfies them. Cite relevant experience of your team, especially if that experience is a close match for what is required in the RFP.

Write a persuasive and winning proposal. While still adhering to required form and structure, the proposal is your chance to shine. Using guidelines from this book on persuasive writing, develop the most compelling case that your team is the best choice to take on the planned work.

Pay close attention to pricing. The pricing of your proposal will likely be decided at senior levels in your organization with the aim of achieving a proper balance between being able to deliver on the proposed work and the profitability of your organization.

Deliver your proposal in person. If you have a choice about how to deliver the proposal, choose to deliver it in person so that you have another opportunity to show personally your commitment to winning this contract. If you can deliver a presentation about your proposal, make it as persuasive and convincing as possible that your team is fully capable and committed to customer satisfaction. Have attending team members observe the reactions of the agency to the presentation: who attended, who asked questions, what questions were asked, who was taking notes, follow-up action items, and so on.

Debrief your team. After your proposal presentation, meet with your own team and critique your performance. If appropriate under the solicitation rules, follow up with the agency to thank them for the opportunity to make a presentation. Also, if allowed, address any action items or respond more fully to any questions that arose at the presentation.

Debrief your customer. If you are not awarded the contract, look for opportunities to learn from the experience for next time. Ask the customer what did and did not go well. To get candid responses, an executive at your organization will often want to contact an agency counterpart to ask for feedback.

Develop a proposal knowledgebase. Although RFPs vary, your organization will want to develop a knowledgebase of its proposals. The content can be helpful to new proposal teams.

SUMMARY ▮▮▮▮▮▮

This chapter has examined communicating with your customer and the communications aspects of internal consulting and responding to RFPs—all critical subjects for a successful IT professional.

EXERCISES ▮▮▮▮▮▮

1. Your company manufactures parts for the automobile, aviation, and railroad industries. As a manager of your company's IT department, you have never worked as an internal consultant. Now you are exploring how to provide consulting services to other departments in your company. Develop a persuasive presentation to your colleagues in the business division of your company seeking to become their consultant. What IT capabilities may be of interest to them?
2. Suppose that you are planning to become a consultant to companies that design and develop software products for business intelligence.
   a. What steps should you take to know your customers?
   b. On what topics would they likely need consulting support?
3. What are the success factors of doing internal consulting in IT?
4. The following are old Greek words: *ethos, pathos,* and *logos.*
   a. Search your dictionary or the web to find out what these words mean, if you don't know their meanings.
   b. How would you apply these words in the context of becoming an IT consultant?
5. Study a current RFP from the examples of library information systems at the Integrated Library System Reports web site, http://www.ilsr.com/sample.htm. Answer the following:
   a. What is the profile of a company that would be a likely respondent to this proposal?
   b. What are the capabilities needed of likely respondents?
   c. From searching the web for IT companies, assemble a team of companies that have the needed capabilities you identified.
   d. If you are part of a class or other learning group, divide up into teams of 4–5 people. Each team should prepare a 15-minute persuasive presentation of their proposal in response to this RFP.

ENDNOTES ▮▮▮▮▮▮

1. TCMnet.com. "Gartner Says Worldwide IT Services Revenue Grew 6.2 Percent in 2003," downloaded from http://www.tmcnet.com/usubmit/2004/Jun/1050267.htm, August 24, 2004.
2. Swanson, Dan. "Auditing System Conversions," Institute of Internal Auditors, downloaded from http://www.theiia.org/itaudit/index.cfm?fuseaction=forum&fid=5495, December 3, 2004.
3. News.com. "Sarbanes-Oxley Cheat Sheet," downloaded from http:// news.com.com/Sarbanes-Oxley+cheat+sheet/2030-7349_3-5465172.html, December 3, 2004.
4. World Transformation. "Rapport," downloaded from http:// www.worldtrans.org/TP/TP1/TP1-36.HTML, February 29, 2004.
5. Ibid.
6. Hiebert, Murray. "Checklist for Establishing Rapport," downloaded from http://www.consultskills.com/rappchek.htm, February 29, 2004.

7. Italo, A. "Effective Communication with Customers," downloaded from http://www. mindspring.com/~italco/com.html, February 29, 2004.

8. Dimakos, I. "Issues Concerning Consultant-Customer Interactions: Things I Learned at the Information Center," downloaded from http://www2.sas.com/proceedings/sugi22/TRAINING/PAPER323.PDF, February 29, 2004.

9. Ten Step. "Manage Issues/Techniques," downloaded from http://www.tenstep.com/4.2ManageIssues.htm, February 29, 2004.

10. Wesselius, Heico. "Internal vs. External Consulting," downloaded from http:// www. vault.com/community/v_community_main.jsp ?mod=article&vcm_page=1&ch_id= 252&article_id=2184397&mod_id= 363& listelement=3, February 22, 2004.

11. Wagner, Felice C. "Steps to a Successful RFP Response," downloaded from http://www. imakenews.com/sugarcrestreport/e_ article000014193.cfm, February 25, 2004.

12. Garlock, Nicole. "Proposal Writing Authority," downloaded from http:// www.proposalwritingauthority.com/ rfp-response.html, February 25, 2004.

Index

Page numbers followed by *f* indicate figures; *t*, tables.